cp²

OP
50⁰⁰

40 —

WOMEN ARTISTS
OF RUSSIA'S NEW AGE

Edited by Anthony Parton

WOMEN ARTISTS OF

With 284 illustrations, 83 in colour

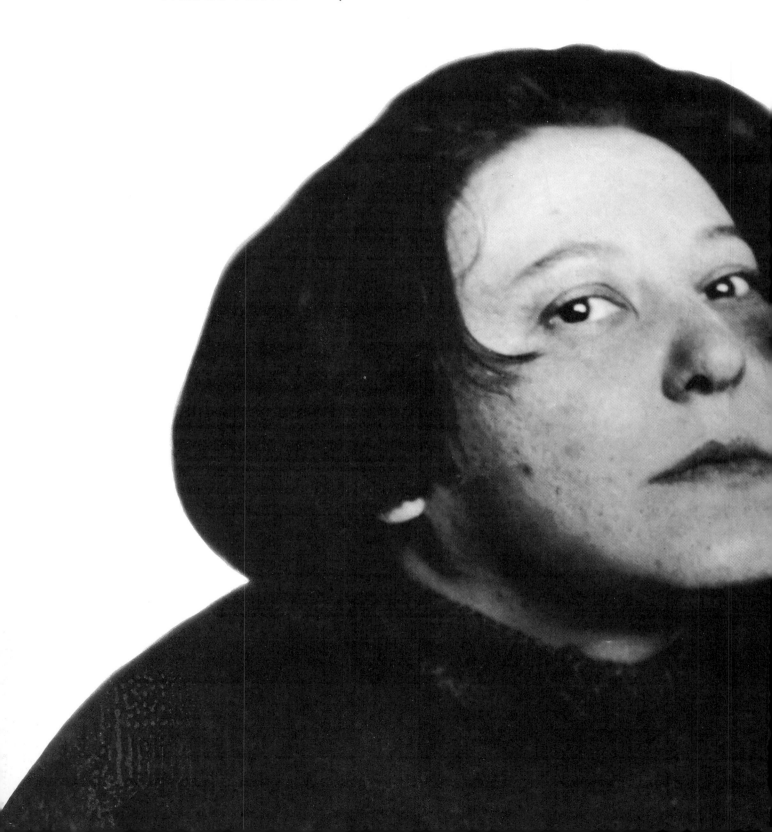

M.N. Yablonskaya

RUSSIA'S NEW AGE
1900 - 1935

RIZZOLI
NEW YORK

TITLE PAGE: Varvara Stepanova
(left) and Lyubov Popova.
Photograph by Rodchenko

Edited and translated from the Russian by Anthony Parton.
Translation of documents and preliminary draft by Felicity O'Dell Vnukova.

First published in the United States of America in 1990 by
Rizzoli International Publications, Inc.
300 Park Avenue South, New York, NY10010

Copyright © Thames and Hudson Ltd, London, 1990

Library of Congress Cataloging-in-Publication Data

Yablonskaya, M. (Miuda)
    Women artists of Russia's new age, 1910–1935 / M.N. Yablonskaya ;
    introduced and edited by Anthony Parton.
        p.   cm.
    Includes bibliographical references.
    ISBN 0-8478-1090-9
    1. Art, Russian.   2. Avant-garde (Aesthetics)—Russian S.F.S.R.—
History—20th century.   3. Constructivism (Art)—Russian S.F.S.R.
4. Women artists—Russian S.F.S.R.   I. Parton, Anthony.   II. Title.
N6988.I14   1990
704'.042'094709041—dc20   89-42692
                                                              CIP

Printed and bound in Singapore

CONTENTS

FOREWORD

It was the Russian Futurist poet Benedikt Livshits who so aptly referred to the women artists of Russia's New Age as 'Amazons'. For the most part these women of the avant-garde sprang not from the cultural élite of Moscow and St Petersburg but issued like 'Scythian riders' from the far-flung provinces of Russia. In general their aim was to overrun the refined conventions of the West which had taken root there, and to create their own distinctive aesthetic standards. Even the members of the intelligentsia outside the avant-garde circle, such as Serebryakova and Simonovich-Efimova who were brought up within the cultured environments of the Benois and Serov families, later embraced the inspiration offered by rural Russia and painted the peasantry in the provinces. Moreover the sheer force of their respective characters (one thinks particularly of Golubkina and Goncharova), the formal innovations which they championed and the stylistic vitality which characterized their work and which contributed so dramatically to the development of Russian modernism, clearly associated them, in Livshits' mind at least, with their mythological predecessors.

During the late nineteenth and early twentieth centuries these women played a crucial role in the Russian visual arts – more so than in other European countries at

Varvara Stepanova
Reclining Figure, 1919

this time. From the turn of the century onwards they established themselves on an equal footing with their male counterparts not only by force of numbers, but by the lucid expression of their intellectual and theoretical skills, and by the quality and quantity of their artistic productivity. Although the work of these 'Amazons' has already featured prominently in exhibitions and literature devoted to modern Russian art, it is only in recent years that significant scholarly attention has focused on the role of the Russian women artists as a whole. The pioneering exhibition 'Women-Artists of the Russian Avantgarde' hosted by the Gmurzynska Gallery in Cologne in 1979 played a formative role in this respect. With this new appreciation of Russian women artists in mind, Yablonskaya has here taken up her pen to examine the contribution of major as well as lesser known figures in this, the first major publication devoted to the subject.

The author principally considers the period 1900–1935 during which, she argues, women artists conceived a new role for themselves. Adopting a contextual approach for the discussion of their work, the author sketches in their individual temperaments, highlights the most important and exciting aspects of their creativity and observes their development against the rapidly changing background of their times. In charting the thirty-five years of artistic development, from the wistful Symbolist paintings of Maria Yakunchikova to the patriotic sculptures of Vera Mukhina, the author narrates the impact on painters and sculptors alike of the two revolutions of 1905 and 1917, indicates the complexity and importance of the changing intellectual and cultural climate throughout the period, and discusses the dramatic effect of the Stalin years. The result is a carefully considered account of the unique contribution made by Russian and Soviet women artists during one of the most volatile and exhilarating periods of their history.

ANTHONY PARTON

INTRODUCTION

Women have played a particularly significant and distinctive role in the history and development of Russian art. Yet Russia is a country in which this fascinating artistic phenomenon has not as yet been either studied or appraised. There still exists a historical tradition of mistrust towards the idea of 'women's studies', and male chauvinism in Russia is still in evidence. As in the West, it was sexual inequality which promoted such chauvinism, and the struggle for equality continues to this day. In Russian art and literature this struggle began around the turn of the century when the creative qualities of female perception were widely demonstrated. The West, however, has not been slow to recognize the talent of Russia's leading women artists, and there have been a number of interesting exhibitions dedicated to the subject. In following on from these, this book does not claim to be a comprehensive study, but rather attempts to generalize and popularize the work and achievement of the women artists of Russia's 'New Age'.

A recently discovered manuscript by the Russian architect Feodor Rerberg[1] dating from the early years of the century represents one of the earliest attempts to examine the question of the role of the female artist. Rerberg asks whether or not male and female approaches to art are identical, and concludes that they are not. The nature of women's creativity, he says, is different from that of men, but both should be recognized as being of equal importance and usefulness. Rerberg continues: 'The role of women in the arts is significant, and will become even more so when women themselves become fully conscious of it, when they are fully aware of their own strength, and cease imitating the work of men. They must stop being ashamed of their own feminine souls and sympathies, and use all their strength to reveal their beauty of spirit, which is finer and more sensitive than that of men.'[2]

Rerberg's 'pre-avant-garde' thoughts on this subject are all the more appropriate as our starting-point because his manuscript represents the only attempt in Russian art theory to question the nature of women's creativity. However striking the art of women may have been, little has changed since Rerberg's day. The creative achievements of women artists are still evaluated according to male criteria — 'a masculine talent', 'a male strength of expression', 'virile art' and so on. Moreover, contemporary women in the artistic professions fight to be called 'artists' (*khudozhniki*) rather than 'women artists' (*khudozhnitsy*)[3] despite the fact that their keen emotional responses and graphic and pictorial analyses are no less valuable than those of men.

Natalya Goncharova
Illustration of the poem 'Vila and the Wood-goblin', from Kruchenykh's and Khlebnikov's *World Backwards* (*Mirskontsa*), 1912

Sonia Delaunay in her studio, 1924

Women had begun to make their names in European art from the eighteenth century onwards, but their work was not particularly characteristic of their sex and appears somewhat secondary to the works executed at that time by men. The famous pastellist, French Royal Academician and portraitist Rosalba Carriera (1675–1757) executed many works in the then-popular rococo style which made it possible for her to succeed in a predominantly male environment without challenging prevailing social ideologies. The same can be said of Elisabeth Louise Vigée-Lebrun (1755–1842), who was a pupil of Greuze and was elected a member of the Academies of Art in Paris, Petersburg and Rome. The work of the Swiss artist (and Royal Academician) Angelica Kauffmann (1741–1807) is similar to that of Joshua Reynolds. In the nineteenth century the American painter Mary Cassatt (1844–1926) was famed for her devoted interest to the works of Courbet, Manet and Degas, and the work of Berthe Morisot (1841–1895) was heavily influenced by Renoir. However in the early twentieth century we notice a change of emphasis, in which the art of the Ukraine-born Sonia Delaunay (1885–1979) is representative. At an early stage in her career she moved to the West, where at first her easel painting was influenced by Post-Impressionism, and subsequently by the Simultaneist theories of her husband Robert Delaunay. However it was her embrace of a variety of media and a 'handicraft' emphasis that represented a new characteristic. Sonia Delaunay became famous for her easel painting, costume and fabric designs as well as for her contribution to modern book design. She was aware of her own strength, and consciously conceived a new role for herself. It was at this point that women's creative talents made their appearance as an artistic phenomenon, and the worth of women's work ceased being evaluated in terms of its similarities to that of men.

It was no accident that women's creative abilities found a distinctive expression around the turn of the century. Women were growing more aware of themselves and were entering employment. Suffragette movements championed the equality of the sexes, and the intense emotional and psychological upheaval of the times brought to the fore an incandescent quality in the work of women artists. The work of the German Expressionist artist Käthe Kollwitz (1867–1945) is particularly notable in this respect, as is that of the Russian artist Natalya Goncharova. Then, again not by chance, women sculptors made a particularly important contribution to twentieth-century art. A significant factor in this was the tactile, object-based nature of the medium. The English sculptor Barbara Hepworth (1903–1975), for instance, reveals a profound interest in the expressive qualities of direct carving. It is characteristic that Anna Golubkina and later Sarra Lebedeva and Vera Mukhina in Russia, alongside such European sculptors as Hepworth in England, encompassed all the discoveries born from the crisis of European sculpture in the early twentieth century.

In addition, Russian women artists at the turn of the century revealed an organic involvement in national handicrafts and applied arts. Particularly important in this respect were Elena Polenova (1850–1898) who founded the famous artists' colony and school of applied art on Savva Mamontov's estate of Abramtsevo, and Princess Maria Tenisheva who organized arts and crafts activities on her estate of Talashkino near Smolensk. Both women were instrumental in the rediscovery and development of traditional arts which until then had been in a state of decline. In this respect the work of Russian women artists who were previously little known is now attracting more attention worldwide. Maria Yakunchikova is such an example. Her work is hardly known in the West, but it is with her that we can first trace the expression of a specifically female creative perception. In her paintings Yakunchikova combined an intensely emotional vision of the world with its concrete and tactile depiction. Moreover Yakunchikova was one of the first women in Russian art to work simultaneously in diverse artistic fields such as easel painting, book design, pokerwork and oils, embroidery and toy making. She assisted Elena Polenova to form the influential Abramtsevo collection of peasant artifacts.

It was Zinaida Serebryakova who took over the baton of creativity from Yakunchikova. This artist's independence and her attempt to search out something new were the characteristics that linked her with the Russian avant-garde movement, in which women artists had the final word. Natalya Goncharova, Olga Rozanova, Lyubov Popova, Alexandra Exter, Varvara Stepanova, Nadezhda Udaltsova and their colleagues attacked everything that was old and past its time.

Anna Akhmatova

It is important to note that in Russia at least women artists have become stronger and more active at times of great social tension. Moreover it is possible to define certain landmarks in the development of collective life according to the acuteness of the creative life of women. It is true to say that a real consciousness of their role came to women at times of intense social turmoil. As the poet Alexander Blok wrote: 'Painting, music, literature, philosophy, religion, social activity, even politics, are indivisible in Russia. Together they form a united and powerful force which carries the precious burden of our national culture.'[4] Poets no less than artists were engaged in the revolutionary struggle. Not since the time of Pushkin and Lermontov had Russia known such poetic fervour. It was expressed by Symbolist poets such as Blok, Konstantin Balmont, Andrei Bely, Valery Bryusov, Maximilian Voloshin and Innokenty Annensky, Acmeists such as Nikolay Gumilev and Osip Mandelstam, and Futurists such as Velimir Khlebnikov, Alexei Kruchenykh, Vasily Kamensky and Vladimir Mayakovsky. Russian poetry, moreover, was shaken for the first time in its history by the appearance of women poets. It is sufficient to name two of the brightest stars among them – Anna Akhmatova (1889–1966) and Marina Tsvetaeva (1892–1941) – for this new phenomenon in Russian culture to be brilliantly exemplified. The work of Akhmatova and Tsvetaeva illuminates the essence of the time and reveals the conditions in which the visual arts too were created. In 1917, for example, Akhmatova found herself caught up in the very vortex of Revolutionary events, and in her poetry crystalizes the dilemma of the choice between self-preservation

Marina Tsvetaeva

and patriotism which many artists and writers of the time experienced. Whereas the foreboding of catastrophe in the work of her contemporary Alexander Blok takes on a historical and philosophical dimension, for Akhmatova the dilemma remains a matter of personal fate, and is stated in a tone and form that are intimate.

The words of the great poet Marina Tsvetaeva also characterize the work of women artists of the period when she writes: 'Poets will best serve their time when they allow their time to speak through them . . . the "time" is what is significant, that by which it will be judged . . . "Contemporariness" is in itself a matter of selection. What is truly "of its time" is also outside its time — is eternal.'[5] For Tsvetaeva, what is 'contemporary' is a revelation of the dialectic characteristic of the time. Like the art of Natalya Goncharova, her writing is imbued with the power of the primitive even though it may also be theoretically profound and rationally organized. Like the art of the time, her style and language combine the prosaic with the dramatic and symbolic. In her essay 'The Poet and Time' she cites the following poem: 'A writer, if only a wave — the ocean is Russia — /Cannot but be perturbed when the element is perturbed. /A writer, if only a nerve of a great people, /Cannot but be struck when freedom is struck.'[6] It was as the nerves and voice of their time that women artists drew, painted, embroidered, sculpted, constructed and designed, as we shall see in the following chapters.

The first peak of women artists' achievement was reached in the pre-Revolutionary period, and the second was the Constructivist period of the 1920s. During the late 1920s and early 1930s women artists led two contrary developments — one of an intimate and personal character, as with the art of Antonina Sofronova, the other more publically affirmative, as with the work of Sarra Lebedeva and Vera Mukhina. The mid-1930s, however, marked another new stage, when the general development of Soviet culture suppressed female perception, and for a period its contribution ceased to be distinctive.

1 WOMEN ON THE BRINK OF MODERNISM

Maria Yakunchikova
Anna Golubkina
Zinaida Serebryakova

Zinaida Serebryakova

Anna Golubkina

Maria Yakunchikova

Maria Yakunchikova

Where there is no mystery of feeling, there is no art. A person for whom everything is simple, attainable, comprehensible, can never be an artist.

VALERY BRYUSOV[1]

At the turn of the century women's participation in Russian artistic life followed a pattern which is well exemplified in the lives and work of Maria Yakunchikova and Elena Polenova. They were both members of the Symbolist generation, and approached their work as if it was the expression of internal desires and moods. In this they reflected the prevailing artistic trends of the day in Western Europe, and yet their work was imbued with a distinctive Russian character drawn from their immersion in traditional folk-art forms. It was they who took the initiative in rescuing many traditional Russian arts and crafts from the complete oblivion which then threatened them, and their collection of Russian handicrafts, folklore and fairy tales provided the subject matter and inspiration for their creative life and work.

Maria Vasilievna Yakunchikova was born in Wiesbaden in 1870, and grew up in Moscow surrounded by members of the Russian artistic intelligentsia. Konstantin Stanislavsky, Anton and Nikolai Rubinstein and the Mamontovs were frequent visitors to the family home. In addition marital ties within the family introduced Yakunchikova to other cultured individuals. Her maternal aunt was married to the famous art collector Pavel Tretyakov, and in 1882 her sister, Natalya Vasilievna, married the artist Vasily Polenov in the first ceremony performed in the newly completed church at Abramtsevo where both had worked.

It was at this time that Yakunchikova first revealed her flair for art. 'Maria Vasilievna always loved to draw,' recalled Natalya Polenova, 'and her special talents appeared when she was about twelve. Some watercolour sketches, mostly landscapes drawn with a child's idealized imagination, have been preserved'.[2] A year later Yakunchikova began to study painting and drawing privately with the artist N. A. Martynov, and in 1885 she began attending classes at the Moscow School of Painting, Sculpture and Architecture.

The first works of art to impress Yakunchikova were the landscapes of the painter Isaak Levitan whom she met at painting evenings organized at the Polenov household during 1887–9. Here she also came to know the painters Konstantin Korovin, Sergei Ivanov, Valentin Serov, Mikhail Nesterov, and the icon-collector Ilya Ostroukhov. Maria Yakunchikova's early enthusiasm was for landscape-painting, and her oils on this theme recall the advice of Konstantin Korovin who wrote that 'landscape must not simply be depicted without purpose, it must tell the story of the soul, respond to the heart's feelings. It is an art something like music.'[3]

Yakunchikova's landscapes were always imbued with these qualities. They echo the sad and poetic note struck by Levitan and evoke a wistful and nostalgic atmosphere, expressive perhaps of the artist's own melancholy. She had contracted tuberculosis, and the recurrence of the disease necessitated many visits abroad to warmer climates.

During 1888 Yakunchikova travelled to Austria and Italy, and a year later to France and Germany. She was struck not only by the changing landscape, but also by the urban townscapes which were more industrialized than those of Russia. It was characteristic that Yakunchikova's father kept a cow which daily joined a herd to amble through the central streets of Moscow to its pastures. Whenever Yakunchikova travelled she wrote letters to her sister in which she described places principally in terms of their pictorial characteristics and overall colour harmonies. From Venice she wrote that 'the water in the canals is light-blue and soapy, a wonderful shade. The streets and canals are of such an indescribable beauty that it gives me a lump in my throat. The colours are unique and are simply represented by the word 'Venice'. The predominant colours are bluish-green, a yellowish-green, russet and a peach-pink. The main feature is the peculiar flatness of the buildings with their pointed Gothic windows, the bridges, the flights of steps and the streets which are so narrow that one can hardly walk along them with an open umbrella.'[4] Berlin was different again, 'just as in the children's books'.[5] In this respect it is interesting to compare the underlying colour structure of paintings such as *Moscow in Winter, Middle Kislovka* of 1889 (State Tretyakov Gallery), with the pictorial characteristics of the other European cities which she depicted on her travels, and which were so different from Moscow in their atmosphere, urban civilization and spiritual qualities.

Yakunchikova was often troubled by a sense of transience and this pervaded both her work and letters. *The Flame* of 1897 can be read as personally symbolic, for her life, like a flickering candle light, could so easily be extinguished. In her letters Yakunchikova gave expression to similar feelings: 'One must hurry on with life or everything will pass. All the so-called details at present pre-occupying me will have slipped away. Another mood will begin, new circumstances . . . another period of my life will start and I shall regret my unrecorded past.'[6] It was this feeling of nostalgia and her acute sense of the inevitable metamorphosis of life which characterized her work, and identified Yakunchikova with the evocative and sombre moods of Symbolism.

The Parisian context was formative in this respect. Although Yakunchikova studied at the Académie Julian, working in the studios of the academic painters Bouguereau and Fleury, she was also exposed to the then-popular Art Nouveau, and acquainted herself with contemporary artistic developments. Works such as the *Bois de Boulogne* of 1896 were filled with sinuous lines derived from Art Nouveau, and symbolic swans reminding one of Wagner's *Lohengrin* or the old Russian legend of the Swan Princess. Other paintings feature deserted mansions or old churches and convey the haunting atmosphere achieved at this time by the

Maria Yakunchikova
Park at Saint Cloud, 1898

4

1

15

Russian Symbolist painter Borisov-Musatov. Moreover her remarkable picture entitled *Fear* (Polenov Estate Museum), portraying a frightened girl rushing through a nocturnal forest, clearly alludes to Edvard Munch's *The Cry* of 1895 (National Gallery, Oslo) and, as John Bowlt points out, can be interpreted as an overture to the nervous and convulsive time of Russian Symbolism.

Russian Symbolism developed towards the end of the 1890s and was a particularly complex phenomenon. Influenced by a wide variety of literary sources such as Baudelaire, Maeterlinck, Wilde, Nietzsche and Ibsen, it also embraced mystic philosophy, the romantic existentialism of Dostoevsky's prose, the poetry of Tyutchev and Fet and the *Stürm und Drang* of German Romanticism. Russian Symbolism was romantic in its constant search for eternity in the finite, and in its subordination of reason and will to feeling and mood. Yakunchikova readily made the 'intuitive leap', and her approach to reality completely changed.

Having adopted the Symbolist aesthetic Yakunchikova began to experiment with graphic work, for the qualities of wood-engraving, etching and lithography lent themselves well to the subject-matter which preoccupied the Symbolists, while the new technique involved suited Yakunchikova's tactile and graphic propensities. Yakunchikova's first coloured etchings were produced during 1893–5, and employed complex imagery and novel subject-matter. In *Death and Flowers* a linear skull with its fantastic lines seems to fuse with a colourful pattern of flowers which symbolize life. This theme is repeated in three versions, with pale-blue, pink and pale-green backgrounds, to suggest three different emotional responses to the inevitable conjunction of life and death. The etching *The Unattainable* which features a girl with raised arms trying to fly after swallows wheeling in space is more external. However as Mikhail Kiselev points out, both *Fear* and *The Unattainable* are self-portraits and this justifies our reading of them as reflections of Yakunchikova's own emotional and psychological condition.

In her painting *The Depiction of an Intimate World* of 1894 (I. S. Weber Collection, Chêne Bougerie, Switzerland) the image again presents the mysterious combination of inner and outer worlds in the ambiguous juxtaposition of real objects with the reflection of Yakunchikova's own ephemeral and rather sad face in the window pane. The painting is both a personal expression and a representative work of Russian Symbolism. However it is interesting to note that the work of Yakunchikova, although it gave a bow to European Symbolism, remained essentially Russian. Yakunchikova was bound to her country, her house and her favourite corner of the garden, and in her diary proclaimed that it was only in studying these that one could understand the universal and the eternal.[7]

Moreover Yakunchikova never aligned herself with any European group. Having visited Paris in 1894 she wrote to Polenova that 'The Rose + Croix [a group of French Symbolists] has now become a show-booth of Symbolists, where empty-headed charlatans are gathered to shock the Parisian public with blood and depravity.'[8] She also dismissed the work of Symbolist artists such as Redon by dismissing the very basis of their works. Of his *Chevalier Mystique* she writes: 'The

Maria Yakunchikova
*From the Window of an Old
House,* 1897

knight has come with the head of his murdered mistress to the door of the temple, but the chimera guarding the entrance is shaking its head and saying that one cannot achieve immortality through punishing the vices of others (the subject is taken from a poem), but it is not so, it is not so.'[9]

Yakunchikova was no stranger to such visionary images, which Konstantin Balmont described as having 'a hidden content beyond the subject-matter'.[10] However she increasingly devoted herself to painting the subject of the forest, and the pokerwork-and-oil studies of aspen and fir trees are among her finest works. *The Window* of 1896 is no more than a pretext to depict the languid branches of the firs outside, while *Aspen and Fir-tree* of the same year presents an essentially stylized and synthetic view of nature. Yakunchikova maintained an organic link in her work with nature and natural forms. Even inanimate stone pillars seem to creep with vegetation. In this the work of Yakunchikova can be compared with that of her contemporaries, and in particular Elena Polenova.

At this time Yakunchikova had grown particularly close to Polenova, and the two artists seem to have shared a creative dialogue. As Yakunchikova sought symbolic expression in her stylized paintings of trees so Polenova's arts and crafts work was characterized at this time by stylized plant motifs which had the power, she believed, to convey inward states. In short, both artists shared the desire for symbolic depiction and followed a similar creative path. Polenova's desire to find visual expression for her inner experience is revealed in her correspondence with Yakunchikova, and there was no conflict in Polenova's mind that a style so subjective could at the same time express that 'Russian spirit' which she felt was in

2

3

the best tradition of the Russian arts and crafts. According to Wendy Salmond, 'her conviction that the modern Russian artist could, through direct subjective intuition, attain access to the world-view of the Russian peasant and capture that essence in new forms became the real cornerstone of the so-called Neo-nationalist movement'.[11]

It was under Elena Polenova's influence that Yakunchikova first developed her interest in Russian history, national design and the ancient Russian architecture such as churches and monasteries which so often occur in her paintings. It was also through Polenova's encouragement that in 1887 Yakunchikova herself began to collect folk artifacts, and wrote excitedly to her sister: 'I have already explored seven villages and have found thirteen objects . . . I am only sorry I can't show you my wooden pieces.'[12] During the early 1890s Yakunchikova divided her time between Russia and France, spending the mild winters in Paris and the warm summers on the Polenov and Mamontov estates where she immersed herself in the study of folk art and handicraft production.

When Yakunchikova returned to Paris in 1894 she organized an exhibition of applied art by women artists, and a year later undertook the organization of folk art exhibitions and began work on her astonishing series of pokerwork panels. Without neglecting easel painting, Yakunchikova also took up book-illustration and embroidery. The World of Art group commissioned graphics from her, and in 1899 she designed the cover of their magazine. Her illustration in delicate blues and yellows of a swan on a lake with borders of juniper berries and the title of the magazine *Mir Iskusstva* in ancient orthography proved one of the most evocative designs that the cover of the journal ever carried.

With Yakunchikova's pokerwork panels and embroideries we can observe the close relationship which was developing at this time between the fine and

Dresser designed by Maria Yakunchikova at the Exposition Universelle, Paris, 1900

Maria Yakunchikova in 1895

decorative arts. Each artist worked in a wide variety of media and the 'work of art' was now giving way to the product of 'artistic activity'. Besides easel painting, graphic art, pokerwork and embroidery, Yakunchikova also created remarkable textile and furniture designs, toys and ceramics. A toy model of a Russian town dating from 1899 is particularly notable, as are a child's bed with decorated panels and ten plates decorated with landscape motifs.

Following the death of Elena Polenova in 1898 Yakunchikova took charge of the embroidery workshops at Abramtsevo, and helped her sister-in-law Maria Feodorovna Yakunchikova to carry out Polenova's plans for an exhibition of Russian handicrafts at the Exposition Universelle in Paris in 1900. It was for this exhibition that Yakunchikova executed an enormous embroidered panel, *Little Girl and Wood Spirit* (I. S. Weber collection, Chêne Bougerie, Switzerland). Executed in gold, white and deep browns, this work more than any other testifies to

Yakunchikova's Symbolist leanings as well as to 'her powerful style' and the 'extraordinary scale and consistency' of her embroideries.[13]

Yakunchikova died two years later at Chêne Bougerie at the early age of thirty-two. Her untimely death was mourned by the 'World of Art' group, who dedicated a special memorial issue of their magazine to her work,[14] and by her one-time tutor, the artist and art critic Sergei Glagol, who proclaimed Yakunchikova 'the pride of our young Russian art'.[15] Yakunchikova's life may have been brief, but the path it lighted was one that other women artists would soon follow.

DOCUMENTS

Yakunchikova to Elena Polenova – 31 May 1889
. . . What if it were possible to get outside one's fate and one's deserts, to cut the threads binding us to our lives, to step aside, be forever an observer rather than a participant? Well? I think that this would be quite a bearable condition although what a difficult one![16]

Yakunchikova to Elena Polenova – 1889, Paris
Professors Bouguereau and Fleury take turns, each seeing us once a week for a month; they never correct anyone, they just give instructions and fairly general ones at that; we could manage without them. The models change every week. . . . There is the greatest freedom, you can do what you want – draw, use oils, watercolour, charcoal, pencil, work in an album or on a large sheet of paper. Once a week, on Saturdays at three o'clock, there is an anatomy lesson; a wonderful professor talks like a book but is so eloquent that you can't get it into your head . . .

[Fleury] seems to be regarded as some kind of god. He comes down on Fridays after correcting our work and sits on a stool waiting for Elise to give him some cognac . . . while everyone sits round him, watching his lips. . . . He has a habit of sniffing in front of a bad picture. They all seem to be afraid of that. I don't know any of his other qualities.[17]

Yakunchikova to Elena Polenova – 28 October 1889, Paris
. . . I think that if I ever paint a picture, it will be in Russia and not here.[18]

Elena Polenova to Yakunchikova – 22 May 1892
. . . I very much sympathize with and approve of your involvement in ceramics and etchings, these are wonderful. It is dry and dull to draw only for paintings and as studies. It is somehow lifeless, and where there is art there should be life – it is necessary to move around, to bustle, so as not to get bored or come to a standstill.[19]

Konstantin Somov to Alexander Somov – 1897
She is now an interesting artist, which is very unusual for a woman. She draws well, she has a fine and individual feeling for colour, her technique is masculine. . . . I haven't yet seen what she is going to send, but it is good that tomorrow I shall go to her and see. She is also interesting as a person, she is understanding, and not indifferent.[20]

1 **Maria Yakunchikova**
Bois de Boulogne, 1896

2 **Maria Yakunchikova**
The Window, 1896

3 **Maria Yakunchikova**
Aspen and Fir-tree, 1896

4 **Maria Yakunchikova**
The Flame, 1897

5 **Maria Yakunchikova**
*Church of the Old Estate of Cheremushka,
near Moscow*, 1897

6 **Anna Golubkina** *Manka*, 1898

7 **Anna Golubkina**
*Portrait of the artist's grandfather,
Polikarp Golubkin, 1892*

8 **Anna Golubkina**
*Portrait of the patron and art-collector
Savva Morozov, 1902*

9 **Anna Golubkina**
Walking Man, 1903

10 **Anna Golubkina**
Little Fox, 1902

11 **Anna Golubkina**
Karl Marx, 1905

< 12 **Anna Golubkina**
*Portrait of the writer Alexei
Mikhailovich Remizov*, 1911

13 **Anna Golubkina**
Old Woman (Old Age), 1907

14 **Anna Golubkina**
Female portrait, 1908

15 **Anna Golubkina**
*Portrait of the writer Alexei
Nikolaevich Tolstoy, 1911*

16 **Anna Golubkina**
*Portrait of Professor Vladimir Ern,
1914*

Anna Golubkina

Her pictorially formless shapes of bronze or marble suggest the union of two opposing elements, inert matter and rebellious spirit struggling to free itself from its fetters.

ELENA MURINA[1]

Sculpture played a distinctive role in Russian art of the early twentieth century, and it is notable that it was a woman who was the pioneer and leader in this field. After a long period of crisis it was Anna Golubkina who almost single-handedly introduced a renaissance in the medium of sculpture. Golubkina was one of the new generation of artists who searched for fresh expressive possibilities with which to convey contemporary life and, although the names of Pavel Trubetskoy and Sergei Konenkov are justly revered, it was the work of Golubkina which stood out as the brightest phenomenon in the sculpture of the period. When the poet Maximilian Voloshin characterized the Russian genius as being 'exclusively moral' and inflamed by 'the fire of conscience'[2] it was Anna Golubkina that he had in mind, for it was she who expressed these qualities in her work more consistently and strikingly than any other artist of her time.

Anna Semyonovna Golubkina was born in the town of Zaraysk in the region of Ryazan in 1864. Her father was a market gardener, but the poverty of the large family precluded any formal education. Golubkina was never schooled, but instead educated herself using the library of a Zaraysk merchant. Her artistic training began in 1889 when she was taught by the sculptor S. M. Volnukhin whose work represented the highest achievement of Russian sculpture in the nineteenth century. Two years later, in 1891, she studied with the painter Sergei Ivanov at the Moscow School of Painting, Sculpture and Architecture, and in 1894 she began work in the studio of V. A. Beklemishev at the Higher Art Institute which was attached to the St Petersburg Academy of Fine Arts.

Golubkina derived a lively approach to clay and plaster from her studies with Volnukhin and Beklemishev, but her early works such as the posthumous portrait of her grandfather *Polikarp Golubkin* of 1892 are above all descriptive. Golubkina quickly felt the limitations of this method, which conveyed neither the stirring nature of the times nor her intense thoughts about the fate of mankind. 'Beklemishev is a very great artist,' wrote Golubkina in 1894, 'but I don't agree with him. I can only concede that he introduces psychology into sculpture, which has scarcely ever happened before. I have looked and listened and been endlessly surprised. Finally, I have concluded that one must work in one's own way, be it good or bad. Beklemishev doesn't force his will on his pupils, but nonetheless you have to be stubborn to remain yourself. In all my work there is a certain lack of restraint. They say that this will result in something good but that hasn't happened

Anna Golubkina in the 1890s

7

Anna Golubkina in her Paris studio, in front of *Old Age* (left) and other works

yet . . . I want to stay independent . . . I am sick of all the imitations.'[3] The artist's increasing perception of sculptural qualities together with her progressive thinking did indeed lead to innovatory conclusions in later years, beginning with her *Walking Man* of 1903 in which she expresses an abstract idea in vigorous concrete form.

Golubkina's path could not but cross with that of Auguste Rodin, and in the autumn of 1895 Golubkina left the St Petersburg Academy of Arts for Paris. However she failed to enter Rodin's studio, and studied instead with the Italian sculptor Filippo Colarossi. Although Golubkina shared her Parisian lodgings with two other young Russian women artists, E. S. Kruglikova and E. N. Shevtsova, she found herself at a complete loss in the city. She had no money, nowhere to go and no-one to go with, and within a year she had returned to St Petersburg.[4]

It was only on her second visit to Paris in 1897 that Golubkina made the acquaintance of Rodin, and while she could not afford to study with him, Golubkina managed to set up her own studio and occasionally consulted him. However Rodin was not so much her teacher as a kindred spirit and example. Golubkina was able to accept Rodin's powerful influence while remaining creatively independent and pre-eminently a Russian woman artist. For example both sculpted the subject of *Old Age* working from the same model. A comparison of the two sculptures reveals Golubkina's independence at this point particularly well. In the Rodin one feels regret for the ephemeral nature of physical beauty while Golubkina subordinates her form to the sorrow of human destiny caused by the endless chain of suffering which has moulded the Russian people. Elena Murina wrote of Golubkina that 'her talent, temperament and perception corresponded to her time, which demanded that the artist should transcend the detail of daily life and perceive human life on a more general level'.[5]

Golubkina treated the theme of childhood in a similar manner. In a marble bust entitled *Manka* of 1898 she relied on the language of plasticity to translate her perception of the tragedy of life. As her subject she chose a child with rickets, and in her sculpture Golubkina presents the over-large forehead, swollen eyes, and the lips still childishly full but trembling with affliction. An air of suffering permeates all of Golubkina's portraits in this early period. They evoke the difficult life people faced at the time, their disturbing visions of the future, the contradictions they experienced, their hunger for good and intolerance of evil.

The painter Nikolai Ulyanov, who taught with Golubkina during 1901–3, referred to her as 'an Antigone, an Electra, dominated by the idea of retribution'. Vengeance certainly became one of the main themes of Golubkina's work and is particularly evident in her sculpture *Walking Man* of 1903. This work invites comparison with Rodin's famous sculpture *The Striding Man* of 1877 (Musée Rodin, Paris). However, whereas Rodin at this stage was primarily interested in proportion, anatomy, and the rendering of movement, Golubkina evokes a threatening and menacing quality. Her *Walking Man* seems to arise, like a primordial creature, out of the very earth itself and, taking its first stumbling steps, it confronts the future threatening revenge for the human condition into which it has been born.

Throughout her life Golubkina returned to the theme of old age, and during the first decade of the century her portraits of old people acquire a Rembrandt-like strength. *Old Woman* of 1906 (State Tretyakov Gallery) appears in two versions both of which are equally important in revealing something of Golubkina's working methods. In the first version she reveals her interest in the unique physical features of her model, while in the second Golubkina attempts to generalize the image and make a universal statement about the condition of old age. In conveying the 'universality' of her message Golubkina relies on both the nature of the material she is using and on various compositional features. In her book *Some Words on the Sculptor's Craft*[6] Golubkina writes at length about the significance of the material used to create particular works. Clay is used for the first stage of her perception and plaster for fixing that stage. However in the final execution, the nature of the medium itself, be it stone, metal, wood, or even marble, contributes to the work's meaning. Marble, being sculpture's most durable material, naturally evokes a timeless quality. Moreover Golubkina discovered that 'the universal' could be achieved through simplified forms and stylization. In *Old Woman* the headscarf frames a contemporary face and suggests time and wisdom. The model turns into the concept 'old woman' and the concrete portrait into a symbolic statement about old age.

Golubkina's passionate humanistic convictions led her to play a role in the revolutionary events of 1905. In that year she completed the first Russian portrait of *Karl Marx* and donated the fee she received to a fund for homeless workers.

31

Moreover her own home was used as a temporary hospital and canteen. Golubkina was watched by the police for a time, and then in 1907 she was arrested for distributing documents calling on the peasantry to 'overthrow the Tsar and the Government'. In court Golubkina admitted to the offence but announced that she did not consider it a crime. Nonetheless she was imprisoned and went on hunger strike as a mark of protest.[7]

These events clearly affected her, and in 1907 she wrote to Rodin: 'I had hoped to create something splendid and enduring that would demonstrate my gratitude to you. . . . Now I no longer have any hope of creating what I wanted, and so I am writing to you. . . . Your words had great significance for me. Previously all my teachers with the exception of one of the oldest, the Moscow sculptor Ivanov, had told me that I was on the wrong path. Their condemnations troubled me but could not change me because I did not believe them. When I saw your work I thought "if this artist were to say the same, then I should listen to him". You cannot imagine the joy I felt when you, the best of artists, told me what I myself already felt, and gave me the chance to be free. . . . I am writing now because we are passing through very stormy times and no⁄one knows what turn events will take. Everyone is being imprisoned and I have been in prison once. While I live I shall always venerate you as a great artist and the person who gave me the possibility of life.'[8]

Following her release from prison Golubkina rented a studio in Moscow where she worked for the rest of her life, and in the decade before the revolution she became famous for her portrait busts of the leading intellectual and literary figures of her day. Her portraits include a remarkable brooding bust of the writer *Alexei Mikhailovich Remizov* of 1911. Here Golubkina chose wood as an appropriate

12

Anna Golubkina, second left, with her relatives in the yard of their home in Zaraysk in 1908

Anna Golubkina, on the left, in her Moscow studio in 1903

material and emphasized the chiselled furrows of the surface. This technique revealed the soft yet resistant qualities of the wood and so suggested the complex and contradictory nature of the writer. Her portrait of another literary figure, the Russian and Soviet writer *Alexei Nikolaevich Tolstoy*, expresses his essentially serene nature. This in fact was the first of Golubkina's works to represent an optimistic view of life, but there again, Tolstoy was no ordinary model. The sculptor Efimov noted that Golubkina would often talk about the 'ordinary' behaviour of her models. 'I pointed', Efimov remembered, 'to the wooden bust of Alexei Tolstoy. "And what about that one?" "Oh, him. He guzzled oysters."'[9]

15

Her portrait of the Symbolist poet and critic *Andrei Bely* of 1907 is one of the most strongly symbolic. Golubkina herself said 'I did not make the person, I made the poet'. On the other hand the portrait of Professor *Vladimir Ern* of 1914 received a more sober and classical treatment appropriate to the scholarly intellectual he was. Ern later described his sittings for Golubkina who was, he said, 'coarse in her speech, direct, from a peasant background. She is often hungry but gives away 500 roubles at a time. She mutters rather than speaks. She looks so seriously and deeply that you feel awkward, and then she smiles with a wonderful child-like smile. . . . It seems to me that sculpting is for her a way to perceive people.'[10]

16

During 1914–15 Golubkina arranged a personal exhibition in Moscow to raise funds for the war-wounded. In all she displayed 150 of her sculptures, representing her work over almost a quarter of a century. 'At last', wrote a contemporary, 'Russian sculpture has reached that joyful stage where it can have its own exhibitions. Up till now sculpture was only an adjunct to painting: statues were simply there like pieces of furniture. Golubkina's chisel does not reveal the beauty of human life nor the joys of a happy existence. She has devoted her strength and talent to revealing the abnormal life of the city which forces men to heavy physical toil and drives women to vice. The stamp of want and degeneration is impressed on the faces of children. Russian sculpture has never been so close to contemporary life. It has never before seized the heart of the viewer so profoundly as at this exhibition, organized during the war-time suffering to help the victims of the conflict. It is nonetheless a festival of Russian sculpture which is a welcome addition to our lives.'[11]

17–19

When serious illness interrupted her work on large-scale projects Golubkina began working on a small scale. During the early 1920s she executed delicate cameos such as *Neptune, Female Face* and *Borzoi*. Small as these relief sculptures were, Golubkina compressed into them the same ingenuity and power which characterized her larger pieces. Golubkina also taught in these years, and contributed all her strength and zeal to post-Revolutionary art. In 1923 she published her book *Some Words on the Sculptor's Craft* in which she presented not only her professional experience but also her moral stance. For example, she writes that artists are totally reflected in their work, down to their smallest thoughts, and any falsity or deliberate pursuit of success will show as a flaw in their work.

Anna Golubkina
Portrait of the writer L.N. Tolstoy, 1927

20

As Golubkina's illness progressed, in the hardest time of her life, she created her most harmonious sculptures. Particularly notable is her portrait bust of *Lev Tolstoy* of 1927 in which Golubkina forsook a naturalistic representation in favour of a powerful and flowing sculpture which conveyed the scale of the writer's personality. In contrast the sculptor's last and unfinished work *Little Birch-tree* is both charming and graceful in its supple uprightness. It is significant that as her parting statement to the world Golubkina should bequeath an image not of vengeance, old age or sorrow but that of a young girl fanned by a gentle breeze, an image of youth and clarity. Perhaps Golubkina had finally realized that the future did not belong to either the old or the vengeful but to children such as these.

As Elena Murina aptly concludes, Golubkina eludes categorization: 'How can one be a revolutionary influenced by decadence, a Realist inspired by Symbolism, a daughter of the people who speaks in mystical tones?'[12] These apparent contradictions can only be explained by the fact that Golubkina's work reflects the complex times through which she lived, and it is this which contributed to the intensity and depth of her approach, and to the strong and organic qualities of her work.

DOCUMENTS

Golubkina to her friend Elena Glagoleva – 1907, Zaraysk
You ask if you can do anything to help me? This is what you can most certainly do. You know some rich people, get them to buy something of mine. My marble things are in Moscow, at Nikolay Pavlovich Ulyanov's. . . . If you manage to do this, I shall be extremely happy. You know, previously I simply hoped, but now the lid has slammed very tightly over me. . . . Prison is nothing, I am not afraid of that . . .[13]

Golubkina to the artist Lidya Gubina – 1909, Zaraysk
. . . You need to spend two days in the Louvre, one looking at the sculpture, the other at the paintings. Don't forget the Mona Lisa, you could easily walk right past it.

Don't forget the portraits by Titian and Van Dyck, then go straight on to the Venus de Milo without stopping. Have a look at the Roman busts beside her. The Luxembourg, the Trocadero, the sculptures of the Renaissance. Downstairs in the Louvre are Michelangelo and Carpeaux. The Luxembourg is small, you'll be able to see everything at one go. Climb up Nôtre Dame. It isn't worth going to the Zoological Garden or to the Cluny Museum, it would only confuse your impressions. You won't get tired in the London museums; everything is displayed so well. Look there at the encrusted boxes from where all the Burlyuks were born. The main great thing there is the Assyrian sculpture. They've also got stuff from Egypt but it's a bit broken. In Berlin, Gubina, there is Egypt, Pekin, the Japanese and Holbein. In London there's Westminster Abbey. Well, Rodin, you'll see for yourself. In the evening get on a horse and have a ride – keeping your eyes open . . .[14]

Golubkina to the artist and designer Alexandra Khotyaintseva – September 1913, Moscow
. . . You know that I've been teaching some courses and some workers have rejected my teaching because I am so demanding. You know in art I can't let anything slip and I am afraid that some kind of incident will take place again. Where art is concerned I turn into a different person, and can't answer for my own behaviour.[15]

Golubkina at home: reminiscences of Adrian Efimov, son of the artist Nina Simonovich-Efimova, who lived as a child in the building where Golubkina had her studio
On 7 September 1987, sixty years from the date of Anna Golubkina's death, about twenty of her friends gathered in her studio-museum. The Museum Director, Nelli Alexandrovna, asked us to talk about Anna Semyonovna as we sat round the table with the samovar.

In the studio in which we are sitting there is no contrast between what I see and what I remember. There's still the same wallpaper, the same shelves on the walls, the stands for sculptures, the podium. Yet there's something not quite right. Perhaps it's the atmosphere, the smell? Then it used to smell of fresh clay, of plaster. Anna Semyonovna would choose her clay in a very expert way – it was the material she used for the majority of her works, it was her 'work companion'. Anna Semyonovna wrote remarkably about clay in her book. It also used to smell of birch wood – a living fire . . . although it is true that Anna Semyonovna frequently could not afford fuel.

My parents would often go to Anna Semyonovna's even after they had moved to a different flat by the Twenties . . . I would sit on the divan and listen. My parents went to Anna Semyonovna as to a wise ascetic. Nina Yakovlevna used to say that going to her meant reassessing oneself, because Anna Semyonovna delved deeply. She would demand complete communication from others although she wouldn't give much away about herself. Ivan Semyonovich used to say that it was impossible to think low thoughts or tell lies anywhere near her. Probably my memory is stronger on sights and smells than on sounds because I cannot remember Anna Semyonovna's words although I know that she used to talk to me. I remember one sentence of hers (though I probably remember it through Nina Yakovlevna):

Anna Golubkina with her nieces in Zaraysk in 1906

'People who come after us — we shall talk to them.' By 'we', she meant her sculptures. Her sculptures see into our souls. People should learn to hear as well as see Anna Semyonovnas's sculptures . . .

Vera Nikolaevna told how when Golubkina was working on her sculpture of *Hummock*, using children as models, she put them in the bath and forgot about washing them, she so admired them covered in soap . . .

She wanted to sculpt the carpenter Bednyakov, but he had a bath, cut his hair and shaved, and so she threw him out . . .

She fell out with Gorky. She waited, got ready, but he did not come. When he next saw her, he said 'I was busy. When shall I come?' She replied 'Now I'm busy.' She was not offended, of course. It was just that something was destroyed in her . . .[16]

Memories of Golubkina by E. B. Levina
The first teachers of my mother [Eva Rozengolts-Levina] whom I remember her talking about all the time were the sculptors Erzya [S. Nefedov] and Anna Golubkina . . . Golubkina was Eva Pavlovna's second teacher. That would have been in about 1920, in either the Free State Workshops or the Higher Arts and Technical Workshops. . . . Mother always used to say that Anna Semyonovna did a great deal both to educate her character and to establish her as an artist. . . . She described her as 'severe looking, reserved, in a simple skirt, almost nineteenth-century peasant style, with a cardigan on top. She smoked a lot. She was masculine.' Then she would interrupt herself to say enthusiastically, 'She was a Tolstoyan, a friend of Chertkov's.'

Mother said that Golubkina at first seemed to ignore her. This upset her, as she thought that Golubkina considered her frivolous — she sometimes missed classes because she was meeting someone. Anna Semyonovna thought a personal life was an obstacle to creativity. Once mother could not restrain herself and called her over. Anna Semyonovna looked at what she had done and said: 'Stop working and don't touch clay until you experience joy.' 'I did not know what joy was, and I did not know what it meant to find it. I thought about this all the time and even stopped going to classes. But once, going into the studio, I saw the work of a woman-friend of mine, it made me ecstatic and after that I wanted to work.' Before long mother was alone with one other pupil in the studio and they were so bound up in their work that they did not notice that a fire had broken out — the heating was from a stove. Anna Semyonovna herself dragged them unconscious out on to the snow. After that Golubkina changed her attitude to her. She would make comments on her work, and mother almost became her favourite pupil. I remember mother saying how Anna Semyonovna taught them to see colour in stone and to feel its breathing. Mother said that Golubkina noticed her aptitude for colour when they were doing some polychrome sculpture.

I can't remember why mother left Golubkina's studio. Perhaps it was because of Anna Semyonovna's illness, or more probably because of her own desire to study painting. One important aspect of their relationship is that after some time Golubkina apologised for her attitude at the beginning. It made a strong impression on Eva Pavlovna that a great sculptor could apologise to a young girl-pupil. She valued this as a sign of her large spirit.[17]

17 **Anna Golubkina**
Borzoi, shell cameo, 1922–3

18 **Anna Golubkina**
Female Face, shell cameo, 1922–3

19 **Anna Golubkina**
Neptune, shell cameo, 1922–3

20 Anna Golubkina
Little Birch-tree, 1927

21 *Evgeny and Maria Lanceray, parents of Zinaida Serebryakova,* in 1877

22 **Zinaida Serebryakova**
Bleaching Linen, 1917

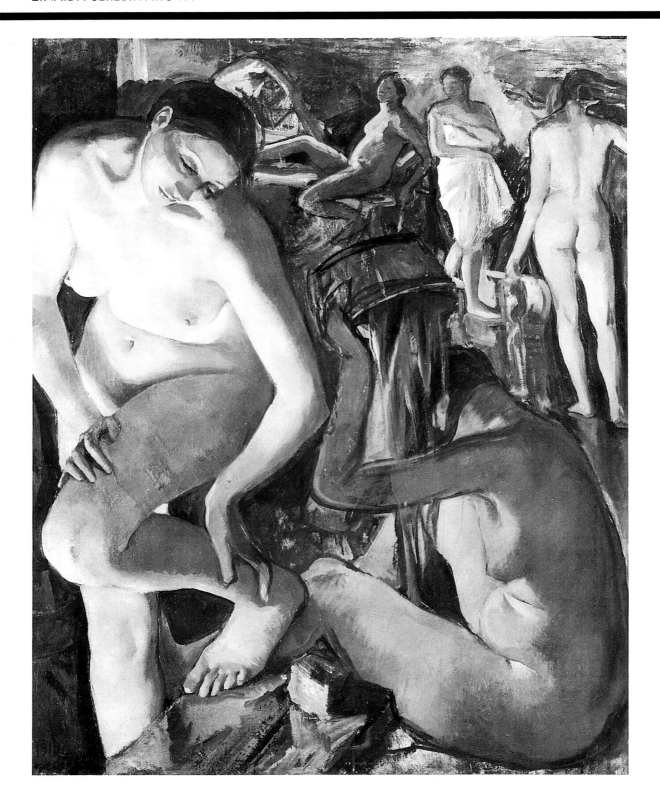

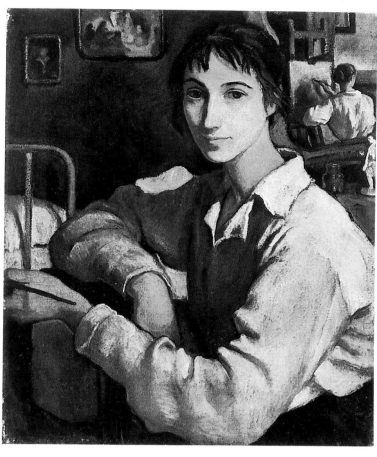

23 **Zinaida Serebryakova**
Bathhouse (study), 1912

24 **Zinaida Serebryakova**
Self-portrait, 1922

25 **Zinaida Serebryakova**
The House of Cards, 1919

26 **Zinaida Serebryakova** *Self-portrait at the Dressing-table*, 1909

Zinaida Serebryakova

All Serebryakova's art is free, and it is full of a gaiety
which reflects the conditions of joyful emotion in
which the artist works.[1]

ALEXANDER BENOIS

Zinaida Serebryakova was born on the estate of Neskuchnoe near Kharkov in
1884, and although she grew up in a milieu very different from Anna Golubkina's
she possessed a similar independence of spirit. Her contemporaries found it difficult
to appreciate the complex interaction between Russian Realism and personal
expression in Serebryakova's work, but perhaps it was Alexander Benois who
characterized her individuality best of all, not only in the above quotation but also
when he wrote: 'Serebryakova's paintings are recognizable among thousands, but
it's not a question of this or that style. Their family resemblance arises from the fact
that all were created in a similar state of excitement and with similar inspiration.
The technical aspect is always subordinated to the emotional.'[2] These qualities in
Serebryakova's art arose from the happiness of her family life, although in her
childhood and maturity she experienced both pain and struggle.

Serebryakova was fortunate to be born into the intellectual and cultured
Lanceray-Benois family which was well known both inside and outside Russia.
Her father was the sculptor Evgeny Lanceray, while her two brothers Evgeny and
Nikolai were also professionally involved with the arts. Evgeny was a talented
painter and graphic artist and a leading member of the 'World of Art' group,
while Nikolai was a well-known architect. On her mother's side was the Benois
family who kept open house for painters, architects, actors and musicians. Her
maternal grandfather, Nikolai Benois, was an architect and her maternal uncles,
Alexander and Nikolai, were both well-known artists and respected members of
the 'World of Art'.

In 1886 when her father died the young Serebryakova went to live in the Benois
household. 'Coming to us at about two,' wrote Alexander Benois, 'she grew up a
long way from my study where all our conversations and ideas occurred. Zina grew
up as a rather ailing and unsociable child, in which she resembled her father, and
not at all her mother or brothers and sisters, who were all merry and sociable.'[3]

Nevertheless this environment was a fertile one, and in 1901 Serebryakova spent
a month in Princess Tenisheva's school at Talashkino which was headed by Ilya
Repin. It was here that her vocation as an artist was established. During 1902–3
Serebryakova visited Italy where she studied the work of the Venetian masters. On
her return she was tutored by the artist Osip Braz, and in 1905 she went to Paris to
study painting at the Académie de la Grande Chaumière. Here she visited the
museums and developed an admiration for the work of Watteau and Fragonard as

21

Zinaida Serebryakova
(Lanceray) as a child in her
mother's arms, among her
brothers and sisters

well as the Impressionists, particularly Renoir, Monet and Degas. On her return to
Russia in 1906 she struck the art world with the maturity of her talent. Benois for
example recalled that 'At about twenty-two, Zinaida Serebryakova to everyone's
surprise turned out to be a fully-fledged artist, she was in the same camp as the rest of
us, following the same directions and having the same tastes. She joined the World
of Art group as a matter of course. We were delighted to welcome such a
fascinating talent to our ranks.'[4]

The World of Art group played a crucial role at this time in preparing the way
for Russian modernism. Led by Sergei Diaghilev, artists such as Benois, Bakst,
Lanceray and Dobuzhinsky tried to promote the concept of 'national art'.
However it was not only Yakunchikova's adoption of folk art principles which
inspired them, but also a broad and cosmopolitan attitude to 'all that had been
created in Russia', including architecture and painting influenced by Western
styles and taste. The group believed that Russian art could only play a vital role in
the European context if artists were widely cultured, and understood not only their
own artistic heritage but also the history of art and the nature of contemporary
artistic developments. The idea of style as opposed to naturalistic representation was
also a central feature of their ideology. For this reason they adopted an 'art for art's
sake' position, and concerned themselves with the formal aspects of painting. In
particular the concept of beauty was important for them. Both Diaghilev and
Benois claimed that they were attempting to rescue art from the critical realist
tradition of the preceding generation, and were trying to 'bring into life the
principle of calm unity – in other words of true beauty' and once again to make art
an expression of people's natural instinct for beauty. In this their work was marked
by a certain retrospectivism, as each artist sought inspiration in the ideal styles from

At the Talashkino artists' colony, near Smolensk. The frieze is by the 'World of Art' artist Nicholas Roerich

the past, Bakst in Greece, Benois in the tastes of Versailles and Evgeny Lanceray in eighteenth-century St Petersburg.

In this context Serebryakova was chiefly influenced by the idea of 'national art' and the concept of 'beauty' which the World of Art were trying to recreate. However unlike her colleagues, Serebryakova found her themes and inspiration in contemporary life and her Russian surroundings, so that for her there was never any question of retrospectivism. Her enthusiasm for self-portraiture is characteristic, and the painting *Self-portrait at the Dressing-table* of 1909 made an immediate and strong impact on her contemporaries. Benois declared that he was amazed by the painting, and described her work as being fresh, direct and captivating, without following any routines or formulae. Serebryakova often returned to this genre, as in *Girl with a Candle* and *Pierrot*, and sometimes used her sister as a model because of their close resemblance.

26

Serebryakova exhibited her *Self-portrait* in the exhibition organized by the 'Union of Russian Artists' in St Petersburg in 1910. This was the first exhibition to which she had contributed, and the fact that the Tretyakov Gallery purchased the *Self-portrait* following the closure of the exhibition marked Serebryakova out as an artist of prestigious talent. Indeed contemporary critics such as Benois saw especial value in her search for 'a healthy and cheerful realism' devoid of any 'modernistic refinements', and declared that 'the simple real-life atmosphere illuminated by youth is joyous and lovely.'[5] Thus, although a contemporary subject and quite unlike the work of her World of Art colleagues, Serebryakova's *Self-portrait* fulfilled Benois' call for beauty in art in a novel and charming way.

The painting also represents an expression of Serebryakova's own personal happiness at this time in her life. In 1905 she had married the railway engineer Boris

Serebryakov and the children she had by this marriage brought her great joy. The same happy atmosphere which is evident in *Self-portrait* also characterizes the series of paintings which feature her children. The delightful painting *At Dinner* of 1914 (State Tretyakov Gallery) is an optimistic and harmonious work but is in no way sentimental, as are portraits such as *Portrait of a Student* of 1909 and those of *E. K. Lanceray* and *N. P. Chulkova* of 1910. Serebryakova's nudes also express her interest in the epic and the ideal. For Benois these paintings of the nude were 'the chief glory of her work, there is nothing quite like them. In these studies of the female body we find not merely natural quality but a special quality familiar to us from literature and music.'[6]

23

The call by the World of Art for 'national art' also found expression in Serebryakova's work in an important series of peasant paintings such as *Mid-day* (State Russian Museum) and *Harvest*. These paintings depict peasant women and peasant labour, and link her work not only with the main thematic tradition of Russian art of the second half of the nineteenth century, but also with the early nineteenth-century artist Venetsianov. Serebryakova was captivated by Venetsianov's peasant paintings in which the harmony of nature finds expression in the ordered and happy peasant life which he depicts. 'I cannot see sufficient of this wonderful artist,' she wrote, and, although Serebryakova's paintings are based on her experience of peasant life at the family estate of Neskuchnoe, she follows in Venetsianov's footsteps by depicting her subjects at rest after labour.

Serebryakova, like her colleagues in the World of Art, also had a keen sense of preserving what was fine in artistic tradition. Consequently the subjects of some of her peasant paintings such as *Bleaching Linen* of 1917 are expressed with all the monumentality of form and rhythmicality of composition derived from her admiration of Titian and Tintoretto, Rubens and Poussin. Executed from a low viewpoint, the picture elevates the simple yet bold forms of the peasants and conveys an almost mythological quality. The painting speaks not only of the 'beauty' which Benois and Diaghilev advocated but also of their attempt to create a national art with its roots in the traditions of the past. It was in works such as these that Serebryakova found her most individual and personal expression. *Bleaching Linen* is clearly allegorical, and follows on from a series of decorative paintings executed in 1916 for Kazan Station in Moscow in which Serebryakova personified the countries of the Orient by beautiful eastern women.[7]

22

Benois wrote that he felt he must overcome his scruples against praising the work of his own niece to state that 'Serebryakova is truly one of the most remarkable Russian artists of our time'.[8] In January 1917 Serebryakova was proposed for the title of Academician of Art, and had she been elected she would have been the first woman in the history of Russian art to receive the honour. However the Revolution intervened and the meeting at which her election was expected was never held.

The revolutionary storm swept Serebryakova aside as it did most artists. In 1918 a fire at Neskuchnoe destroyed not only Serebryakova's house but also many of her paintings which were stored there. Then in 1919 her husband died of typhus.

Zinaida Serebryakova at
Neskuchnoe, 1907

Serebryakova was left to support four children and her ailing mother, and in 1920 the family moved to Petrograd. As the artist Anna Ostroumova-Lebedeva wrote: 'she unwillingly abandoned Neskuchnoe for Petrograd where they lived in extreme poverty . . . Her works were taken by unscrupulous dealers in exchange for food and second-hand clothes.'[9]

During this period Serebryakova continued to paint and draw and executed several portraits and landscapes. Particularly moving and relevant to her personal circumstances was her painting *The House of Cards* of 1919. Here Serebryakova 25 again depicts her children, but now they wear worn and wearied expressions. Clarity has turned to unease, peacefulness to uncertainty. Rather than looking out of the picture as they do in earlier works their attention is centred on the ephemeral house of cards.

Serebryakova's despairing efforts to recapture the ideas of beauty, grace and harmony are evident in the ballet drawings in which she used her daughter Tatyana and other children as models. Such works as *Ballerina in the Dressing Room* (Zilbershtein Collection, Moscow) and *Snowflakes from Tchaikovsky's Ballet 'The Nutcracker'* (State Russian Museum) are executed in the new and more direct technique of pastel on cardboard. As Serebryakova later recalled, 'I use pastels as if they were ordinary crayons, only retouching and sometimes shading'.[10]

In 1924 Serebryakova left Petrograd for Paris to execute a commission for a large mural, and remained there, hoping to be able to earn a livelihood. Unfortunately the circumstances of the times prevented her return and she was to spend the rest of her life in exile among people who, as she wrote, did not understand 'simple Russian art', and in an environment whose art she herself was unable to accept. Her daughter later recalled: 'Mother felt keenly the separation from her homeland. She experienced great difficulties because of poverty, illness and approaching old age. Despite all this she preserved her interest in national art and did not alter her position. She was true to herself to the end of her days.'[11] Serebryakova travelled widely, visiting Brittany, Algeria and Morocco, and continued to paint popular life in a realist style. The common folk always appealed to her, and perhaps the most impressive works of this period were her portraits of the Brittany peasants. However in 1966, a year before her death, the Soviet state officially recognized her contribution to Russian art and organized a large touring exhibition of her work. The art historian Dimitrii Sarabyanov wrote of her that 'sometimes critics wanting to praise a woman artist talk about her 'masculine hand'. Even Benois once called Serebryakova's work 'masculine'. Yet it seems to me that what is most valuable in Serebryakova's work is what comes from her being a woman.'[12]

Zinaida Serebryakova was never a radical or avant-garde artist, and to the last she remained a staunch critic of abstract and non-objective art. Yet the World of Art group of which she had become such an integral member opened the way for modernism through the ideas that it propounded in its magazine and exhibitions. It is a sad fact that the art of the avant-garde which emerged indirectly from their efforts was totally incomprehensible to them. Both Serebryakova and the World of Art failed to recognize that in destroying conventional disciplines, the avant-garde maintained their synthesist traditions although in a different way, and like themselves united the arts more closely. It was the pioneering example of women artists such as Yakunchikova, Golubkina and Serebryakova which focused the aims of the avant-garde and led them on to new means of expression.

DOCUMENTS

Konstantin Somov, painter and graphic artist – 11 February 1915
Shura [Alexander Benois] showed a sketch by Z. Serebryakova for the ceiling of the Kazan Railway Station – it shows a very beautifully depicted, exotic female nude . . . I am thinking of buying it . . .

Konstantin Somov to A. A. Mikhailova – 4 April 1927, Paris
I haven't yet been to her exhibition [at the Galerie Charpentier] but from what she and others have said it is clear that here too she acted clumsily . . . she didn't turn up to hang her pictures herself and when she saw how they had been hung she was terribly displeased.

Serebryakova to T. B. Serebryakova – 22 November 1955, Paris
I long to be with you on the banks of the Moscow River and walking in Kolomenskoe . . . Now I have grown so timid with old age that I cannot take the decision to abandon my Shurik and Katya, and this is a torment for me . . . I have decided to leave some of my most characteristic things (there are terribly few of them) to a collection or museum in the USSR. For here there are such confused ideas about art that they cannot understand simple Russian art. And I am no longer trying to show my things to a completely blind society . . .

2 THE AMAZONS OF THE AVANT-GARDE

Natalya Goncharova
Olga Rozanova
Lyubov Popova
Alexandra Exter
Varvara Stepanova
Nadezhda Udaltsova

Nadezhda Udaltsova

Varvara Stepanova

Lyubov Popova

Alexandra Exter

Natalya Goncharova

Olga Rozanova

Natalya Goncharova

She has the courage of a Mother Superior. A directness of features and views. She rarely smiles but when she does it's delightful. Her gestures are brief and meaningful. Such is Goncharova with her modernity, her innovation, her success, her fame, her glory, her fashion – she has everything to tempt – but no! She did not lead a permanent school, she did not convert a one-time discovery into a method and did not canonize . . . To sum her up? In short: talent and hard work.

MARINA TSVETAEVA[1]

Maria Yakunchikova, Anna Golubkina and Zinaida Serebryakova each in their own way contributed to the revolutionary processes in the art of the early twentieth century. We can see in Maria Yakunchikova's work in several genres the renewal of traditional Russian art combined with the troubled atmosphere of Symbolism. Zinaida Serebryakova represents a harmonious synthesis – the peasant subject-matter of nineteenth-century Russian Realism brought into the twentieth century. Anna Golubkina was a rebel, rejecting the harmonious resolutions to which recent rebellions against academicism had led. She was a prophet of future cataclysms. These women artists were near-contemporaries, and their differences, even oppositions, are the clearest sign of the complexity of the developments taking place. The historical forces of their time were evidently experienced with extreme acuity by women artists, and when mounting pressure required a new analysis of reality, then women artists came to the fore.

Natalya Goncharova was both an artist and an innovator. Her career does not fit our ordinary conception of a woman artist whose painting expresses artistic sensitivity but whose art has a 'domestic and dilettante character'. Goncharova claimed the role of leader of the emergent avant-garde, an initiator of new paths in art, and as Sarabyanov notes, she led the way to a new type of femininity characterized not by weakness but by strength and frenzied preaching.[2]

Natalya Sergeevna Goncharova was born in 1881 in the village of Negaevo and spent much of her childhood at her grandparent's estate at Ladyzhino, in the province of Tula in Central Russia, where the family owned a linen mill. Her family had distinguished connections. Her father was an architect and her great-aunt, also called Natalya Goncharova, had married the poet Pushkin. As a young girl Natalya delighted in the life of the countryside, and especially in the songs, handicrafts and customs of the peasants.

Goncharova's early years have been portrayed with particular understanding by the poet Marina Tsvetaeva, who was a neighbour of the Goncharov family in Moscow and in later years became friendly with the artist in Paris. 'At the age of twelve,' Tsvetaeva wrote, 'Goncharova was carried off to the town. She was carried off like a corpse, for her entire soul was "where the grass grows up through the stones, or better still where there are no stones at all."' In Moscow her hatred of stone was increased when she attended a stone school – High School No. 4 –

where she considered that seven years of her life were completely wasted. When asked by her headmistress what she liked about being there, she replied 'nothing, nothing at all'. Goncharova felt that school harmed rather than benefited her.[3]

One of Goncharova's earliest and strongest recollections was of the song which her nurse used to sing: 'Youth will not return, it will not return again,' for it carried the sense of irrevocability, the nostalgia, which is at the root of all Russian feeling. Yet, as Tsvetaeva wrote, this rather sombre little girl was extremely able. What motivated her was 'neither ambition nor ability, but rather a passion for work'.[4]

After completing her schooling Goncharova decided to continue her studies and enrolled on a medical course. As she herself put it, 'I always loved to be doing things'.[5] She left the course after only a week, 'put off, not by the anatomy theatre which she would have struggled with, but by the masculinity of the other girls on the course'.[6] Then she was attracted by the humanities and enrolled in the historical and philological faculty of Higher Women's Courses, but she quickly left that too, and in 1898 we find her name on the list of those attending sculpture classes at the Moscow School of Painting, Sculpture and Architecture. There she was taught by Pavel Trubetskoy, a distinguished sculptor who had spent much time abroad and was influenced by Rodin. She graduated from her course with a silver medal.

More importantly, it was at this time that she met the young artist Mikhail Larionov who was to have a decisive influence on her life and artistic development. As Tsvetaeva wrote, 'to speak of Goncharova without speaking of Larionov is impossible. It was he who told Goncharova that she was a painter: "You have eyes for colour but you occupy yourself with form. Open your eyes to your own eyes."' Goncharova became a painter. 'I suddenly realized', she remembered, 'that painting could do everything that sculpture could not.'

Initially Goncharova painted in a gentle Impressionist style, and at the invitation of Sergei Diaghilev she exhibited some of her earliest works in the 'Russian Art Exhibition' at the Salon d'Automne in Paris 1906. Goncharova then passed through a brief Symbolist phase. She worked closely with artists such as Pavel Kuznetsov and Vasily Milioti who were members of the Blue Rose group, and showed wistful and nostalgic landscapes in exhibitions such as 'The Wreath' organized by Larionov, Alexandra Exter, and the brothers David and Vladimir Burlyuk in 1907. The real breakthrough in Goncharova's art occurred after 1908. It was then that the wealthy industrialist and art patron Nikolai Ryabushinsky financed the 'Golden Fleece' exhibition which introduced Moscow to modern and contemporary French painting. Some two hundred Post-Impressionist and Fauve works were exhibited, and following this revelation of crude form and bright colour Goncharova adopted a more primitive and expressionist approach.

Goncharova readily admitted that she had learned a great deal from her French contemporaries, and her cycle of paintings *The Fruit Harvest* of 1909 betrays this new-found influence. In these bright scenes of peasant life all the strength of expression is concentrated in the spontaneous brushwork, the variegated use of colour as well as the simple yet majestic forms of her peasants. These works have all

29–32

the exotic and primitive power of Gauguin combined with the heavy sculptural forms to be found in the early Cubist figure-paintings by Picasso which were then on display in the Morozov and Shchukin collections in Moscow.

The French had stimulated Goncharova's artistic awareness. Through them she realized the significance and value of the artistic traditions of her own country, and these began to take priority in Goncharova's work. The figures in *Washing Linen* of 1910 are more akin to the crudely sculpted forms of the old stone babas which decorated the southern Russian steppes than to French example. Moreover a comparison with Serebryakova's work on a similar theme highlights Goncharova's violent emotional spontaneity. At this time Goncharova often painted cyclical works based on the life and labour of the Russian peasantry. Tsvetaeva describes these works as 'the seasons in labour, the seasons in joy: harvest, ploughing, sowing, the apple-picking, wood-gathering, reaping, old women with rakes, planting potatoes, peddlers and peasant-farmers all interspersed with images from icons'.[7] Tsvetaeva's observation is important in pointing to an underlying mysticism in Goncharova's peasant paintings. For Goncharova daily life is observed in epic, religious or even apocalyptic terms. The influence of the Russian north with its atmosphere of ascetic exaltation can be felt in these works, and as Tsvetaeva later noted, Goncharova's favourite themes were resurrection and life depicted in the allegory of the harvest and the Russian peasant life.

The essence of Goncharova's art lies in the fact that she was a deeply national painter. In her thirst to discover a new painterly language she turned wholeheartedly to the folk tradition. This approach culminated in her first mature works of 1910, which dealt with specifically Russian subjects and revealed the bold impact upon her of Russian artistic traditions such as the icon and the popular print (*lubok*). This style, which Goncharova elaborated in conjunction with her companion Mikhail Larionov, became known as Neoprimitivism, and represented a unique development on Russian soil of the Expressionist tendencies which were then flourishing in the West.

A key example of Goncharova's work at this time was her cycle *The Evangelists* of 1910. Here Goncharova offered a contemporary and painterly re-interpretation of traditional Russian art-forms. The characteristic poses and compositional compression of the figures within the narrow vertical format of the canvas recall the archangels and saints in the deesis tier of an ancient church iconostasis. However, the execution of each Evangelist reflects the additional refinement of Goncharova's vivid Expressionist approach. The overall impact of these works is redoubled by a system of contrasts in the colouring and design. Cool greens and greys are played off against warm ochres, while the abstracted silhouettes which point towards Heaven and the Word of God are earthbound by reason of the powerful brushwork and texturing which contributes to a sense of their materiality. Yet for all their traditional iconography, these Evangelists take the monumental form of the Russian peasantry of Goncharova's own day, with whom she mixed freely during summer visits to Ladyzhino.

Goncharova's Neoprimitive work claimed her a place at the very forefront of the avant-garde, and in the years before the First World War she became known as a vigorous champion of Russian artistic traditions. In 1910 Goncharova and Larionov played an important role in the formation of the 'Knave of Diamonds'. This was a group of young avant-garde artists which included Lentulov, Mashkov, Konchalovsky, Falk and Kuprin, who were influenced by the early Cubism of Picasso and Braque as well as the crude forms and bright colours of Fauvism. Their first exhibition in Moscow in 1910, in which Goncharova participated, caused public consternation and was later regarded as the first manifestation of avant-garde activity in Russian art. Two years later, however, Goncharova publicly dissociated herself from them because of their reliance on Western models, and proclaimed that the principles of Cubism could equally be found in the old stone babas and wooden dolls sold at Russian fairs. At this time Goncharova and Larionov played a formative role in the organization of the 'Donkey's Tail' group which included the painters Kazimir Malevich and Vladimir Tatlin. This self-styled 'leftist' group set itself up in opposition to the 'conservative' Knave of Diamonds, and soon became associated with everything that was seen as scandalous in modern art. (Several of Goncharova's religious compositions were censored and officially removed from the first exhibition.)

In 1913 Goncharova held a large one-woman exhibition in Moscow in which she showed over seven hundred paintings dating from all periods of her career. In the preface to her catalogue the artist declared: 'I turn away from the West because for me personally it has dried up, and because my sympathies lie with the East. The East means the creation of new forms . . .'[8] Tsvetaeva writes: 'Now is the time and place to talk about Goncharova bringing the East to the West. She brought painting that was not only Russian but also Chinese, Mongol, Tibetan, Indian. And not only painting. From her hand, her contemporaries took the earliest and most ancient of things.'[9] Goncharova and Larionov understood the vital contribution of Eastern art to the development of traditional Russian culture, and in 1913 they organized an exhibition in Moscow entitled 'Original Icon Paintings and Popular Prints' which included Persian miniatures and Japanese and Chinese prints. However as Sarabyanov notes, 'Goncharova drew ever nearer to the West, but not as a pupil, more as an opponent fully aware of her own strength.'[10]

At this time Goncharova also began to collaborate with the two avant-garde poets Velimir Khlebnikov and Alexei Kruchenykh, and during 1912–13 she illustrated several books of their verse. Most famous are her illustrations to *A Game in Hell*. The book comprised one long poem written jointly by the authors which described a card game between the sinners and the devils in Hell. Kruchenykh tells us that the poem had its origin in the story of a *lubok*. Likewise Goncharova's illustrations draw on infernal and demonic imagery to be found not only in the old prints, but also in Russian icon- and fresco-painting. They are executed in an expressive manner which is heightened by the contrasts of light and shade, and this adds to their 'chimerical' nature, which is perfectly matched to the content of the

Natalya Goncharova
Illustration to Kruchenykh's book
Hermits (Pustynniki), 1912

poem. Goncharova also supplied Neoprimitive illustrations to Kruchenykh's and Khlebnikov's book *World Backwards* of 1912 as well as to Kruchenykh's book

38–9   *Hermits* of 1913.

Goncharova worked closely with other members of the literary and painterly avant-garde, and in the two years before the First World War she also became known as an abstract and non-objective artist. This was a period of phenomenal activity for Goncharova in which the artist turned her attention to the claims of

42–3   Italian Futurism and became excited by electricity and movement. She subscribed to Larionov's theory of Rayonism, signed his manifestos, and executed a

40   remarkable series of Rayonist landscapes in which reflected rays of light, sharp as ice-crystals, shatter both the figurative forms and pictorial space of the painting. According to Apollinaire the success of these abstract and non-objective works lay in Goncharova's ability to sift and synthesize the best from 'Fauvism of all varieties, Cubism of all systems and Futurism of all nationalities'. In his opinion it was this that gave Goncharova a total creative freedom and ultimately a completely unique individuality.[11]

In these years Goncharova was a formidable advocate of Russian Futurism. She organized provocative exhibitions in both Moscow and St Petersburg, was

vociferous in debates about 'the new art', published offensive manifestos, and was frequently reported in the press for her violent propagandist activities. The once-quiet Impressionist now burgeoned into an Amazon of the avant-garde. She became involved with Larionov in Russian Futurist theatre, and during 1913 and 1914 painted motifs on her face and body, performed with Larionov in a Futurist cabaret called 'The Pink Lantern', caused public disorder in a manner that usually demanded police intervention, and even starred with Larionov in a Russian Futurist film called *Drama in the Futurists' Cabaret No. 13*.

This Futurist phase was of a relatively short duration in Goncharova's career but it was sufficient to attract the attention of Diaghilev, the director of the Ballets Russes, who invited her to make stage designs for his production of *Le Coq d'Or* which was to be staged at the Paris Opéra in 1914. Several of Diaghilev's associates felt uneasy about inviting her participation, but Goncharova's final designs were a triumphant success of Neoprimitivism. They combined the rich and striking colour-harmonies of Russian folk art with the simple yet expressive qualities of the popular print and icon, and represented a complete synthesis of Russian traditions. Goncharova put her heart and soul into this commission. She visited the archaeological museums to study the ancient costumes of tsars and boyars and, in

Natalya Goncharova
Illustrations for Kruchenykh's and Khlebnikov's *A Game in Hell* (*Igra v adu*) 1912. Above right, the 'devils' card-game' described in the poem

44–7

the words of the choreographer Fokine, produced 'something unexpected, beautiful in colour, profoundly national and at the same time enchanting'.[12]

After the opening-night Natalya Polenova wrote from Paris to her husband: 'Goncharova arranged the entire stage in the style of our Russian dining-room furniture and especially in the style of the painted trays. The curtain opened on to darkness and then suddenly the lights illuminated a fiery landscape – a fiery town, a yellow sky, a red sun in the form of a face, red trees with huge blossoms. Everything was so unreal that the characters seemed like puppets. The audience acknowledged the design with thunderous applause and cries of 'C'est épatant!' and so on. Despite its crazy brightness there was nothing in any way gaudy about it.

'The second act began with night. This was our blue Tarusa trays very beautifully arranged. In the middle of the act the tent of an eastern queen rises from the ground. A crescent moon appears behind it. This decorative construction hides the entire corps de ballet. It comes out of the tent with miraculous arabesques. It is all very beautiful!'[13]

Le Coq d'Or brought Goncharova both fame and success in the West, but she took both in her stride. Goncharova was always an unassuming person, and as Marina Tsvetaeva records: 'fame visits her but is never admitted. It stays beyond the door. Goncharova is scarcely acquainted with her name. Her name crosses the ocean in full crates, resounds at exhibitions and appears in headlines. Goncharova sits (or rather stands) at home working . . . but chases her name away. "Don't stand beside me, don't jog my elbow, don't get in the way. There's the canvas. You don't

Natalya Goncharova
Jacket designs for Alexei Kruchenykh's and Velimir Khlebnikov's *World Backwards* (*Mirskontsa*), 1912

Natalya Goncharova
The Tsar's Palace, design for *Le Coq d'Or*, 1914

exist."' And she quotes Goncharova as saying: 'The theatre? I wanted to go to the East, I went to the West. I happened to encounter the theatre. Imagine it, a theatre design is commissioned from you, it is successful, not just for you yourself but also on the stage. Then comes another commission. . . . You can't refuse, and each is a test of skill. But theatrical work never was and will never become my favourite.'

On the outbreak of war Goncharova returned to Moscow where she contributed to the war effort by designing an album of patriotic lithographs entitled *Mystical Images of War*. If the 'pure painting' of the avant-garde including Goncharova's abstract experimentation had been distancing itself from reality, this folio demonstrates that behind the mask of 'pure art' lay a traditional synthesis of the philosophical, the religious and the social.[14] The war inevitably drew artists from individuality to a sense of national duty. As Mayakovsky wrote: 'the upheaval demands either something new or a solid support in tradition'. It was the latter that Goncharova provided.[15] Goncharova's lithographs are based upon apocalyptic, religious and national imagery, and to these subjects she brought the refinement of the icon tradition, the boldness of the popular print and all the technical expertise gathered as an illustrator of Russian Futurist books. As Alexander Blok noted: 'The concepts of duty, of what should be done in art have been added to the artist's concern with form and content.'[16]

48

In 1915, however, Goncharova forsook blood-stained Russia and travelled to Switzerland with Mikhail Larionov to take up Diaghilev's invitation to join the Ballets Russes. For several years Goncharova toured Europe with Diaghilev working as a stage designer. In Switzerland she made designs in the style of icons for an unstaged ballet called *Liturgie*; in Spain she was captivated by the mantilla's of the Spanish ladies, which inspired her series of paintings entitled *Espagnoles*, and in Rome she worked with Larionov on the designs of the ballet *Contes Russes* and collaborated with the plethora of artists, writers and composers who surrounded Diaghilev. These years of wandering finally drew to a close in 1919 when Goncharova settled permanently in Paris with Larionov.

During the 1920s and 1930s Goncharova became an active participant in what has become known as the School of Paris. She attended artistic soirées and was

Natalya Goncharova
Lithographs from the album
Mystical Images of War, 1914

familiar with painters such as Matisse, Derain, Picasso, Delaunay and Léger, as well as writers such as Jean Cocteau and the Dada poet Tristan Tzara. As a gifted graphic artist, she designed posters and illustrated books of verse, novels and even musical scores. She exhibited widely, took on students and continued to paint with unabated energy, producing mainly abstract and stylized paintings of bathers, flowers and landscapes. However in these Paris years Goncharova built her international reputation not as a painter but as a stage designer. She worked not only for Diaghilev and the Ballets Russes but also for Boris Romanov's Russian Theatre in Berlin, Michel Fokine's ballet company in America, and during the years of the Second World War her collaboration was sought by a wide range of ballet companies both at home and abroad.

After *Le Coq d'Or* her most famous commission was that for Diaghilev's staging of Igor Stravinsky's ballet *Les Noces* in 1923. Initially Goncharova planned a series of sumptuous costumes for this work, but then she radically simplified both the design and colour scheme so that they harmonized perfectly with the Neoclassicism of Stravinsky's score and the bold simplicity of Bronislava Nijinska's choreography. In the simple form and colouring of her costumes and set-designs Goncharova conveyed the mixed emotions of joy and sorrow which pervaded the ballet, and evoked again that sense of 'Russian nostalgia' which Tsvetaeva identifies with Goncharova's work.

Throughout her entire working life Goncharova remained a Russian artist. Perhaps this is why her non-objective experiments of the period before the war do not seem to fit in with the general course of her work, or were an episodic phase of

Natalya Goncharova
Sketch of costumes for *Les Noces*, 1923

her career. Yet they were crucial for artists such as Rozanova, Popova, Exter and Udaltsova.

Goncharova's ties with the nineteenth century were as vital as her ties with the twentieth. For it was the distinctly Russian spirit of artists like the genre painter Venetsianov which inflamed her Neoprimitive paintings as well as her work for the theatre. Goncharova's success was to encapsulate the very spirit of Russia in visual form, and rather than taking after her great-aunt the first Natalya Goncharova, the artist took more after her great-uncle, the poet. With Pushkin, Goncharova could truly say 'I am the People'.

DOCUMENTS

L. P. Bezobrazov to Ya. K. Grosh — 17 May 1880
The linen factory on the Goncharov estate in the Medynsky district of Kaluga Province was where Pushkin lived after his marriage to Natalya Nikolaevna Goncharova — our great grandmother — the beauty for whose sake he was killed in a duel by the Frenchman Dantes. Here there was once a linen factory but there is now no trace of it. It is a large trading and industrial settlement with a market which has served quite a large hinterland. Here is the Goncharov Stationery Factory. The site of the linen factory is wonderful. The estate with its magnificent old house is situated on the very banks of the river. The wooden wing is to this day called Pushkin's house. The poet lived in it after his marriage whenever he came to visit the Goncharovs. The wooden walls of this wing, which in itself looks like a small stately home, were painted by Pushkin, but no trace of his drawings now remain . . .[17]

Goncharova on 'Cubism', from her impromptu speech at the 'Knave of Diamonds' debate in 1912
Cubism is a positive phenomenon, but it is not altogether a new one. The Scythian stone images, the painted wooden dolls sold at fairs are those same Cubist works. True, they are sculpture and not painting, but in France, too, the home of Cubism, it was the monuments of Gothic sculpture that served as the point of departure for this movement. For a long time I have been working in the manner of Cubism, but I condemn without hesitation the position of the Knave of Diamonds, which has replaced creative activity with theorizing. . . . Contrary to Burlyuk, I maintain that at all times it has mattered and will matter what the artist depicts, although at the same time it is extremely important *how* he embodies his conception.[18]

Goncharova's preface to the catalogue of her one-woman exhibition, 1913
In appearing with a separate exhibition, I wish to display my artistic development and work throughout the last thirteen years. I fathomed the art of painting by myself, step by step, without learning it in any art school. . . . At the beginning of my development I learned most of all from my French contemporaries. They stimulated my awareness, and I realized the great significance and value of the art of my country — and through it the great value of the art of the East. Hitherto I have studied all that the West could give me, but in fact my country has created

everything that derives from the West. Now I shake the dust from my feet and leave the West, considering its vulgarizing significance trivial and insignificant — my path is toward the source of all arts, the East. The art of my country is incomparably more profound and important than anything that I know in the West (I have true art in mind, not that which is harboured by our established schools and societies) . . .

If we examine art from the artistic monuments we have at our disposal without bearing time in mind, then I see it in this order:

The Stone Age and the caveman's art are the dawn of art. China, India and Egypt with all their ups and downs in art have, generally speaking, always had a high art and strong artistic traditions. Arts proceeding from this root are nevertheless independent: that of the Aztecs, Negroes, Australian and Asiatic islands — the Sunda (Borneo), Japan, etc. These, generally speaking, represent the rise and flowering of art.

Greece, beginning with the Cretan period (a transitional state), with its archaic character and all its flowering, Italy right up to the age of the Gothic represent decadence. Gothic is a transitional state. Our age is a flowering of art in a new form — a painterly form. And in this second flowering it is again the East that has played a leading role. At the present time Moscow is the most important centre of painting.

I shake off the dust of the West, and I consider all those people ridiculous and backward who still imitate Western models in the hope of becoming pure painters and who fear literariness more than death. Similarly, I find those people ridiculous who advocate individuality and who assume there is some value in their 'I' even when it is extremely limited. Untalented individuality is as useless as bad imitation, let alone the old-fashionedness of such an argument.

I express my deep gratitude to Western painters for all they have taught me.

After carefully modifying everything that could be done along these lines and after earning the honour of being placed alongside contemporary Western artists — in the West itself — I now prefer to investigate a new path.

And the objectives that I am carrying out and that I intend to carry out are the following:

To set myself no confines or limitations in the sense of artistic achievements.

To make continuous use of contemporary achievements and discoveries in art.

To attempt to introduce a durable legality and a precise definition of what is attained — for myself and for others.

To fight against the debased and decomposing doctrine of individualism, which is now in a period of agony.

To draw my artistic inspiration from my country and from the East, so close to us.

To put into practice M. F. Larionov's theory of Rayonism, which I have elaborated (painting based only on painterly laws).

To reduce my individual moments of inspiration to a common, objective, painterly form . . .

To apprehend the world about us in all its brilliance and diversity, and to bear in mind both its inner and outer content.

To fear in painting neither literature, nor illustration, nor any other bug-bears of contemporaneity; certain modern artists wish to create a painterly interest absent in their work by rejecting them. To endeavour, on the contrary, to express them vividly and positively by painterly means.[19]

27–8 **Natalya Goncharova**
The Evangelists, 1910

29–31 **Natalya Goncharova**
The Fruit Harvest, 1909

<32 **Natalya Goncharova**
The Fruit Harvest, 1909

33 **Natalya Goncharova**
Fishing, 1909

34 **Natalya Goncharova** *Haycutting*, 1910

35 **Natalya Goncharova** *Peasants Dancing*, 1911

36 **Natalya Goncharova** *Washing Linen*, 1910

37 **Natalya Goncharova** *Nativity*, 1910

38–9 **Natalya Goncharova** Illustrations for Alexei Kruchenykh's book *Hermits*. Pages 2 and 9

40 **Natalya Goncharova** *Yellow and Green Forest. Rayonist Construction,* 1912

41 **Natalya Goncharova** *Weaver*, 1912–13

42 **Natalya Goncharova** *Aeroplane over Train*, 1913

43 **Natalya Goncharova** *The Cyclist*, 1912–13

44–7 **Natalya Goncharova** Designs for *Le Coq d'Or*, 1914. Above: Curtain

48 **Natalya Goncharova** 'Angels over a City'. From a portfolio *Mystical Images of War*, published in 1914

49 **Olga Rozanova** Illustration for Alexei Kruchenykh's book *War*, 1916

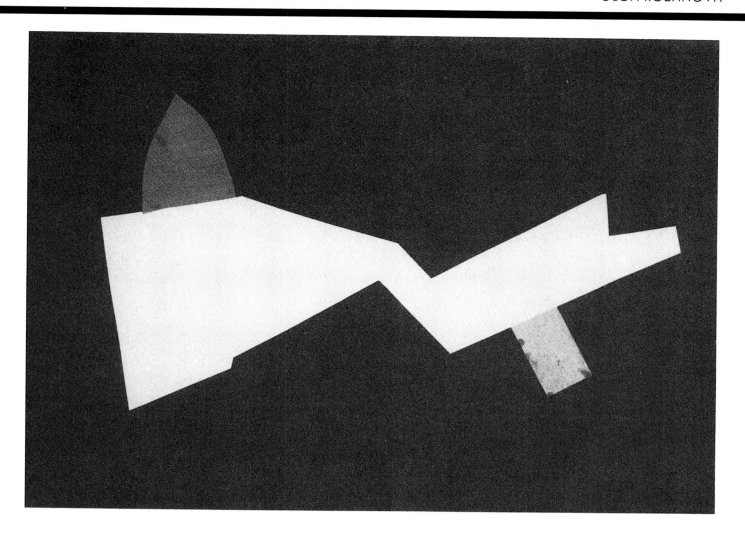

50 Olga Rozanova and **Alexei Kruchenykh**
Universal War, 1916. Collage no. 9
from a cycle of poems and collages

51 **Olga Rozanova** *Untitled* (*Green Stripe*), 1917

Olga Rozanova

After elucidating the essential values of the New Art,
one cannot help noticing the unprecedented diversity
and quantity of artistic trends.

OLGA ROZANOVA

As the revolutionary situation in the arts grew stronger, so the search for new forms
of expression intensified. The rapid development of Russian art from Impressio‚
nism to Cubism is in itself an illustration of the fact that 'Russian artists, like the
very soul of the people they glorify, have never been noted for their prudence. . . .
For them and for the people, in their deepest dreams, it is all or nothing.'[1] The poet
Alexander Blok's observation well characterizes the women artists of the Russian
avant‚garde, and none better than Olga Rozanova, who in her first published essay
echoed Blok when she declared: 'There is nothing worse in this world than the
unchanging face of an artist.'[2] As the art‚historian Vasilii Rakitin has written of
her, she was 'artistically independent to the point of audacity. She followed the
current ideas of her time, yet defiantly violated even the canons of cohesive sects of
innovators. Rozanova absorbed everything and depended virtually on nobody.
She loved to contravene herself, and enter heart and soul into the new. It was only
her premature death that finally stopped Rozanova's forward march.'[3]

Olga Vladimirovna Rozanova was born in 1886 in the town of Melenki in
Vladimir Province in Central Russia. From the age of eighteen she studied
painting in Bolshakov's studio‚school, and she also worked for a short time in the
Stroganov Institute in Moscow. In 1911 she moved to St Petersburg where she
attended Zvantseva's well‚known art school, and it was here, in this new circle,
that her creative life first began to flow. She came to know Mikhail Matyushin, an
artist with the strongest innovatory tendencies, as well as the painters of the 'Union
of Youth' (1910—14), a confederation of young avant‚garde artists who entertained
a rather free aesthetic ideology in distinction to the conservativism of the established
exhibition societies of the day. Rozanova became an active member of the group,
and found herself in the company of such individually minded artists as Pavel
Filonov, and the well‚read and widely travelled Latvian artist Waldemar Matvejs
(Markov) who became its leading theoretician.

The Union of Youth exhibited together and organized theatrical events,
published three important almanacs to which Rozanova contributed and
illustrated several books of verse in association with the literary avant‚garde. The
group also forged links with the Muscovite avant‚garde, and so it came about that
Rozanova was introduced to the latest experiments of Natalya Goncharova,
Mikhail Larionov, Ilya Mashkov and David Burlyuk. The creative activity which
took place among the Union of Youth was both challenging and intense, and for

Olga Rozanova
Hairdresser's, 1915

Rozanova it removed any need she might otherwise have felt to seek the then-traditional training abroad. She became an energetic contributor to the Russian avant-garde, and was never to travel outside the boundaries of her homeland.[4]

In these years Rozanova was close to the aesthetic of Russian Futurism, and her artistic energies found expression not only in easel painting and graphic design but also in her role as propagandist. Her manifesto 'The Bases of the New Creation and Reasons Why It Is Misunderstood', in which she considered and precisely defined her tasks as an artist (p. 97), was conceived as a polemical response to a scornful article in the press by Benois, attacking the New Art.[5] She became involved in public lectures and discussions on the subject of contemporary art, contributed graphic works to Union of Youth publications, and worked actively on the organization of a large number of exhibitions.

In contrast to Yakunchikova and even Goncharova, whose range of activities had a more specifically personal tone, Olga Rozanova was a pioneering social activist. The poet Benedikt Livshits recalls in his memoirs that 'Rozanova occupied the central place in the Union of Youth. She was an outstanding individual. She was someone who really knew what she wanted in art, and who advanced towards her goal by paths that were different from everyone else's. Despite their differences of opinion, artists such as Goncharova and Exter, who were uncompromising in their tastes, took her very seriously.'[6]

In the eyes of her contemporaries Olga Rozanova did not look like a 'pure' Futurist. Her contemporary and colleague Varvara Stepanova said of her that, 'although she has Futurist and Cubist periods, Rozanova does not take the essence from these tendencies, but only their means of expression, which makes her neither a Cubist nor a Futurist . . .'[7] Moreover, one of the greatest critics of the period, Abram Efros, observed the intuitive and lyrical qualities of Rozanova's work at this time. These characteristics are especially apparent when we compare her work with that of Goncharova. Although Rozanova's example was to a certain extent modelled upon Goncharova's innovatory role as both an artist and propagandist, Efros notes that 'Rozanova is like Goncharova's reverse side'. He compares the 'loudness' and 'rollicking nature' of Goncharova's Futurism with the 'very quiet' talent of Rozanova, Futurism's intimate painter.

Rozanova's approach is well illustrated by such early easel works as *The Poet* (State Tretyakov Gallery) or *The Oil Stove* (both 1912). Other works, however, are more overtly Futurist. Both *Factory and Bridge* of 1913 (Hutton Gallery, New York) and *Man in the Street* of 1913 (Thyssen-Bornemisza Collection, Lugano) are characterized by the jolting rhythms of broken images which are scattered over the picture surface, and which evoke the dynamism of modern life. Her most advanced work of these years was the canvas *Dissonance* of 1913 (Hutton Gallery, New York), a brightly coloured abstract work in which the composition is shattered into fragments by heavy diagonal lines which at once recall the Italian Futurist 'lines of force' and the formal vocabulary of Goncharova and Larionov's Rayonist paintings.[8] To underline Rozanova's proximity to the Futurist aesthetic

55

it is important to note that *Factory and Bridge*, *Man in the Street*, *Dissonance* and a painting called *The Port* of 1913 (Hutton Gallery, New York), were shown in the First Free Futurist Exhibition in Rome in 1914 and were formerly owned by Marinetti, the leader of the Italian Futurists.

As an active member of the Union of Youth Rozanova also came into close contact with Kazimir Malevich, who showed works at several of their exhibitions. During 1913 Malevich felt the impact of French Cubism, and a year later began to experiment with the collage technique pioneered by Picasso and Braque in their *papiers collés* and 'synthetic' Cubist works. Malevich's paintings such as *Woman at a Poster Column* of 1914 (Stedelijk Museum, Amsterdam) imitate these aspects of French Cubism, in that Malevich incorporates into his canvas newspaper cuttings, photographs and flat painted planes which lie one over the other to suggest a collage effect. As these were among the most exciting works to be executed in Russia in 1914, it was natural that Rozanova should begin to investigate this path.

The transition from Futurism to Cubism was marked by a series of canvases which include *Metronome*, 1913–14, and the more analytical *Sideboard with Dishes* of 1914. One of the most characteristic works of this period is *Writing Desk* of 1914. Looking at it, and at a number of similar works, it becomes evident that its artistic structure consists of a system of collages. *Writing Desk* is clearly a programme piece. The *Workbox* and *Hairdresser's*, both dating from 1915, are two further examples of Rozanova's work from this period which are based upon the collage approach. Rozanova seized on this idea and developed it further, bringing it to its apotheosis in her cycle of collages for *Universal War*.

The mechanical synthesis of planes of colour underlying Rozanova's completely figurative composition would form the foundation for further abstract experiments by herself and her colleagues. During 1915, Malevich systematically removed any figurative imagery from his paintings and unveiled a mystical, non-objective style of painting which he named 'Suprematism'. Rozanova followed Malevich along this path, and in 1915–16 she produced her first non-objective paintings. She also played an active role in the organization of the 'Supremus' group which had gathered around Malevich. The aim of this group, which included Popova, Exter, Udaltsova, Klyun and others, was to promote Suprematism in the various arts, and to that end Malevich and Rozanova were appointed editors of a proposed magazine.

However, despite her closeness to Malevich and other artists in his circle, and the fact that some of her works such as *Suprematism* of 1916 are named after his innovatory style, Rozanova remained completely independent, and the titles of works such as *Non-objective Composition* of 1916 make the distinction clear. Light in her work was now especially important. Form became the carrier of energy.

It was Stepanova who clarified the difference between Malevich's Suprematist works and those of Rozanova. In her review of Rozanova's posthumous exhibition Stepanova noted that 'Malevich constructed his works on the composition of the square while Rozanova constructed hers on the basis of colour.'[9] In many of her

56, 53

54

52

61

60

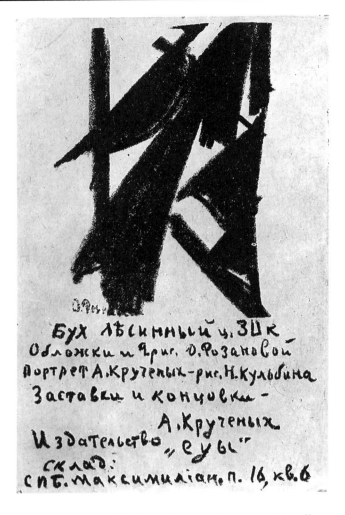

Olga Rozanova
Cover designs for Kruchenykh's
and Khlebnikov's handwritten
poem-book *A Forestly Rapid*
(*Bukh lesinnyi*), 1913

canvases she depended on a modification of black and its combination with yellow and dark or light blue. Her system of distributing colour on the surface of her canvas created an effect that was not only dynamic but also decorative. But this was not to be Rozanova's final development, for before her untimely death in 1918 the artist embarked on a significantly new approach. In the remarkable *Green Stripe* of 1917 Rozanova bisected the cream-painted ground of a canvas with a viridian stripe and in one stroke anticipated the development of American colour-field painting in the 1950s and 1960s. In this the work of Rozanova differs considerably from experiments being carried out either in France or in Italy at the period.

51

Equally innovatory was Rozanova's creative approach to the design and illustration of Russian Futurist books. Russian Futurism was particularly characterized by the deep and creative interdependence of the poets and painters. On one hand the artists of the Russian avant-garde illustrated many almanacs of poetry by Kruchenykh and Khlebnikov, while on the other the linguistic theories developed by the poets informed the development of painterly practice. Thus Kruchenykh's theories and techniques of 'transrationalism' which proclaimed the liberation of words from their conventional meanings and resulted in a kind of abstract sound-poetry, found their equivalent in Malevich's Suprematism in which colour and form were likewise freed from their descriptive functions.

Just as Natalya Goncharova's co-habitation with Mikhail Larionov was a partnership of deep creative 'mutual understanding', so too was Rozanova's work with and later marriage to Alexei Kruchenykh. During the second decade of the twentieth century they collaborated on a whole series of transrational books, so inaugurating a new stage in the development of book design which formed the bridge between the deluxe editions published by the World of Art and Constructivist and Soviet book design of the 1920s and early 1930s.

Rozanova began her career as a graphic artist in 1913 when she illustrated the third and final *Union of Youth* almanac, and in the same year no less than six volumes of poetical and theoretical works by Kruchenykh and Khlebnikov, including the important manifesto *The Word As Such*, and such bizarre books as *A Forestly Rapid*, *Explodity*, *Let's Grumble*, *The Devil and the Wordmakers* and *A Duck's*

Olga Rozanova
Illustrations for Alexei
Kruchenykh's *Explodity*
(*Vzorval*), 1914

Olga Rozanova
Cover for *Transrational Book*
(*Zaumnaya gniga*), with poems
by Alexei Kruchenykh and
Aliagrov (Roman Jakobson),
1915

59

49

Olga Rozanova
Illustrations for Alexei
Kruchenykh's *War*, 1916

Nest of Bad Words. Initially Rozanova approached her graphic work for these books in a Futurist spirit. Her lithographs for *Explodity* are characterized by daring lines which fracture the page, while her hand-coloured lithographs for *A Duck's Nest of Bad Words* are completely integrated with the text of the poem, and reveal her extraordinary sense of colour and line.

In 1914 Rozanova illustrated two more works by Kruchenykh and Khlebnikov. These included a second edition of their Neoprimitive poem *A Game in Hell*, which had originally been illustrated by Goncharova, and a book of transrational poems entitled *Te li Le* (pls. 62–4), pages from which were shown in the First Free Futurist Exhibition in Rome. However, as Rozanova grew away from the rhetoric of Futurism and towards the language of Cubism in her easel paintings, so her interest in collage techniques was carried over into her approach to book design. In 1915 Rozanova worked on two volumes published by Kruchenykh, and she introduced collage elements into both. The cover of the famous *Transrational Book* was decorated with a red paper heart with a white button sewn on to it. Although the illustrations were not collages but 'coloured graphics' depicting the abstract potentialities of playing-card images, Rozanova had already treated this theme in a series of preliminary collages such as *The Four Aces*.

The second volume, entitled *War*, can be seen as more significant in her development, and Khardzhiev records that Rozanova considered this volume to be her greatest achievement in the art of printing.[10]

War comprised four sheets of linocut text and a series of ten linocut illustrations in which schematic and abstracted figures acted out the horrors that were reported from the front. As with the old Russian popular print (*lubok*) a short descriptive

Olga Rozanova
Illustrations for Alexei
Kruchenykh's *War*, 1916

text was sometimes used as a compositional element in its own right. However Rozanova also designed two coloured-paper collages, one for use as an illustration, one to decorate the cover (pls. 57–8). Both incorporated abstract geometrical shapes, in imitation of Malevich's Suprematism with which Rozanova was growing familiar.

In Rozanova's letters to A. A. Shemshurin, who had offered to finance the publication of *War*, she describes her approach to the graphics. She notes that the lino-engraving technique is derived from her work on *Transrational Book*, in which the images were printed as coloured outlines and then coloured in by hand, thus producing a rich and original texture. Although some reprints for *War* came out untidily, Rozanova found it pleasant 'to distribute a means of printing that is laconic and not trivial'. She went on to admit how keenly aware she was of her shortcomings in these books, but recognized that they were 'the best in printing technique that I have done up till now. They are not only technically stronger than anything I have done before but also have more content and are more original.'[11]

Rozanova's linocut illustrations for *War* were produced a year after the publication of Goncharova's folio *Mystical Images of War*, which was evidently a unique catalyst in Rozanova's thinking. It is useful to compare Rozanova's linocuts with Goncharova's lithographs. Despite certain common tendencies, such as their clear reliance on the tradition of popular prints, Rozanova's and Goncharova's works are quite distinct: each artist treats the folk-image tradition in a different way. Goncharova draws directly on the icon and popular print tradition, whereas the images which Rozanova creates are less traditional. They are subordinated to a more subjective perception. As Evgeny Kovtun has pointed out,

48, 49

'in this book there is nothing of the stylization so marked in Goncharova's cycle'.

Rozanova's poetic perception (which in the two collages for *War* also achieved a non-objective expression) is in comparison with Goncharova's literariness a sign of a 'second stage' of development in the avant-garde movement. The fusing of the national and European contributions now brought Russian avant-garde art to a point of parity with European art.

Rozanova's unique contribution to book design, however, can best be appreciated by a study of her 1916 non-objective collages accompanying 50 Kruchenykh's poems on the theme of *Universal War*. Here Rozanova concentrated all her experience as a designer and illustrator of transrational books, and in this series of collages on coloured paper she achieved a completely new synthesis between painting and poetry, the word and the image. Kruchenykh's cycle of twelve poems comprised columns of words and letters which each corresponded to one of Rozanova's eleven non-objective collages. For the painter and the poet this was the height of mutual creative work: Rozanova 'created words' just as Kruchenykh contributed to several of the collages, thus expressing the powerful strength of their cooperation.

Rozanova's success in transposing the abstract qualities of Kruchenykh's poems into the medium of collage depended in large measure upon her acceptance of Kruchenykh's theories. In breaking down syntax and in his use of part-words and letters Kruchenykh destroyed literal meaning in his poems and found himself free to experiment with a wide range of associations aroused by both the sound of his poem and its image on the paper. In Kruchenykh's transrational theories of language the letters of the alphabet have their own semantic meaning. Thus Kruchenykh maintained that 'consonants mean everyday life, nationality, weight. Vowels are the opposite – they are the language of the universe. The consonants are colours, the vowels are lines. . . . A word is visible. The first thing is its image and not its semantic meaning. It is not read, it is looked at as if its meaning were incomprehensible. Thought and speech lag behind experience, that's why artists are free to express themselves not only in the general language of ideas, but also in a personal language without any distracting significance, a language which is not devoid of meaning but is transrational.'[12] Similarly, in his essay *On the Spiritual in Art*, Kandinsky writes that 'just as each word pronounced (tree, heaven, man) gives rise to an inner vibration, so it is with each plastically represented object. To remove its potential for arousing such vibrations would be to impoverish the arsenal of means of expression.'[13]

In *Universal War* Rozanova threw off any tendency toward figurative content. Suffering was converted into a conscious and generalized rejection of war – together with a prophecy of its future inevitability.

In the foreword of the book Kruchenykh proudly declares: 'these coloured pastings derive from the same source as transrational language – the liberation of creativity from unnecessary comforts. . . . Transrational language holds out its hand to transrational painting.'

52 **Olga Rozanova**
Workbox, 1915

53 **Olga Rozanova**
Sideboard with Dishes, 1914

54 **Olga Rozanova**
Writing Desk, 1914

55 **Olga Rozanova**
The Oil Stove, 1912

56 **Olga Rozanova**
Metronome, 1913–14

57 **Olga Rozanova** Cover of Alexei Kruchenykh's *War*, 1916

58 **Olga Rozanova** Illustration for Alexei Kruchenykh's *War* 1916. Page 4

59 **Olga Rozanova**
The Four Aces, 1915–16

60 **Olga Rozanova**
Non-objective Composition, 1916

61 **Olga Rozanova**
Suprematism, 1916

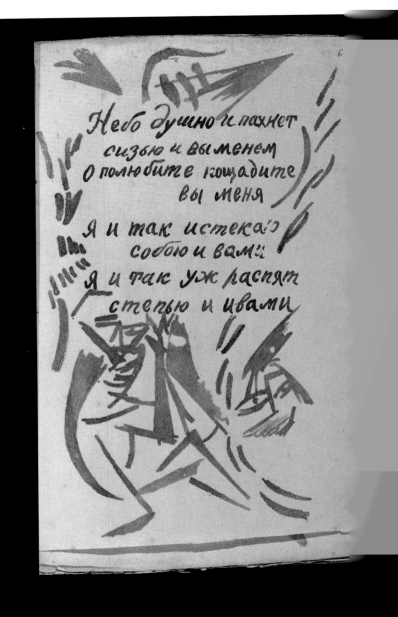

62–4 Olga Rozanova
Illustrations and jacket (below left) for Kruchenykh's
and Khlebnikov's transrational book *Te li le*, 1914.

Universal War was created entirely by hand. The collages were of fabric and semi-transparent paper, all save one set against a dark-blue ground, the colour of the universe. *Universal War* marked the peak of Russian Futurism. 'In everything that was then done,' the artist writes, 'in all our works and searching there was severity. . . . We had all become abnormally tired of the approximate conventionality of aestheticism and no less tired of the trotting races of the Futurist Derby. . . . For a long time we had been aware of an oncoming crisis and we lived on, either blindly or hungrily, or unwillingly or impatiently. We reset the pages, the days, the months with the same sequence with which the life of the town or the fate of the war went on outside our windows. . . . We believed that our art was simple, understandable and necessary. . . . The war did its business with us: it tore away the pieces of the past from us, that which should have belonged to us, it shortened one thing, it lengthened another . . . and, changing the world to a new speed, it gave a malignant background to our lives, against which everything seemed tragic or insignificant.'[14]

Consequently Rozanova welcomed the Revolution when it came in 1917. She immediately threw herself into the socio-artistic activity that followed, becoming a member of the Arts Department of the People's Commissariat of Enlightenment (IZO Narkompros) and of Proletkult. With Rodchenko, she headed the sub-department dealing with production art. She participated in the creation of the Free State Studios (Svomas) which were training-institutions for the arts set up in various provincial towns. In 1918 she visited applied arts centres as a member of the Commission for the People's Commissariat for Enlightenment, and she reorganized the workshops in Bogorodsk (wooden toys) and Ivanovo (textiles).

In 1918 Rozanova suddenly died of diphtheria.

The first small solo exhibition of her works was put on by IZO Narkompros later in the same year. Ivan Klyun, in introducing the exhibition, wrote that Rozanova, 'having attentively studied life, could sense the nerve which tomorrow would inform the spirit of the age.' Rozanova herself had said in 1913: 'Each moment of the present is unlike the world of the past, and the keys of the future carry inexhaustible possibilities for new revelations.'[15]

DOCUMENTS

Vladimir Markov on Rozanova — 1914
. . . Each pure pigment has its own structure, its muscle, its texture . . . Rozanova seizes colours which have the brightest, most dissimilar structure, she takes black, red and green . . .[16]

Rozanova: 'The Bases of the New Creation and the Reasons Why It Is Misunderstood', 1913
. . . To reflect it is necessary to perceive, to perceive it is necessary to touch, to see. Only the intuitive principle allows us to know the world.

And only the abstract principle – calculation – as the consequence of the active aspiration to express the world, can build a picture. This establishes the following order for the process of creation:

1 The intuitive
2 The individual transformation of the visible
3 Abstract creation

. . . Only modern art has advocated the full and serious importance of such principles as pictorial dynamism, volume and equilibrium, weight and weightlessness, linear and plane displacement, rhythm as a legitimate division of space, design, planar and surface dimension, texture, colour correlation, and others. Suffice it to enumerate these principles that distinguish the New Art from the old to be convinced that they are the qualitative – and not just the quantitative – new basis that proves the 'self-sufficient' significance of the New Art. . . .

Messrs art critics and veterans of the old art are being true to themselves in their fatal fear of what is beautiful and continually renewing itself; they are frightened and tremble for the little caskets of their meagre artistic achievements. In order to defend publicly this pitiful property and the positions they occupy, they spare no effort to slander the Young Art and to arrest its triumphant procession. . . .

It is high time that we realized that the future of art will be assured only when the thirst for eternal renewal in the artist's soul becomes inexhaustible, when wretched individual taste loses its power and frees the artist from the necessity of continually rehashing. . . . It is high time that we put a stop to the critics' ribaldry, and asserted honestly that only 'Union of Youth' exhibitions are the pledges of art's renewal. Contempt should be cast on those who hold dear only peaceful sleep and relapses of experience.[17]

Rozanova's statement for the unpublished magazine 'Supremus', 1918
We propose to liberate painting from its subservience to the ready-made forms of reality and to make it first and foremost a creative, not a reproductive, art.

The aesthetic value of an abstract picture lies in the completeness of its painterly content.

The obtrusiveness of concrete reality has hampered the artist's work, and as a result, common sense has triumphed over visions fancy free; but visions fainthearted have created unprincipled works of art, the mongrels of contradictory world-views.[18]

Olga Rozanova
Collages, nos. 1 and 2 from the cycle *Universal War*, 1916

Lyubov Popova

. . . A series of preparatory experiments towards
concrete material constructions.

LYUBOV POPOVA

The career of Lyubov Popova was only a little longer than that of Rozanova, but
the extra five years accorded her saw the full blossoming of her creative talent. A
prodigally gifted artist, she progressed from the pictorial surface to real space, from
easel painting to design. With Popova we come to the remarkable story of the
avant-garde artists who ultimately rejected the fine art tradition, and under the new
banner of Constructivism turned towards the art of production. Popova witnessed
extraordinary changes in the social, political and artistic character of the times, and
was able to respond to them in an individual and striking way. Even now Popova's
work in both painting and stage design look completely contemporary.

Lyubov Popova photographed
by Rodchenko

Born in the village of Ivanovskoe near Moscow in 1889, Lyubov Sergeevna
Popova was the daughter of a rich Moscow merchant, who like Goncharova's
father owned a linen factory. The young Popova grew up on the family estate of
Krasnovidovo and was taught at home by teachers from the factory-school. In 1902
the entire family moved to Rostov, where Popova spent several years at High
School, and then in 1906 the family took up residence in Moscow. Popova's
parents were both cultured personalities and patrons of the arts. They encouraged
her artistic propensities, and during 1907–8 she entered the private studios of
Stanislav Zhukovsky and Konstantin Yuon in Moscow. In this context Popova
was introduced to a mild form of Impressionism which both masters practised. Her
earliest works reflect their teaching, and their concerns with painting the motifs of
the Russian countryside, village landscapes, laundresses, fields with haystacks and
still-lifes. Popova's art during this period was completely traditional. In Yuon's
studio Popova met Lyudmilla Prudkovskaya (Udaltsova's sister) and during the
summer of 1908 they worked together at Krasnovidovo. A year later the artist
undertook her first visit to Kiev, where her attention was attracted by ancient
Russian painting and the works of the Symbolist artist Mikhail Vrubel.

At this time the artistic life in Russia began to blossom. Young artists were
breaking away from the old exhibition societies and mounting their own
exhibitions, and the 'Golden Fleece' was introducing contemporary Western art
into Russia. In this context Popova's art began to mature. Her father subscribed to
The Golden Fleece magazine, and in the years around 1910 we can read the
influence in Popova's work of Goncharova, Gauguin, Van Gogh and Cézanne.
However Popova was prevented from taking an active role in the Russian art world
at this time by the fact that she was frequently on the move.

Lyubov Popova
Female Nude, c.1913

In 1910 she visited Italy with her family, where she studied the impressive works of Giotto and Pintoriccio. In the summer she travelled to Pskov and Novgorod, and in 1911 she visited St Petersburg for the first time and was overwhelmed by the collections in the Hermitage. Then in autumn 1911 she toured the ancient Russian cities of Rostov, Yaroslavl, Suzdal, Pereslavl and Kiev. Naturally Popova's impressions of ancient Russian art and architecture gained on these visits were to influence her future work. Like most of the avant-garde of the time, Popova was slowly coming to terms with the rich painterly traditions of her country, and her subsequent path of bold formal experimentation was acted out against the appreciation of her cultural roots.

On her return from Kiev, Popova set up a studio in Moscow with Prudkovskaya, Udaltsova and Vera Pestel. Later, in the autumn of 1912, Popova and Udaltsova became members of the famous 'Tower' studio organized by

Vladimir Tatlin, where Viktor Bart and Alexander Vesnin also worked. At this time Popova filled her sketchbooks with drawings of nudes in which she investigated the structure of the human form. In this she was similar to Tatlin, who also laid emphasis on figure-drawing. Popova's paintings of studio nudes also date from this period, and display a modelling of form which reflects her knowledge of the techniques of both Vrubel and Cézanne. Progressive artists at this time were particularly interested in Cézanne, and the collectors Sergei Shchukin and Ivan Morozov both had impressive collections of his canvases on display in their homes.

It was under the influence of these collections that in 1912 Popova, Udaltsova and Pestel set off for Paris. On the advice of Alexandra Exter, who knew the city and its studios particularly well, the young artists joined the Académie 'La Palette' where the Cubist painters Le Fauconnier and Metzinger taught. The sculptor Vera Mukhina was in Paris at the same time; Popova and she had become friendly and together visited the studios of painters and sculptors such as Archipenko. In Paris Popova's earlier attempts at an analysis of the human form were refined and deepened by her exposure to Cubism, and on returning to Moscow in 1913 to work with Tatlin and Morgunov her painterly approach had undergone a transformation.

Popova's painting *Composition with Figures* of 1913 is entirely characteristic of her development at this point, and vividly recalls the example of Metzinger. It is large, brightly coloured; the figures are set in an interior with a view on to a landscape. The reduction of the figures to basic volumes and the overall fragmentation of the painted surface reveal Popova beginning to master the Cubist idiom. An attractive painting, it engages our eye because of the contradiction between surface and depth, straight line and arabesque, and the dynamism of the diagonals played off against the static quality of the still-lifes.

Lyubov Popova (on the right)
with Udaltsova (left) and
Udaltsova's sister (centre)
65

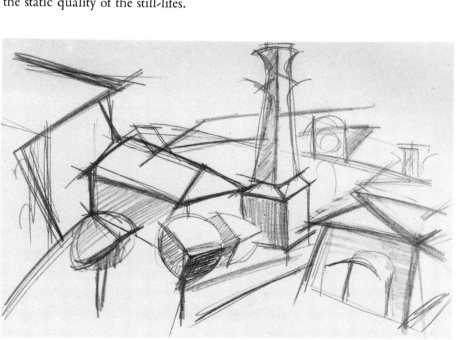

Lyubov Popova
Cityscape with Chimney, 1912

Popova visited Paris once again in 1914 just before the outbreak of war. This time she was accompanied by the sculptors Vera Mukhina and Iza Burmeister, and the three young women toured France and Italy together. Mukhina recalled that 'Popova's reaction to Italy was very intense, impassioned. If she's sensitive to a particular question, for example, the correlation of colours, she fixes all her attention on that, looks for that everywhere. If she doesn't find the answer to that question in a great artist she passes him by.'[1] This period provided the inspiration

69   for the painting *Italian Still-life* of 1914 which displays both Cubist and Futurist influences. The painting adopts the form of a Cubist still-life with some collage lettering, although the use of complete words such as 'Des Canons' and the stencilled reference to the Futurist magazine *Lacerba* adds a content and dynamism to the painting which is specifically Futurist. In addition, Popova always contributes to these works a decorative unity created by the interlacing curves and planes, rhythmic repetitions and sonorous combinations of red, dark blue and yellow.

All that she had seen, thought and experienced took Popova in 1914 to the

65   Knave of Diamonds, where for the first time she showed works such as *Composition with Figures*. As with the other Knave of Diamonds artists, a crucial aspect of her works was the dynamic texture of her canvases and their picturesque and decorative qualities. Her independent and mature period in painting began immediately after the 1914 exhibition. Now she began to attract other artists towards her. She became a focus for artistic activity, and organized a weekly meeting at her home where Udaltsova, Vesnin and the artist and critic Grishchenko presented papers. From this point on Popova began to exhibit widely, mainly in shows of Futurist tendencies. In March 1915 she contributed to 'Tramway V' along with Malevich, Tatlin, Puni, Rozanova, Udaltsova and Exter; in December to 'The Last Futurist Exhibition: 0.10', where Malevich showed his famous *Black Square*; in March 1916 to 'The Store' (p. 115), and later in the year to the 'Knave of Diamonds' in essentially the same company.

As Popova adopted a more central role within the avant-garde, so she was exposed to the innovatory and rapidly developing ideas of her colleagues. The years 1914–16 marked an exciting and striking transformation in Popova's art as she gave way to the painterly trends inspired by Cubo-Futurism. Works such as her *Violin* (State Tretyakov Gallery) of 1915 or *Still-life with Tea Tray* of 1915 (private collection, Moscow) include collages, insets, various stuck-on patches and so on. Collage gave Popova, as it did Rozanova, the chance to express in a tactile way the subject of a painting and at the same time to show things in real space. At this time Popova also experimented with what she called 'sculpto-paintings', fascinating and gaily coloured pictorial reliefs in which painted collage-elements protrude from the picture surface, presenting real volumes instead of just painterly ones. Several of these 'sculpto-paintings' such as *Portrait of a Lady* of 1915 (Ludwig Collection, Cologne) were exhibited at the 1916 'Knave of Diamonds' exhibition.

Although the 'sculpto-paintings' produced interesting results, perhaps Popova's most significant work in this period were her portraits and figure compositions such as *Portrait of a Philosopher* of 1915, a painting of the artist's brother. The work again recalls French example, and particularly the painting *Man in a Café* by Juan Gris. Popova's innovation, however, was to merge the figure, surrounding objects and the background into the overall painterly surface. The spatial fusion created by the interconnecting planes was to form the basis of Popova's later launch into non-objectivity. As Popova herself said: 'The principle of abstracting parts of an object is followed with logical inevitability by the abstraction of the object itself. This is the road to non-objectivity.'[2]

Also important in Popova's development was her interest in Synthetic Cubism, which by 1916 had resolved itself in paintings such as *Grocery Shop* which stressed the interrelated and formally harmonious structure of planes. From here, as in the case of Rozanova, it was only a small and logical step towards the Suprematist form of non-objectivity inaugurated by Malevich. Popova's approach to colour is interesting. For the Italian Futurists colour came from the objects in their pictures. For Popova and her colleagues, colour had importance in itself.

Popova moved decisively into non-objectivity when in 1916–18 she painted a series of *Pictorial Architectonics* which were subsequently exhibited at the 'Knave of Diamonds' exhibition alongside Suprematist works by Malevich and others. Popova firmly identified herself with this development by joining the 'Supremus' group (p. 98) which met in Udaltsova's studio. Several sketches for the *Supremus* logo designed by Popova still exist in the Costakis Collection.

These *Pictorial Architectonics* of 1916–18 manifest an interest in the presentation of surface planes with an energy of inner tension, as the coloured masses, lines and volumes all interrelate to create a formal unity. Initially they took the form of fairly static compositions comprising overlapping planar forms, but very soon they acquired a startling dynamism as Popova tilted the planes at angles and made them slice into each other. In these later paintings surfaces pulsating with colour seem to move around internal spatial axes.

Although Popova's *Pictorial Architectonics* bear a fleeting resemblance to Malevich's Suprematism they differed in three important aspects. Firstly Popova entertained a different approach to the pictorial space. Malevich's squares and rectangles float against the infinity of the background-plane and freely spill over each other, while Popova firmly integrates her planes and fixes them fast in a tight and restricted space. The treatment of space in these works does not suggest the cosmic infinity of Suprematism, but rather gives a sense of construction and formal interrelationship within the frame of the picture. Secondly, whereas Malevich completely relinquishes texture in his Suprematist paintings, Popova brings it to the fore and exploits it, as when using it to emphasize the volume of cylinders in her *Pictorial Architectonic* of 1916 or to contribute to the tension and dynamism of her *Composition* of 1918. Thirdly, for Malevich colour was primarily of symbolic significance, while for Popova it was an aspect of painting which had to be

71

Lyubov Popova
Cover design for the journal
Supremus, 1916–17

66
72

Lyubov Popova
Spatial Force Construction, 1921

articulated like any other, and a solution found to its harmonious relationship with form. In these works her colours form an architecturally accurate but at the same time emotionally resonant harmony.

It is appropriate that Popova should choose the term 'architectonic' with which to describe her non-objective paintings, suggesting as it does the architectural and constructive processes to which these works are subject, and the logical interrelation of the parts. As Sarabyanov says: 'with titanic energy she "moves out" surfaces into the space of the picture, placing one on the other, welding and strengthening. She builds, and her pictures rise up like the façades of magnificent buildings.'[3]

In particular, Popova's aspiration towards integration of colour, form and structure in her *Painterly Architectonics* seems to have been inspired by her study of Islamic architecture. Popova had already been interested in ancient Russian architecture, when in 1916 she visited Samarkand and studied the ancient complex of mausolea known as 'Shah-Zinda'. From Samarkand she wrote to Vesnin: 'The architecture is absolutely amazing! It is exclusively decorative. The façade does not reflect the planes and forms of the whole building but the measurements, the evenness of proportions, the decorativeness of colour and ornament . . .'[4] Islamic architecture achieved a non-figurative expression of the essential balance of the universe, and it was this harmony which Popova sought to evoke in her own *Painterly Architectonics*, several of which were entitled 'Shah-Zinda'. Clearly the fusion of impressions gained from icon paintings and eastern architecture helped the artist to find a new quality in her art of this period.

In March 1918 Popova married the Russian art-historian Boris von Eding, and in November gave birth to her son. In the following summer the family visited Rostov on Don where tragedy struck. Eding contracted typhus and died, and Popova was infected with both typhus and typhoid fever. She returned to Moscow seriously ill and sold off her paintings. During 1919 Popova failed to execute a single canvas and only picked up her brush again in 1920 to paint four *Painterly Constructions* (State Tretyakov Gallery). Here the repeated motifs of lines and circles seem to move on intersecting planes with a freedom hitherto unknown.

Popova's final painterly development took place in 1921–2 when she executed several *Spatial Force Constructions*. These were her last easel works, and having executed them Popova gave up painting. Following the Revolution of 1917 artists began to regard easel painting as an essentially bourgeois and élitist activity which had to be replaced by construction in real space. This point of view was chiefly elaborated by the Constructivists, who proclaimed death to art.[5] Alexei Gan, one of the main theorists of Constructivism, proclaimed: 'Art is finished. It has no place in the working apparatus. Labour technology, organization – that is today's ideology.'[6] As Popova was closely involved with the Constructivist ideology, so she too turned away from easel painting, and in the catalogue to the exhibition '5 × 5 = 25' of 1921 she described her *Spatial Force Constructions* as 'merely a series of preparatory experiments towards concrete material constructions'. From this point on, the artist moved into design and left painting far behind her.

65 **Lyubov Popova** *Composition with Figures*, 1913

< 66 **Lyubov Popova**
Pictorial Architectonic, 1918

67 **Lyubov Popova**
Pictorial Architectonic, 1916

68 **Lyubov Popova**
Costume design for
The Locksmith and the Chancellor
by Anatole Lunacharsky,
performed in 1921

107

69 **Lyubov Popova**
Italian Still-life, 1914

70 **Lyubov Popova**
Grocery Shop, 1916

71 **Lyubov Popova**
Portrait of a Philosopher
(Popova's brother), 1915

72 **Lyubov Popova**
Composition, 1918

73 **Lyubov Popova**
Untitled, c. 1917

74 **Lyubov Popova**
Suprematist design for
embroidery workshop
(Verbovki)

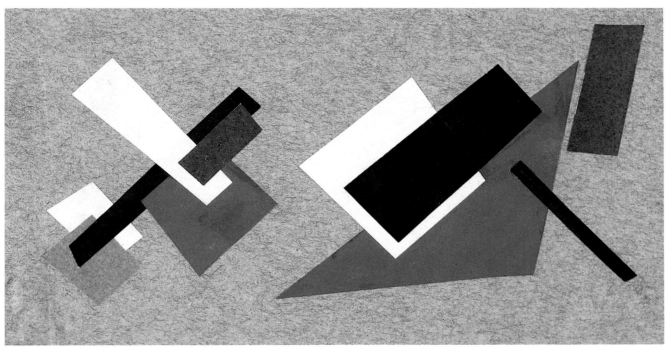

75 **Lyubov Popova** *Dynamic Composition*, 1919

Popova welcomed the Revolution as an inevitable progressive happening and involved herself in its processes. In 1918 she became an active member of Svomas (Free State Studios, after 1920 known as the Higher Artistic and Technical Studios, or Vkhutemas) where she taught a foundation course on colour. Here she began to approach art from a different perspective, analyzing the problem of art in its direct functioning with the everyday environment. Popova was not alone in this; a similar approach was adopted by her most progressive colleagues including Rozanova, Stepanova and Udaltsova.

As the writer Ilya Ehrenburg pointed out, the times now demanded, not art in its traditional form, but the creation of beautiful things 'to turn life into an organized process and thus to annihilate art'.[7] In articles and speeches from those years the idea was constantly expressed that painting had become 'somehow old-fashioned, compromised and inappropriate in an industrial-production age' and that 'all the problems of decorative art should be concentrated only on the relationship between the artist and the machine, between the artistic and the machine method of working with materials'.[8] During 1920 Popova worked at Inkhuk (Institute of Artistic Culture) which was then a hot-bed of Constructivist theorizing. Like her colleagues, Popova agreed with the dictum that 'Art has died once and for all . . . it is no longer necessary to anyone'.[9] Everywhere appeals were heard to 'abandon easel painting and go over to the production of things of material culture'.[10] The last years of Popova's artistic activity were thus taken up completely

Lyubov Popova
Collage jacket for *Towards New Shores*, 1923

Lyubov Popova
Cover for the magazine *Musical Virgin Soil*, No.1, 1923

Lyubov Popova
Fabric design

68

with design-work. She produced graphics for contemporary books and magazines such as *Musical Virgin Soil*, and in 1923 she was appointed head of the Design Studio at the First State Textile Print Factory in Moscow and made many visually striking and novel designs for clothing.

Perhaps Popova's greatest Constructivist contribution was in the field of stage design. Her first experiments in this medium date from 1920, when she made designs for Tairov's production of *Romeo and Juliet*. These, however, were passed over in favour of others by Exter. Popova was then commissioned as a designer for the Children's Theatre in Moscow which was founded and organized by the artist and puppeteer Nina Simonovich-Efimova. Several designs by Popova still exist for Pushkin's hilarious *Tale of the Priest and His Dunderhead Servant*. Popova's interest in puppets continued, and in 1921 she planned to set up a puppet laboratory in Moscow in association with Alexandra Exter and Ivan Efimov.

Popova's first designs to be produced in a conventional theatre were those for *The Locksmith and the Chancellor*, a play by Anatole Lunacharsky, the Commissar of Enlightenment, which was performed at the Comedy Theatre in Moscow in May 1921. The designs based upon her 'Architectonic' compositions failed to attract any positive criticism. Increasingly Popova thought of theatre in Constructivist terms, as a form of production with its own specific technology. It was in collaboration with the director Meyerkhold that her theatrical ideology was finally worked out to the full in a number of Constructivist stage works which still today seem remarkably contemporary. It is perhaps these works which are the most widely recognized aspect of Popova's art.

In this medium Popova's greatest success was achieved with her extraordinary stage constructions and costumes for *The Magnanimous Cuckold*, produced by Meyerkhold on 25 April 1922. It seems quite clear that her designs represented a development of the principles first elaborated in her *Spatial Force Constructions*, but now intersecting wooden lattices and platforms with revolving doors and turning wheels were brought to life in three dimensions and in real materials. The free-standing set and movable parts conveyed the idea that industrial development held the key to social progress. The actors likewise adopted Meyerkhold's system of Biomechanics and, discarding unproductive gestures and individual emotion, performed by using impersonal and mechanical actions. Popova and Meyerkhold found themselves thinking as one, and the play was an unqualified success. Popova's revolutionary approach to the design was greeted with enthusiasm and earned her the title of 'mother of scenic constructivism'.[11]

During 1923 Popova continued to work with Meyerkhold and made equally remarkable designs for his production of Trotsky's *Earth in Turmoil*, where she utilized another skeletal framework which included a gantry frame and a screen for the projection of visual material during the performance. However Popova's Constructivist activity was cruelly curtailed by her tragic death in an epidemic on 25 May 1924 in Moscow. Despite her passionate Productivism and her consistent support of Constructivist ideology, what was important in Popova's art 'were not

Lyubov Popova
Stage design for Meyerkhold's production of *The Magnanimous Cuckold,* 1922

the dogmas of ideological directives, but vital creativity itself, its ever-pulsating energy lashing through all consciously and compulsorily erected obstacles and restrictions. Most important of all was the spirit of creative progress, of renewal and inquiry.'[12]

Hand in hand with the times, Popova's short career had charted a remarkable path from representation to construction, and from painting to production, a path along which comrades in arms such as Exter and Udaltsova would follow.

DOCUMENTS

Rodchenko on 'The Store' exhibition of 1916
I got to know Tatlin at Vesnin's where I had gone with Varvara [Stepanova] for a stretcher. Varvara and I were living in a small room, ten square metres, and I had decided to draw something big, but I had no money and no stretcher . . . so I wanted to hire a stretcher a metre-and-a-half by a metre. It was also difficult to buy real canvas, so I bought a cheap calico and primed it, and instead of an easel I fixed it to a bed.

Tatlin looked at my works, approved and said: 'We've organized an exhibition group consisting of Tatlin, Popova, Udaltsova, Exter, Pestel, Klyun, Bruni, Malevich, and you as well if you like, Rodchenko. We've all contributed money towards the exhibition, but as you probably haven't got any, you can contribute work, as I do. I'm the organizer and arranger, and you can be my assistant, and you can also sell the tickets. . . . Do you agree?

Of course, I replied. We rented an empty shop, no. 17 Petrovka, for a month and began to hang our things. The shop had two rooms, one big and the other further in and smaller. In the first room we hung Tatlin's counter-reliefs, Popova, Exter, Udaltsova, Bruni, Klyun and Malevich. In the further one there was Vasilieva, me and Pestel. . . . Tatlin, as I have already said, exhibited counter-reliefs and a few paintings, and Udaltsova showed some Cubist things. Popova, Klyun, Malevich, Pestel also . . .

But Bruni exhibited a broken barrel of cement and glass shot through by a bullet – this particularly upset the public.

Popova, one of the rich, regarded us with condescension, as if she considered us unsuitable company and not of the right class for her. Later, in the Revolution, she completely changed, and became a true comrade.[13]

Statement by Popova

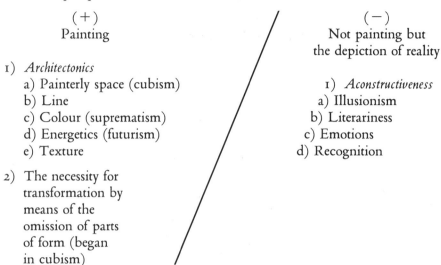

(+) Painting	(−) Not painting but the depiction of reality
1) *Architectonics* a) Painterly space (cubism) b) Line c) Colour (suprematism) d) Energetics (futurism) e) Texture 2) The necessity for transformation by means of the omission of parts of form (began in cubism)	1) *Aconstructiveness* a) Illusionism b) Literariness c) Emotions d) Recognition

Construction in painting = the sum of the energy of its parts.

Surface is fixed but forms are volumetrical.
Line as colour and as the vestige of a transverse plane participates in, and directs the forces of construction.
Colour participates in energetics by its weight.
Energetics = direction of volumes + planes and lines or their vestiges + all colours.
Texture is the content of painterly surfaces.
Form is not of equal value throughout its whole sequence. The artistic consciousness must select those elements indispensable to a painterly context, in which case all that is superfluous and of no artistic value must be omitted.
Hence the depiction of the concrete – artistically neither deformed nor transformed – cannot be a subject of painting. Images of 'painterly', and not 'figurative', values are the aim of the present painting.[14]

Lyubov Popova
Tailpiece from *Musical Virgin Soil*, 1923

Alexandra Exter

A general plan for experiments in colour . . .
ALEXANDRA EXTER

It is interesting that in pre-Revolutionary Russia many of the brightest and most talented of women artists emerged from the Ukraine and Byelorussia – among them Exter, Stepanova and Udaltsova. Perhaps it was the rich traditions of popular and applied art which first shaped their consciousness, and dictated the subsequent path they would follow. In this respect Alexandra Exter is typical of many Russian women artists of the time. The poet Benedikt Livshits was aware of this when he referred to Exter and other women artists as 'Scythian riders' galloping from the south-west to challenge the refined European conventions of Moscow and St Petersburg. As Livshits noted, 'the grafting of French culture on these real Amazons merely endowed them with a great resistance to the "poison" of the West. They did not cut off their right breasts and replace them with a tube of Dosekin paint simply because of aesthetic considerations.'[1]

Alexandra Alexandrovna Exter was born in 1882 in the town of Belostok in the Kiev region of the Ukraine, and played a vital role in the cultural life of Kiev in the years before the war. She received her first art education in the Kiev Art School during 1906–7, and in 1908 studied at the Académie de la Grande Chaumière in Paris. On her return home Exter participated in the famous 'Link' exhibition in Kiev which had been organized by David Burlyuk, Larionov and Goncharova. The exhibition was the forerunner of the Futurist shows, and was the first to call down on its head a storm of protest. Exter's works at this time were what Livshits called 'innocuous pieces of pointillisme timidly repeating Signac's experiments',[2] but they were sufficiently novel nonetheless to draw the bile of the reviewers.

Exter was not an artist to be rigidly bound to a specific ideology or group, and so in the years before the war she associated with many different factions of the Russian avant-garde. Moreover, as Exter moved freely between Kiev, Moscow, St Petersburg and Paris she contributed to many exhibitions both at home and abroad. In St Petersburg she became friendly with Nikolai Kulbin, and in 1910 showed works in his 'Triangle' exhibition. Her acquaintance with young artists in St Petersburg naturally led her to support the formation of the 'Union of Youth', and she contributed to its exhibitions in 1910 and 1913. In Moscow Exter principally aligned herself with the Knave of Diamonds, and during 1910–14 contributed to all their exhibitions. However her friendship with David Burlyuk and the poet Benedikt Livshits introduced her to the Russian Futurist camp, and in 1914 she not only collaborated on several Futurist books but also showed works at Larionov and Goncharova's 'No. 4' exhibition. On her visits to Paris Exter associated with the Cubist painters and poets. She knew Léger particularly well, and was friendly with Picasso, Apollinaire, Delaunay and the Futurist painter Soffici. Because of her Western contacts Exter was always treated with respect by the Russian avant-garde and was often consulted as an authority on Western developments.

Exter's paintings of the pre-war period stand out from those of her colleagues by virtue of the originality of their colouring, architectural rhythms and integrated compositional approach. Generally works such as *Sèvres Bridge* of 1912 are cast in a Cubist mould, but Exter always introduced an interesting structural dynamism of colour and line. Her extraordinary sensitivity to colour relations within her painting also distinguishes her work from that of her Cubist counterparts, and adds an emotive quality which is lacking in the strictly logical and analytical work of Picasso and Braque. As Livshits records: 'One of the Cubists' principles was to modulate the scale of colours and this inhibited Exter's violent, colouristic temperament. More than once Léger chided Asya [Exter] for the excessive brightness of her canvases.'[3]

Exter was far too careful an artist ever to give way wholeheartedly to Italian Futurism, but slowly she digested its impact, and in 1914 she visited Italy and showed works in the 'First Free Futurist Exhibition' alongside those exhibited by Rozanova. Several of Exter's paintings of this period such as *Florence* are dedicated to her Italian interests, and are quite distinct from her previous work. In their bright colouring and architectural references these paintings recall the cityscapes of Robert Delaunay. However Exter's abstract work is totally constructive. *Florence* is built on a precise 'enumeration' of the details of an urban landscape. It is interesting that in this picture Exter uses a Futurist motif by introducing the written word into her painting. However, in this case, the word 'Firenze' does not so much encode the meaning of the image as lead in to the complex multi-layered content of the painting. Paintings such as *Town at Night* of 1915 represent a later development of the cityscape theme and are treated in a more dynamic manner.

Throughout the war years Exter remained in Russia, and her necessary proximity at this time to purely Russian developments is indicated by her painting *Still-life with Egg* of 1915. This approach to painting, in which diverse images are brought together in an apparently contradictory and illogical manner, recalls the transrational paintings of the same period by Malevich, Puni and Rozanova. These had their pictorial basis in the *papiers collés* of Picasso and Braque, but from the point of view of content they were related to the linguistic developments of Kruchenykh and Khlebnikov. These two poets believed that it was only possible to tap the expressive power of words and images by divorcing them from their literal meaning, and this they achieved by breaking them up, removing them from their logical context and juxtaposing them in unusual combinations. It is interesting to compare Exter's approach with that of Rozanova in her *Hairdresser's* of 1915 (p. 82) to see how close in conception the two paintings are.

It is not unusual that Exter should at this time come into the orbit of the Malevich group and respond to similar stimuli. In 1915 she exhibited at 'Tramway V' in Moscow (see p. 239, Chronology: 1915), and a year later became an enthusiastic supporter of the trends initiated by Suprematism and also showed works at Tatlin's 'Store' exhibition (p. 115). Exter's own non-objective canvases such as *Abstract Composition* of 1917 and *Colour Construction* of 1921 are based on a system of planar contrasts. The artist's link with both Tatlin and Malevich is apparent in these works, but, as with Rozanova and Popova, Exter's works are quite distinctive, giving priority to textural, structural and colour relationships.

79, 80

The surfaces of Exter's non-objective paintings are executed in a complex manner, the texture varying with different concentrations of colour. The surface moves and pulsates, evoking precise emotional equivalents such as disturbance, agitation, rebellion and inspiration. However behind this seeming iconoclasm lay a deep love for Poussin. Kovalenko tells us that in Exter's most radical works 'she looked for a dialogue with the art of the past, seeing it not as something to hold one back (as expressed in contemporary manifestos) but as a stimulus to move forwards'.[4] In this respect Exter drew upon Poussin's sense of rhythm, his use of space, his direct but emotionally strong juxtaposition of cold and hot colours. Perhaps it was Exter's enthusiasm for his work which defined her own approach to colour, synthesizing all her analytical experiments on form. According to Tugendkhold Exter had a feeling for synthesis which always predominated over her feeling for analysis, and in her non-objective canvases this was achieved through the uniting structure of colour.

In addition to her sensitivity towards colour Exter at this time became increasingly concerned with the relationship between line and plane. In this respect *Colour Construction* of 1921 represents an active fusion of Exter's principles with those of Constructivism.

80

It is interesting that in this year Exter exhibited with Stepanova, Vesnin, Popova and Rodchenko in the '5 × 5 = 25' exhibition, and showed works under the general title *Plane and Colour Constructions*. In a small declaration she wrote that 'the present works are part of a general plan for experiments in colour. They go some way towards solving questions concerning the mutual relationships of colour, its mutual tension, rhythmicization and transition to a colour-construction, based on the laws of colour itself.'[5]

Alexandra Exter thus travelled the usual path for Russian women artists of the avant-garde – from Cubism and Futurism to Suprematism and Constructivism. However other aspects of her career deserve attention, particularly her vigorous response to the Revolution. In 1918 Exter established her own teaching studio in Kiev, and alongside her pupils engaged in what is known as 'agitational art'. At this time young artists threw themselves into overt propagandizing, and physically transformed their environment with designs and decorations which proclaimed the Revolutionary message. In particular Exter and her pupils were among those responsible for decorating the carriages of the famous 'agit-trains'. These trains were conceived as educational and publicity vehicles with the purpose of taking the Revolution to the furthest corners of Russia. The trains usually had a cinema-carriage which showed film of Lenin or Trotsky, and in addition they were well-stocked with Revolutionary manifestos, pamphlets and leaflets. Initially they spread the knowledge of the Revolution into far-flung towns and villages, but later they were used as propaganda vehicles and were sent out to cheer the cause of the Red Army on the Civil War front. Some of the trains painted by Exter and her pupils bore the striking images of the Revolution and the resounding mottos of its leaders, while others were covered in Suprematist compositions which gave the carriages a festive and somewhat fantastic appearance. In her agitational work Exter revealed her natural gifts as a designer, but these only found full expression in her innovatory work for Tairov's Chamber Theatre.

Tairov was a staunch opponent of the 'naturalist' approach to theatre which had been propounded for several years through Stanislavsky's productions at the Moscow Art Theatre. In its place Tairov proposed a form of 'emancipated theatre' in which all the disparate aspects of a production were completely integrated to create a single whole. Stage design necessarily played an important role in the elaboration of this concept. Tairov required that the staging, costumes and actors should create an overall plastic unity and that the design should express the inner conflicts and tensions of the action taking place within it. For Tairov the key-word was 'rhythm', and the stage design had to form a rhythmical unity with the rest of the production so as to present a unified expression of the dramatic action. As Meyerkhold found himself completely in tune with the artist Popova, so Tairov found in Exter an ideal interpreter of his own theatrical ideology.

Exter's name is associated with many innovatory experiments, and so it is important to emphasize that she also had a traditional side, and a clear spiritual link with the past that found expression not only in her paintings but also in her stage design. In this Exter shared an approach with the Symbolist poet Innokenty Annensky who re-animated ancient myths by freely modernizing them. The method of expressing the deep psychology of the past in contemporary plastic form strongly influenced Exter's perception. It was for this reason that in 1916 Tairov commissioned Exter to make designs for his production of Annensky's play *Famira Kifared*.

81–3

Famira Kifared was based on the ancient Greek myth in which the Thracian bard Famira was blinded by the muses for challenging them to a contest on the lyre, and it represented Exter's first work for the theatre. In her designs she championed a thoroughly novel and modern approach towards the role of visual art in the theatrical context. Her skilful manipulation of the visual aspects of the production to create an integrated visual equivalent to the rhythmical tension between Apollonian restraint and Dionysian revelry marked her out as the leading theatrical designer at this time in Russia. According to Tairov it was Exter's contribution which made *Famira Kifared* the first production to embody his concept of 'emancipated theatre'.

76 **Alexandra Exter** *Sèvres Bridge,* 1912

77 **Alexandra Exter**
Florence, 1914–15

78 **Alexandra Exter**
Town at Night, 1915

<79 **Alexandra Exter**
Abstract Composition, 1917

80 **Alexandra Exter**
Colour Construction, 1921

81 **Alexandra Exter**
Famira Kifared, 1916. Sketch for
Fauns' costumes

82 **Alexandra Exter**
Poster for *Famira Kifared*, performed at
Tairov's Chamber Theatre, Moscow, in 1916

84 Alexandra Exter
Romeo and Juliet, performed at Tairov's Chamber Theatre, Moscow, in 1921.
Sketch for curtain

85 Alexandra Exter
Romeo and Juliet, 1921.
Costume for the First Mask at the Ball

86 **Alexandra Exter** *Salome*, performed at Tairov's Chamber Theatre, Moscow, in 1917.
Costumes for the Dance of the Seven Veils

87 **Alexandra Exter** *Salome*, 1917. Sketch for costume

88 **Alexandra Exter** Sketch for *Spanish Dancer's* costume, 1920

89 **Alexandra Exter** Woman's costume from *Dancer's Reverie* series, 1920

90 **Alexandra Exter** *Still-life with Egg*, 1915

Exter's set was constructed from conical forms which represented the cypresses of ancient Greece and cubes which represented rocks. The latter were coloured black and gold and expressed the tension between the Apollonian and Dionysian forces. Exter also relied on coloured lights for contrast, manipulating intersecting beams to produce a coloured 'tactile' space. For Tairov the lighting and staging intensified the drama by reinforcing the actors' gestures and hence charging the atmosphere with emotion. The costumes also played a crucial role in the expression of the overall rhythm of the play. The satyrs, which represented the Dionysian force, were dressed in costumes which emphasized the contrast between line, shape and texture, and were equipped with wigs and false breasts to suggest their carnality. In addition, Exter painted the musculature of the legs of the actors to emphasize their physique, in the manner of Attic vase-painting. Of all the features of Exter's design, it was her use of line which contributed a plastic coherence to her theatrical works.

It is important to note that Exter's approach to stage design was firmly rooted in the bold experimentation undertaken in her easel paintings of the period. As Nakov notes, 'Exter's theatrical creations are parallel to her pictorial evolution and they cannot be disassociated'.[6] Exter, like Goncharova before her, was an accomplished easel painter whose concern with pictorial construction and three-dimensional spatial resolutions led her to experimentation in the real space afforded by the theatre. However, as John Bowlt points out, 'in contrast to many of her colleagues, particularly those who worked in Diaghilev's Russian Ballet, Exter was not drawn into the traditional illusionist and ethnographical aspects of decor and costumes. Rather she was interested by the idea of materially constructed space as an element of composition.'[7]

It was by developing this concept that Exter contributed so much to the evolution of Constructivism. Her designs for *Famira Kifared*, like her non-objective compositions or Tatlin's counter-reliefs, demonstrate a careful structural organization of formal elements which can be identified with the origins of the Constructivist aesthetic. However, it was to be her subsequent designs which led her towards a mature Constructivist approach.

In 1917 Exter made designs for the Chamber Theatre production of Oscar Wilde's *Salome* which proved a tremendous success. Here she introduced a new 86-7 and emotive dynamism into the sets by suddenly revealing curtains of various shapes and colours at specific points throughout the drama so as to heighten the emotional tension. Again, the origins of this approach lie firmly in Exter's paintings of the time, which were conceived not just as experiments in themselves, but as preludes to her use of colour to evoke mood and emotion in the theatrical context. Equally vivid were her sketches for the costumes such as *Dance of the Seven* 86 *Veils*. These, along with the other costumes for the play, were all conceived as plastic expressions of the natures and roles of those who wore them. As Cohen says, 'Salome's appeal had the direct impact of a punch, communicating visual and emotional sensations in a way that was nothing less than modern.'[8]

137

Alexandra Exter
Stage design for *Romeo and Juliet,* 1921

88–9

84–5

Alexandra Exter
Cover design for Yakov Tugendkhold's *The Art of Degas,* 1922

In the following years Exter was commissioned to make designs not only for drama but also for ballet. Her costumes for *Spanish Dancers* and *Dancer's Reverie,* both executed in 1920, are particularly interesting. The two designs indicate that Exter conceived her costumes not as independent creations in their own right but as part of a wider design-concept. The abstract grounds against which the dancers perform reveal Exter's concern with that integrated harmony not only between form and colour, but also between movement, costume and set.

Exter's final and most radical designs for the Chamber Theatre were those for the production of *Romeo and Juliet* in 1921. As in *Salome* the stage and curtain designs (Bakhrushin Theatre Museum) recall her paintings of the period such as *Colour Construction* of 1921. In both Exter's paintings and set designs there are diagonal networks of bars and wedges, and Cohen suggests that these can be read as visual equivalents to the tangled and opposing relationships of the play. The actual set of the play was conceived as a dynamic three-dimensional construction comprising ladders, platforms, rails, and inclined planes which were brought to life by their bold intersection and the bright colours of the beams of light which played on to them. The various vertical levels of the set were transformed into different locations by the rapid furling and unfurling of curtains. Exter's costume designs such as the *First Mask at the Ball* show that she conceived the actor as a kind of living non-objective construction in motion on the stage. This novel and highly original approach guaranteed Exter success among the critics, who were charmed by the way in which she had again modernized a historical drama by casting a Renaissance spirit in contemporary form.

Exter was also interested in film, and in 1924 she worked on the set and costume designs for *Aelita* directed by Protazanov. A decade before, Goncharova had both designed and starred in a Futurist film, but now the technicalities of the medium were more advanced, and Exter prepared a series of striking designs which rank

Aelita alongside other science-fiction film masterpieces of the time such as *Metropolis*.

In 1924 Exter emigrated to Paris where she became an active participant in avant-garde circles, and taught stage design and painting at Léger's Académie d'Art Moderne. Artistic life in Paris was in full bloom and Exter played a vital role within it but, removed from the revolutionary context of the new Russia, her art gradually lost its *raison d'être*. The heroic phase of Exter's career had come to an end.

In 1926 she was commissioned to make designs for a series of forty marionettes which were to star in a film by Peter Gad (not realized). Exter had already made designs for Nina Efimova's puppet theatre in Moscow but she now demonstrated her real ingenuity in the field, and the twenty surviving marionettes testify to her witty artifice and clever kinetics. The marionettes are two feet high, and are constructed from diverse materials including wood, fabrics, tin, metals, cardboard, plastic, glass, ribbon and threads. Their sophisticated design embraces Bakstian elements, Cubist motifs, Suprematist shapes and Constructivist mechanics, and their structure is perfectly attuned to express their respective characters. The *Robot* is composed of brightly coloured cubes and cylinders and assumes a stocky form while *Longhi II* is notable for her dress created by freely hanging lozenges which introduce a charming caprice into her movements. *The Red Lady* and *The American Policeman* adopt the bold and garish aspect of contemporary life, while the cast of *Harlequins* and *Columbines* from the *Commedia dell' Arte* gesticulate at each other wildly.

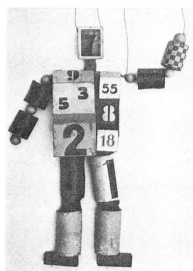

Alexandra Exter
Puppets, 1926

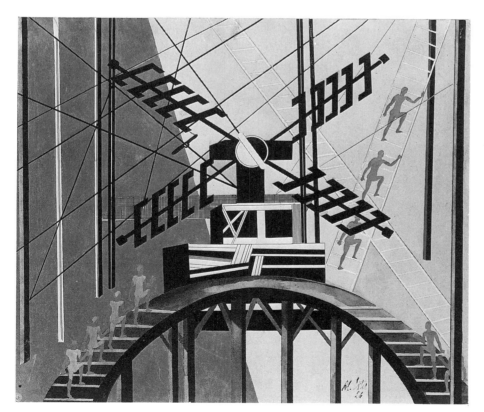

Alexandra Exter
Gymnastique, 1926

Many members of the Russian and French avant-garde were particularly interested in marionettes at this time, but those by Exter, especially, create a synthesis of painting, design, structure, movement, textured surface and colour. We are reminded of the words of George Sand when she said that the marionette was a child of its creator, for these marionettes, as John Bowlt says, extend the very psychology of Exter herself.[9]

Livshits had described Exter as an Amazon of the avant-garde, and the validity of his characterization can be weighed only when we consider the breadth of her artistic achievements. Exter was a crucial figure in the dialogue between Russia and the West, both before and after the Revolution. She made bold contributions in every field of artistic practice. As a painter she had earned the respect of the French Cubists, Italian Futurists and the Russian avant-garde. As a stage designer she not only set the tone for the development of the Revolutionary theatre, but also decisively influenced those whom she taught in her Kiev studio. Her pioneering aesthetics were taken up by the stage-designers Alexander Vesnin, Mikhail Andreenko, Isaak Rabinovich, and the painters Tyshler and Tchelichev. But more than this, Exter left her mark on her women contemporaries who were working in the fine, dramatic and applied arts. Her departure for Paris might have created a hiatus in Russia but new Scythian riders were ready to advance the cause which Exter had championed.

DOCUMENTS

Exter: 'Simplicity and Practicality in Clothes', in 'Red Cornfield' – Moscow, 1923
The pace of contemporary life demands the least expenditure of time and energy on production. To contemporary 'fashion', changing according to the whims of businessmen, we must oppose clothes which are both practical and beautiful in their simplicity. The dress for general consumption must be made from the simplest geometrical forms, such as the rectangle, the square, the triangle; the rhythm of colours varies the impact of the form. They are quite utilitarian since they are constructed from a combination of parts and, in putting them on or taking them off, the wearer dramatically modifies both the form and its purpose. Made in the most ordinary materials – cotton canvas, satin and silk, and worsted material – these clothes are easily changed and do not wear out, and the wearer can always alter both the silhouette of the clothes and their colours, since the separate parts are made in different colours.

By removing the wrap of an outdoor costume we have a holiday dress, and by taking off a white blouse we come to the underfrock – the working costume. A dark undershirt acts as a simple housedress which allows free movement, but add the overshirt and it becomes a holiday costume. A man's working jacket with leather pockets and cuffs made for the summer from coloured canvas is designed to give freedom of movement for every form of manual labour, for which the leather pockets hold the tools.

All the designs are simple in their outlines, material and construction so as to minimize the number of seamstresses required for their manufacture.[10]

Varvara Stepanova

We are practitioners, and in this lies the distinctive
feature of our cultural consciousness.

OSIP BRIK[1]

Olga Rozanova had followed in the footsteps of Natalya Goncharova and
consolidated her discoveries, but then moved towards Suprematism. Popova in her
turn had passed through a period of Suprematist experimentation to the
architectonic structuring of pictorial space, and it was only her early death which
prevented her from taking the next logical step. It was this step which artists such as
Stepanova took when they forsook the easel and moved into artistic design of the
most varied kinds, believing whole-heartedly in the connection between art and the
construction of the new life. Stepanova was a younger artist than either Rozanova
or Popova, and reached her artistic maturity in the years following the Revolution.
She witnessed both the birth and extinction of the Constructivist ideology, and
was able to participate throughout in its natural 'overflow' into design.

Varvara Feodorovna Stepanova was born in 1894 in Kovno. At school, she
was a gifted pupil, and concluded her high school education by winning a gold
medal. She first studied painting at the Kazan Art School in 1911, and it was here
that she met her future husband Alexander Rodchenko, with whom she worked
closely throughout her life. In 1912 Stepanova moved to Moscow and studied
under Konstantin Yuon, and in 1913 attended the Stroganov Institute which
taught courses in applied art. This was to be important in her future development,
for of all the leading members of the Russian avant-garde who concerned
themselves with industrial design in the 1920s, only Stepanova had received an
official training. From the age of nineteen she exhibited independently at
exhibitions such as the 'Moscow Salon' of 1914, but during the war years, in order
to earn a living, she took a job as a secretary in a metal-products factory.

In the years following the Revolution Stepanova became particularly interested
in poetry and wrote several transrational poems in the manner of Alexei
Kruchenykh. It was at this point that her mature creative life really began.
Following Rozanova's death in 1918 Stepanova illustrated Kruchenykh's play
Gly gly, combining indian ink drawing with collage. Here Stepanova worked out
a system of mounting figurative and photographic fragments which heralds the
future graphic designer. At this time Stepanova also illustrated editions of her own
and Rozanova's transrational poems. Indicative of her technique of 'graphic
poetry' is her unusual work on the books *Zigra ar* and *Rtny khomle* of 1918 and
Gaust chaba of 1919. These books comprise sheets of non-objective gouache and
collage images constructed on the basis of intersecting rhythms. The words of the

Varvara Stepanova in 1928,
photographed by Rodchenko

92–3

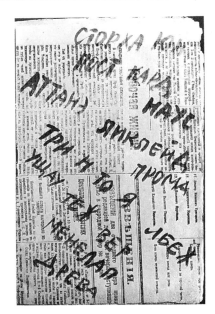

Varvara Stepanova
Gaust chaba, 1918. Script over
newsprint

poems are semantically meaningless and yet they are rich in both their visual and aural qualities. The respective 'textures' of word and image evoke profoundly poetic qualities.

When Stepanova exhibited these graphic works at the 'Tenth State Exhibition: Non-objective Art and Suprematism' in 1919, she declared in the catalogue: 'I am linking the new movement of non-objective poetry – sounds and letters – with a painterly perception that instills a new and vital visual impression into the sound of poetry. I am breaking up the dead monotony of interconnected printed letters by means of painterly graphics, and I am advancing toward a new kind of artistic creation. On the other hand, by reproducing the non-objective poetry of the two books *Zigra ar* and *Rtny khomle* by means of painterly graphics, I am introducing sounds as a new quality in graphic painting.'[2]

Stepanova's technique of graphic poetry follows on from the traditions established by the pre-Revolutionary Futurist books which had attacked the notion of a book as a beautiful and aesthetic object and had established a solid link between poetry and art. However it is interesting that Stepanova's work, as she herself recognized, demonstrates something new in this area. Books such as *Gaust chaba* have been called 'anti-books' because they utilize cheap newspaper whose printed text is denied its communicative function by Stepanova's superimposition of her manuscript text in watercolour. Her poems were entirely transrational while the underlying newspaper was quite prosaic. In addition, the newspaper text was placed sideways with the collages and poems diagonally over it so that it was essentially incomprehensible. As a final act of subversion Stepanova placed the title page at the end of the book. In the conventional sense of the word the book was thoroughly unreadable, and as Kovtun notes, the only way in which works such as *Gaust chaba* related to the concept of a book was in the fact that the pages could be turned.[3]

At this time Stepanova was an advocate of non-objectivity, and wrote a persuasive article on the subject for the catalogue of the 'Tenth State Exhibition' in which she declared: 'Non-objective creation is still only the beginning of a great new epoch, of an unprecedented Great Creation, which is destined to open the doors to mysteries more profound than science and technology.'[4] However her easel work of the period remained essentially abstract, chiefly an animated cycle of paintings entitled *Figures*. A photograph of Stepanova's studio taken in 1922 shows over thirty of this series displayed on the wall. *Figure with Drum* of 1920 like other works from the same cycle creates a convincing synthesis of drawing and painting. The constructive images of the figures are created by the vital and complex lines outlining the geometrical shapes which form them. Also noticeable in these works, and an important aspect of Stepanova's future development as a textile designer, is her sense of texture and her love of the tactile qualities of the paint. Several of these paintings were exhibited at the 'Nineteenth State Exhibition' in Moscow in 1920, while others made their appearance at the 'Erste Russische Kunstausstellung' at the Van Diemen Gallery in Berlin in 1922.

Varvara Stepanova
Figure, 1920

Varvara Stepanova and Alexander Rodchenko in their studio. Photograph by Rodchenko

The *Figures* series contributed enormously to Stepanova's standing in the post-Revolutionary Russian art world, and during the 'Nineteenth State Exhibition' they attracted a great deal of favourable criticism. Stepanova wrote in her diary: 'At the opening Shor got almost embarrassingly carried away. . . . Osmerkin admitted that I'm a real painter and that he never thought I could paint like that. . . . In general everyone congratulated me as if it were my birthday. Shemshurin thought I overworked my paint – in total contrast to Rodchenko (using paint straight from the tube is the sign of an innovator) – but it makes the subject of the painting boring, something which according to him is in general typical of women's art. Chagall noticed an enormous difference in the way we both work . . . like Shemshurin and Shor he was really intrigued as to what I'll do next.'[5]

Of the many exhibitions in which Stepanova participated at this time perhaps the most important was '$5 \times 5 = 25$' which was held under the auspices of the Institute of Artistic Culture (Inkhuk) in Moscow in September 1921. Stepanova participated under the pseudonym of Varst, along with Popova, Rodchenko, Exter and Alexander Vesnin. Each artist was represented by five works which were conceived as a 'farewell to pure painting',[6] and in the catalogue each explained his or her own credo. Popova declared her works to be 'preparatory experiments towards concrete material constructions', while Stepanova for her part

99   exhibited works in the style of *Figure with Drum* and in the catalogue declared the death of composition in art, by stating: 'Composition is the artist's contemplative approach to his work. Technology and industry have confronted art with the problem of construction as an active process and not as contemplative reflection. The sacred value of an artwork as something unique has been destroyed. The museum which was a treasury of this entity is now transformed into an archive.'[7]

The exhibition marked a turning-point in the development of Constructivism, for from that moment forward members of the group increasingly turned away from easel painting to embrace the new aesthetics of Productivism. Like many other innovative artists, Stepanova was concerned with the problem of how to instill her ideas most quickly and broadly into contemporary art, and she found her solution in her work on textile design, theatre design and graphic design.

Both Stepanova and Popova regarded clothing and textile design as a logical extension of their commitment to Productivism, and according to Rowel and Rudenstine, during 1922–3 they formulated a theory and methodology linking the two: 'First and foremost they emphasized the functional aspects of clothing, and while they clearly invested a good deal of imagination in the execution of their designs, they rejected what they considered to be purely 'aesthetic' considerations.'[8] The subject of workers' clothing had already been debated at IZO Narkompros in 1919, after which the Constructivists declared war on the concept of 'universal dress' and advocated instead the concept of *prozodezhda* – the design of specialized clothing for workers of a specific category engaged in specific activities, such as labour or relaxation. The nature of Constructivist clothing was also raised at debates within Inkhuk in the early 1920s, at which Stepanova succinctly declared her programme in stating: 'A basic principle governs clothing constructed today: comfort and expediency. There is no one single type of clothing, but rather specific clothing for a specific productional function.'[9]

Stepanova particularly enjoyed designing specialist clothing for surgeons, firemen and pilots, but some of her most remarkable designs include those for sports 102   clothing in which she combined an economy of material with bold colour-contrasts for easy identification on the sports field. Stepanova thus fulfilled the basic idea of production art as stated by Osip Brik, in which 'the outward appearance of an object is determined by its economic purpose and not by abstract aesthetic considerations'.[10] In late 1923 or early 1924 both Stepanova and Popova began to work in the First State Textile Print Factory in Moscow, translating their experimental designs into practical clothes for daily wear. Stepanova created 150 101   designs of which over 20 were finally put into production. It is true to say that, through the commitment of artists such as Stepanova, the Constructivist aesthetic really did join forces with industrial mass production, and for once the products of Constructivism actually reached the market to which they were ideologically directed. Here again we touch on the theme of the 'tactile' artistic perception of women artists, which links the post-Revolutionary period with the Tsarist times of Elena Polenova, Maria Tenisheva and Maria Yakunchikova.

91 **Varvara Stepanova's** works in the studio she shared with Rodchenko, 1921

< 92 **Varvara Stepanova** Illustration for the transrational book *Zigra ar*, 1918
93 **Varvara Stepanova** Cover design for *Zigra ar*, 1918

94 **Varvara Stepanova** Cover for the magazine *Cine-Photo* (*Kino-fot*), No. 3, 1922

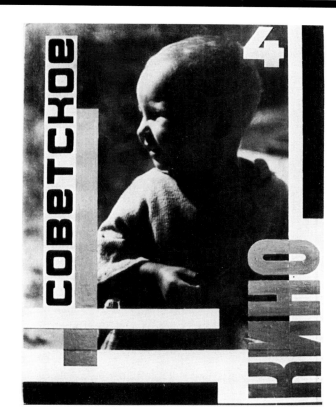

95 Varvara Stepanova
Cover for *Cine-Photo* (*Kino-fot*), No. 2, 1922

96 Varvara Stepanova
Cover for *Soviet Cinema*, No. 4, 1926

97 Varvara Stepanova
Cover for *Soviet Cinema*, No. 1, 1927

98 Varvara Stepanova
Cover for *Literature and Art* (*Literatura i iskusstvo*), No. 1, 1930

149

99 **Varvara Stepanova** *Figure with Drum*, 1921

100 **Varvara Stepanova**
Textile design, 1924

101 **Varvara Stepanova**
wearing a dress of her own
design, 1924

102 **Varvara Stepanova**
Sketches for sports costumes,
1920s

103–5 **Varvara Stepanova**

The Death of Tarelkin, 1922. Designs for clothes and apparatus: overalls and a table (above), and the swing (above right). Right, children on the swing

106–7 *An Evening of the Book* (*Krasnaya Nov*), 1924. Below: the cover of the programme, right: scene at the 'Evening', with the characters

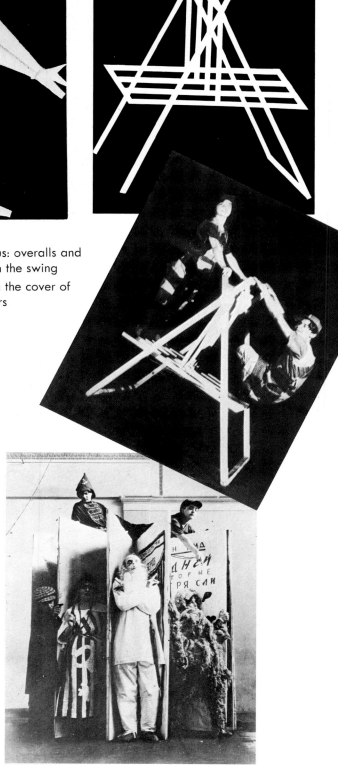

Like her precursors Stepanova was also deeply involved in social and didactic activities. While working in the Textile Factory Stepanova was simultaneously a professor in the Textile Faculty of Vkhutemas where she taught the principles of clothing and textile design. Moreover, throughout the 1920s Stepanova occupied many administrative and teaching posts in the new artistic organizations which flourished following the Revolution. She was a Deputy Head within IZO Narkompros (1918–22), the Academic Secretary of Inkhuk (1920–1), she was on the Decorative Arts panel of the Union of Art Workers (1920–2) and taught in the Fine Arts Studio of the Krupskaya Academy of Communist Education (1920–5).

Varvara Stepanova
Charlie Chaplin Turning Summersaults, 1922

At the same time Stepanova began to work with the theatre director Vsevolod Meyerkhold and designed the stage decor and costumes for the anti-Tsarist play *The Death of Tarelkin* which was performed in Moscow in November 1922. Stepanova's Constructivist designs for the play are clearly related to those by Popova for *The Magnanimous Cuckold* produced earlier in the year. In fact Meyerkhold readily admitted that there was a rivalry between the two artists, with Stepanova consciously trying to outshine Popova in this area.[11] For the set-designs Stepanova created individual constructions which were painted white and distributed across the stage. Each piece was constructed from standardized wooden slats, and some were collapsible so as to perform two or three separate functions. There were grid-like chairs, screens made of struts and a meat-grinder which represented the police station. The open grid-like structure of each piece of staging clearly revealed the means of construction and were conceived as 'instruments for playing on the stage', or, as Stepanova preferred to call them, 'apparatus-objects'.[12]

Stepanova's costume designs also demonstrated her desire to maximize expression through economy of means. Here Stepanova found herself in line with the technicalities of Meyerkhold's production, in which make-up was rejected and conventional acting-procedures were replaced by his concept of Biomechanics. As Alma Law notes in her essay on the production: 'Today we can appreciate this extraordinary production as a landmark, and as one of the most fascinating pages in the history of theatrical Constructivism. At the time however *Tarelkin* pleased 103–5 almost no-one.'[13]

Stepanova was also noted for her contribution to the design of contemporary magazines. In 1922 the artist worked on cover designs for the journal *Cine-Photo* 94–5 (*Kino-fot*) and during 1923–5 she was a regular contributor to the magazine *LEF*. The latter was the organ of a group of Futurist poets and Constructivist artists and critics known as the 'Left Front of the Arts' which was founded in 1923 by the poet Mayakovsky. Although this group held meetings and organized events, its most successful endeavour was the publication of its journal which publicized its ideology of 'Communist Futurism', and declared its aim to 'de-aestheticize the productive arts'. The most important contributors to *LEF* were the critics Osip Brik and Boris Arvatov, artists such as Popova, Rodchenko and Stepanova, and writers such as Mayakovsky, Kruchenykh and Viktor Shklovsky. Even writers such as Boris Pasternak who were not members of the Left Front of the Arts submitted work for publication. Between them Stepanova and Rodchenko were crucial to the publication of the magazine. Rodchenko designed the covers of each issue, while Stepanova worked on the magazine in a technical capacity, and also supplied illustrations of her work (her sports costumes were reproduced in the second issue of April/May 1923), and articles dedicated to Constructivism in action. For the third issue of *LEF* in June/July 1923 she wrote an article 'On the Work of Constructivist Youth' hoping to dispel criticism that the magazine was only interested in purely formal concerns.

106–7 In their renewed commitment to social and political concerns Stepanova, Rodchenko and Mayakovsky contributed to several Government campaigns of the day, most notably that to promote universal literacy. It was in this context that in 1924 Stepanova organized her famous 'Book Evening', a stage performance held in the Club of the Krupskaya Academy of Communist Education. The subject of the performance was that of a battle between pre/Revolutionary and post/Revolutionary literature during which characters, dressed in costumes of Stepanova's design, stepped out one by one from the pages of a huge book. The 'Book Evening' proved to be a particularly successful venture, and was enthusiastically reviewed in the press. This period was also marked by an especially close relationship with Mayakovsky, in which Stepanova executed the posters for Mayakovsky's texts while Rodchenko illustrated his publications.

By 1925, however, *LEF* was in decline following repeated attacks alleging that the magazine was generally incomprehensible to the masses, and in this year its publication was terminated by the State Publishing House. During 1927–8, however, Mayakovsky resurrected the journal under the title of *New LEF* and it gave voice to the same writers and artists who had contributed to the original magazine a few years before. Stepanova and Rodchenko again collaborated on both the content and production of the journal, but it proved unpopular and publication soon ceased. By this time, however, Stepanova had received commissions to execute design work for more conventional publicist magazines, and during 1926–32 she collaborated with the journals *Soviet Cinema*, *Literature and Art*, *Red Students*, *Books and Revolution*, *Contemporary Architecture*, *Abroad*, *The Class Struggle* and *Work Shift*, and in 1933 she made the imposition and design for *Collective Farm Newspaper*.

96–8

At the height of Stepanova's activity in 1925 she had gained international recognition through her contribution to the Exposition Internationale des Arts Décoratifs in Paris. Here Stepanova's work was exhibited in the 'Theatre', 'Textile', 'Graphics' and 'Book Industry' sections, and all together the exhibits revealed how successfully easel art had been abandoned in favour of the Constructivist approach to production art. As Osip Brik concluded, the success of artists such as Stepanova was to realize that 'the textile print is the same product of artistic culture as the picture is, and there is no basis for advancing a dividing line between them'.[14] In addition Brik was speaking specifically of Stepanova and

Popova when he said that 'Only those artists who once and for all have broken with easel craft and have recognized productional work in practice can grapple successfully and productively with the problems of contemporary artistic culture and their solution.'[15] In Constructivist terms, then, Stepanova was recognized as being completely successful, but in the late 1920s the times were changing. The Constructivists were increasingly criticized for pursuing formal investigations, and in the 1930s Stepanova and Rodchenko gave up their intense experimentation and concentrated mainly on the production of photographic albums such as *15 Years of Soviet Cinema*, *10 Years of Uzbekistan*, *Moscow Rebuilds*, *The First Cavalry*, and *Soviet Aviation*. Here Stepanova executed important tasks such as the imposition of a text, page layout and general mock-ups of a publication. The artists' ability to work with script, montage and collage was not new but now it was the nature of the times which demanded it. The mediocritization of the arts which commenced in the second half of the 1930s was becoming more pronounced, and the earlier tendencies of multi-talented artists such as Stepanova were felt to be beyond the limits of Soviet art and even outside its history.

DOCUMENTS

Rodchenko to Stepanova — 20 March 1915, Kazan
Varya!
... I'm freeing art (even Futurist art) from what it has so slavishly held to so far ... I prefer to see ordinary things in an unusual way ... I have found a uniquely original way. I shall make things live like souls ... I shall make people die for things, but things will live. I shall put people's souls into things and things will become souls.
Your Rodchenko[16]

'She was a true artist': Stepanova by her colleague the artist Solomon Telingater
In 1923–4 Stepanova was in Moscow, meeting people who could not but leave a mark on her work, who could not but influence her . . . great people like Mayakovsky, Meyerkhold, and Rodchenko to whom she closely tied her life, as well as a whole range of other comrades. Then there was [the journal] *LEF*, and this left a deep mark on her creative work. At that time I was at the Vkhutemas (1920) and our life was marked by the fact that almost every artist wanted to make some new discovery. This was the formative period when Stepanova was finding her feet in her work. . . . There was a large group, headed by Mayakovsky and under his influence, which felt the need to link their work with the demands of the people in their construction of a new society. Thus came the slogan 'art into production'. The artists tried to link their work more closely to production in the broadest sense – to textiles, typography, metalwork etc. Stepanova first worked in textiles, then typography, in making what the people and the state needed.

When an artist doesn't work privately but sets out to fulfil people's everyday needs, then the aesthetic quality of everyday life is improved. In my opinion this is the case with everything Stepanova did. It is typical of her that not only did she link her life to production art, but it became her life. . . . She had the advantage of practical experience, and she could be found at any time of the day or night working over a model or a manuscript. . . . She made many drawings for textiles, and these are expressive and bright. They have much in common with what we love in folk art. How well she worked with typography! . . . She exploited type without using too much emphasis as many artists of the time were fond of doing. . . . What was important always came across to the reader expressively, clearly and, at the same time, simply . . .[17]

Stepanova: Diary — 1920
. . . Yesterday Anti [Rodchenko] got talking about critics — at the moment we have no real criticism because our critics generally don't try to write according to the essence of what they are criticizing, but to make their writing art, something literary. And they think more about the beauty of their words than about what they are saying. That is why the reader is impressed or disturbed — not by the work which the article or book or whatever was written about, but by the article itself.

Vasilich [Kandinsky] probably likes us, although he doesn't particularly appreciate our eternal disorder. Yesterday I went to ask to borrow a cup (Franketti had called and as we have only two cups, there was nothing for him to drink his tea from).

Nanny said I had come for a cup, and Vasilich answered that whatever we wanted from upstairs, she should always give it to us without asking.[18]

Stepanova in 'Vechernyaya Moskva' (Evening Moscow) — 28 November 1928
Until now the work of the artist in the textile industry has been mainly concerned with decoration, with applying designs to prepared fabrics. The artist works like an appendage, and doesn't participate in either new possibilities for dyeing or in inventing new fabrics or materials. At an industrialized factory the artist remains effectively a primitive craftsman. . . . The artist in the textile factory is thus no way comparable in importance with even the designer at a car factory — what costume designs of the last decade can compare for quality with a post-war Ford?

The only correct path would be for the artist to design clothes and then work backwards to the making and dyeing of the fabric.

'Fashion' rarely comes from the pattern of the fabric — it is the shape of a garment that determines the material and patterns used.

It would be a mistake to think that fashion can be abolished, or that it is haphazard or unnecessary. Fashion gives the lines and shapes to suit the particular time. . . . At the moment one sees an amusing phenomenon — that men's clothes are changing more noticeably than women's, which over the last decade reflect only their emancipation. . . . Men's clothes have gone on a rather dangerous diversion, obliterating all traces of wartime dress such as field-jacket pockets. Rationalizing tendencies are confined to sports clothes. A strange dualism has been created in men's clothes which is a characteristic sign of the instability of capitalist society. In European women's clothes this dualism appears in the exclusive model or dress to be worn just once — perhaps not even sewn but pinned together, such a thing has been seen in couture shows.

If the task of fashion in a capitalist society is to reflect the economic level, then in socialist society fashion will be the development of more and more appropriate forms of clothing. All technological advances should influence forms of dress. . . . Most important of all, the artist should get to know the consumer's daily life, and find out what happens after the fabric leaves the factory.[19]

Nadezhda Udaltsova

Our groups opposed contemporary bourgeois society.
The Futurist poets thundered out against the
bourgeoisie in their poetry while we painters
demolished it in our paintings.
NADEZHDA UDALTSOVA[1]

The artist Nadezhda Udaltsova occupied a central position within the Russian avant-garde. In the years before the Revolution she worked closely with artists such as Malevich, Tatlin and Popova, contributed to many now-historic exhibitions, and played a crucial role in the dissemination of Cubism and in the elaboration of Suprematism. Following the Revolution Udaltsova worked tirelessly in her capacity as a teacher and organizer in the new art schools, but, unlike her colleagues in the Constructivist ranks, she remained a fervent supporter of easel painting. Udaltsova was always a decisive and strong-willed artist, and when in the early 1920s the experimental paths of non-objectivity failed to satisfy her demands she was not afraid to return to a figurative approach. In association with her husband the artist Alexander Drevin she journeyed to Central Russia where she executed works in a schematic and almost Impressionist manner. The death of Drevin in a concentration camp in 1938 brought to an end not only a deeply meaningful marital union but above all a creative one as well. Udaltsova faced this with the same fortitude she had displayed in front of the opponents of the New Art almost a quarter of a century before.

Nadezhda Udaltsova with the study for her painting *The Restaurant*, 1915

Nadezhda Andreevna Udaltsova was born in the town of Orel in 1885.[2] Her father was a severe and taciturn military man who paid little attention to his children. Her mother, though, was more gentle and sensitive. Vera Nikolaevna was well-educated and had an interest in the humanities. From their childhood her daughters (of whom there were four) were encouraged to study art, and in her autobiography Udaltsova tells us that 'Among my earliest recollections is one of my sister and I sitting at a big table and drawing with coloured pencils. Drawing was a second life to us. We invented people and children and depicted them as if they were alive. We took the subjects from our own environment and from the books we read.'[3]

When Udaltsova was six she moved with her parents to Moscow. She recalled that her childhood was sheltered and that this contributed to her introverted character. However Udaltsova read a great deal, and graduated from her High School with distinction. Having left school she was attracted by the idea of studying philosophy at university, but chose instead to pursue an artistic career. Like many talented artists of her generation Udaltsova began by training at the Moscow School of Painting, Sculpture and Architecture, and in 1906 she continued her studies at the art school organized by Konstantin Yuon in Moscow.

However her transition to painting was not smooth: 'I was tortured by a duality: my own art vis-à-vis that of others. Mine was dead. Just naive studies from nature. But my encounter with Nikolai Ulyanov clarified a great deal for me.'[4] It was through her teacher Ulyanov and his encouraging words that Udaltsova finally decided to commit herself to a career in painting. Other important events in this formative period of her career included a visit to a posthumous exhibition of paintings by the Russian Symbolist artist Viktor Borisov-Musatov, where Udaltsova was charmed by the originality of his imagery which was 'genuinely created, not copied'.[5] The idea of a figuratively integrated art, in contrast to the traditionally descriptive approach, became important for Udaltsova at this time, and she began to search for a new plasticity with which to express her perception of life. Traditional artistic teaching methods proved inadequate for Udaltsova and her contemporaries, for as the artist later recalled: 'There was a riddle going around at the time: "What is a sparrow?" The answer was, "A sparrow is a nightingale which has graduated from the Conservatory."'[6]

In 1908 Udaltsova travelled abroad, visiting the Dresden Gallery where she was particularly impressed by the work of Tintoretto. On her return to Russia she also came into contact with Sergei Shchukin, and was allowed to study his remarkable collection of modern and contemporary French paintings. Later she recalled: 'My acquaintance with the French paintings in the Shchukin collection made a terrific impression on me: here was art, creation, not a photograph or a tedious and pitiful imitation. Cézanne, Van Gogh, Gauguin: this was the creation of new, unprecedented forms, new visions of the world.'[7]

At this time Russian artistic life had begun to blossom with a richness hitherto unknown. The famous 'Golden Fleece' exhibitions were taking place in Moscow, Nikolai Kulbin and the artists gathered around him were active in St Petersburg, the young avant-garde were beginning to create a stir in exhibitions such as 'The Link' in Kiev, and week by week new studios were opening where artists could paint informally and discuss the latest ideas from the West. In 1909 Udaltsova began to study with Karol Kish who had organized an up-to-date studio where Udaltsova was immediately introduced to the problems of modern art. Later she recalled: 'I am much indebted to Kish. The search for severity of form and restraint in colour enabled me quickly to assimilate the notion of Cubist construction and to develop as a painter. I made the acquaintance of Vladimir Favorsky and Konstantin Istomin. I studied the principles of painting, of space and form.'[8]

In November 1912 Udaltsova visited Paris with her friend Popova whom she had met through her sister Lyudmilla Prudkovskaya (p. 101). The two artists remained in Paris for a year and studied at the Académie 'La Palette' where they were taught by the classical Cubist painters Metzinger, Le Fauconnier and Dunoyer de Segonzac. This represented a crucial period in the development of both artists, for as Udaltsova recalled: 'Thanks to my teachers, Metzinger and Le Fauconnier, my particular aspirations and endeavours began to define themselves. . . . Cognition of the world of phenomena, clarity of construction, the composition of space, the correlation of masses – these were elements which I had sought long and importantely. This was not the monotonous, superfluous copying of models, but a creative art, or so it seemed to me then.'[9]

Udaltsova's studio work at this time included drawings of Cubist nudes such as *Model* of 1913 which in their planar analysis of form bear a strong resemblance to Popova's sketches of the same period. However Udaltsova also executed many informal studies in the streets of Paris, at Versailles and in the museums. Her letters to her husband Alexander Udaltsov are full of such references: 'I walked about Paris sketching old buildings', 'I spent a wonderful morning in the Cluny drawing enamels' or 'I'm just going off to the Louvre to sketch.'[10] Udaltsova's drawing *On the Bank of the Seine* is a particularly fine sketch of this period which could easily have been worked up into a full-scale Cubist landscape in the manner of either Metzinger or Le Fauconnier.

113

112

Udaltsova was 'absolutely enchanted' during her time in Paris: 'That city with the cubes of its houses and the interweaving of its viaducts, with the smoke of its locomotives, with its airplanes and airships up in the sky presented itself as a fantastic pictorial object, as a piece of genuine art. Picasso incarnated the ochre and silver architecture of the Parisian houses in his Cubist compositions.'[11] In addition to studying the most modern of art Udaltsova and Popova also took the opportunity to study the work of the Old Masters: 'I often went to the Louvre studying Poussin, Leonardo, the Dutch school. I was particularly interested in their textures and also in the drawings of the Renaissance artists such as Raphael and Michelangelo. I visited the Musée Cluny where the coloured *vitraux* of Matisse helped me to understand the great master.'[12]

When Udaltsova returned to Moscow in the winter of 1913 both she and Popova began work in Tatlin's 'Tower' studio. Here like-minded artists such as Alexander Vesnin and Alexei Grishchenko encouraged both Udaltsova and Popova to preach the new language of Cubism. A few months later Udaltsova contributed one of her *Cubist Compositions* to the 'Knave of Diamonds' exhibition in Moscow, but it was not until 1915 that she made her real debut among the avant-garde. In this one year alone Udaltsova participated in three major exhibitions and made her name as an accomplished Cubist painter. At the exhibition 'Tramway V' held in Petrograd in February 1915 she exhibited eight Cubo-Futurist paintings alongside the transrational paintings of Malevich, the painterly reliefs of Tatlin and the Cubist works of Popova and Puni. Udaltsova also participated in the 'Exhibition of Leftist Tendencies' in April 1915 and in 'The Last Futurist Exhibition: 0.10', where she showed her Cubist painting *Bottle and Wineglass* (State Tretyakov Gallery) which was afterwards bought by Tatlin and displayed in 'The Store' exhibition of 1916.

The paintings which Udaltsova exhibited at 'Tramway V' had all been executed during 1914 and demonstrated the breadth of her ability. They included works such as *Restaurant Table* (State Tretyakov Gallery) and *The Restaurant* (State Russian Museum) for which the former was a study. *The Restaurant* was

Nadezhda Udaltsova
Musical Instruments, 1915

apparently inspired by Udaltsova's memories of the atmosphere and fashions of Paris, and in trying to suggest the bustle and modernity of the city she relies not only on classical Cubist devices, such as the decorative manipulation of intersecting surfaces and volumes of colour with significant details interspersed, but also on the rhythmical dynamism of Futurist lines of force. The painting may justifiably be called Cubo-Futurist in style, but even here the rigorous Cubist analysis which underlies the composition is sufficient to differentiate the work of Udaltsova from that of her contemporaries such as Goncharova, Rozanova and Popova. The preparatory oil study entitled *Restaurant Table* was thoroughly Cubist, emulating the Analytical paintings of Picasso and Braque in subject, composition, style and the restrained palette of colours used. A drawing for this painting also entitled *Restaurant Table* reflects Udaltsova's interest in the strict analysis of still-life forms, and it is this which distinguishes her from the more intuitive and emotional approach of her colleagues.

114

Following the exhibition Udaltsova was spurred on to paint a whole series of Cubist works in which the methods of Metzinger and Le Fauconnier were gradually replaced by the techniques of Picasso and Braque. *The Kitchen* of 1915 demonstrates the same vertical structure to be found in Picasso's work, as well as the same faceted treatment of form and surrounding space. In other works such as *Blue Jug*, *Musical Instruments* and *Morning* the titles of newspapers jump off the page to occupy an abstract plane, colours remain restrained and objects are again subjected to a rigorous formal analysis. However in these paintings there is also a strong emphasis on the qualities of texture as suggested by Synthetic Cubist works. *Morning* incorporates scraps of newspaper while in *Blue Jug* the paint seems to have been thickened with another medium to give it a rough surface texture. *Musical Instruments* is particularly impressive in this respect. This canvas represents a Cubist formulation and treatment of musical instruments with all their associations, but the painting also includes a portion of simulated framing with the outer sections of the canvas handled in a much coarser and rough manner than the central composition.

109

108, 110

Udaltsova later recalled that when these works were exhibited 'the press constantly and justifiably condemned our activities, flung mud at us. "Boors" and "hooligans" were the commonest adjectives used to describe us.'[13] In response the artist wrote an essay entitled 'How the Critics and Public Relate to Contemporary Russian Art' in which she took critics such as Alexander Benois firmly to task: 'One feels like crying out: "How long is this going to last for? How much longer is artistic innovation going to encounter only ridicule, mistrust, insults? In science the law of evolution is acknowledged, so why should art be doomed to stand still and go on with the same old truths?"'[14] This essay was as powerful in its polemics but as persuasive in its reasoning as Rozanova's defence of the avant-garde published two years before (p. 97) Again the women artists of the avant-garde demonstrated their ability not only to defend their point of view but also to present a lucid interpretation of the theoretical basis for their artistic achievements.

108 **Nadezhda Udaltsova** *Cubist Composition: Blue Jug,* 1915

109 **Nadezhda Udaltsova** *Cubist Composition: The Kitchen*, 1915

110 **Nadezhda Udaltsova** *Cubist Composition: Morning*, 1915

111 **Nadezhda Udaltsova** *Decorative Composition*, 1916

112 **Nadezhda Udaltsova**
On the Bank of the Seine, 1912

113 **Nadezhda Udaltsova**
Model, 1913

114 **Nadezhda Udaltsova**
Study for *Restaurant Table*, 1914

115 **Nadezhda Udaltsova**
On the Threshing Floor, 1932

116 **Nadezhda Udaltsova**
In an Armenian Village Garden,
1933

117 **Nadezhda Udaltsova**
In an Armenian Village Garden,
1933

118 **Nadezhda Udaltsova** *Horseman in the Forest*, 1931

119 **Nadezhda Udaltsova** *Building the Haystack, Altai*, 1931

Rodchenko recalled that 'Udaltsova would often arrive and talk quietly and ingratiatingly about Cubism. . . . She understood Cubism more than anyone else and worked more seriously than the others.'[15]

During 1915 and 1916 Udaltsova's proximity to Tatlin led her to execute a series of *Painterly Constructions* (State Tretyakov Gallery). In these she overlapped textured abstract planes so as to suggest the basis of a relief construction somewhat in the manner of Tatlin. At this time there was a general tendency in Russian art to experiment with reliefs and the constructive properties of materials. According to Malevich, Udaltsova actually executed a relief, and we know that she was sufficiently close to Tatlin to edit a pamphlet he published for the exhibition '0.10'.[16] However Udaltsova's conception remained principally a painterly one, motivated by interest in the constructive use of colour and texture on the canvas.

It was for this reason that Udaltsova did not follow Tatlin's 'Constructivist' lead to its logical conclusions, but turned instead to embrace the more painterly movement of Suprematism. In 1916 she participated with the Suprematist artists at the 'Knave of Diamonds' exhibition in Moscow, and during 1916–17 she became a member of the 'Supremus' group. At this time she grew friendly with Malevich and executed many Suprematist compostions. Although not directly Suprematist, her *Decorative Composition* of 1916 indicates the nature of the changes taking place in her work. A new pictorial dynamism is evident, as well as a new appreciation of the qualities of colour and its different characteristics when applied to canvas or a sheet of paper. *Decorative Composition* is also characteristic in that it is executed in gouache, which became an important medium for the artist in 1916. Malevich, however, seems to have been unimpressed with her work of this period and, with all the weight of a teacher marking a report, declared: 'Did not fully understand Suprematism. Sensed everything in terms of objects.'[17]

111

At this point the Revolution intervened in Udaltsova's career, giving it a decisively new goal and bias. In her memoirs Udaltsova recalled that 'my colleagues and I gladly accepted the October Revolution and, from the very beginning, we went to work for the Soviets and then for the People's Commissariat for Enlightenment. I played a vital role in the reorganization of the art institutes and, beginning in 1918, worked in various departments and studios.' At first Udaltsova joined the Free State Studios where she worked as an assistant to Kazimir Malevich, and then became the head of her own studio. When in 1920 the Higher Artistic and Technical Studios were organized as Vkhutemas, she became a professor and senior lecturer, and remained on the staff until 1934. During this period Udaltsova also taught painting courses at the Textile Institute and then the Institute of Printing in Moscow.

In the Revolutionary years Udaltsova was considered to be one of the most progressive personalities of her time, in both a creative and a social sense. Even the newspaper *Anarchy* cried 'Hail to the creator Udaltsova for her barbarously painted abstract canvases.'[18] However, she was also one of the most uncompromising artists of her age. In 1920 she became a member of the Institute of Artistic Culture

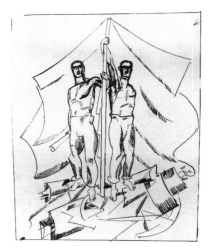

Nadezhda Udaltsova
Democratic Republic, 1917

Nadezhda Udaltsova
Holding the Banner, 1917

Nadezhda Udaltsova
Shaman, 1931

(Inkhuk) and was naturally attracted by the discussions which took place within its ranks on the fate of easel art. Like her colleagues she took an active part in the debate, but when the Institute endorsed the Constructivist line and declared the end of easel painting, she objected and resigned her membership.

Udaltsova's intense teaching and organizational work within the art schools necessarily curtailed her painterly practice, but it is significant that in the early 1920s her new aspirations in art drew her away from the radical avant-garde and closer to the former Knave of Diamonds artists such as Ilya Mashkov, Petr Konchalovsky and Aristarkh Lentulov. Of all the various groups at the time the Knave of Diamonds was most successfully involved in solving the pictorial problems of art. It was thus a natural development for Udaltsova to align herself with them and to exhibit alongside them at the 'Exhibition of Paintings' in 1923, for as the art critic Tugendkhold noted: 'Its very title tells of its reaction against exhibitions of objects, constructions and the like.'[19] Udaltsova's paintings at this exhibition differ notably from her previous works. Her *Self-portrait* of 1923 (State Tretyakov Gallery), for example, relies for its expressive potential on a complex modulation of blue, black and white. According to Malevich this painting was 'saturated with the painterliness of the Cézanne style' and represented a new phase in which 'her painting begins to take on forms again as if this person had never painted before'.[20]

There is little doubt that Malevich saw Udaltsova's creative development at this point as being hopelessly regressive, and analyzing her works of 1924 he notes another 'backward' step in that her art 'changes to a realism of the Impressionist kind and to a Claude Monet approach'.[21] However, Udaltsova was theoretically astute, and seems to have understood that her non-objective art now needed the introduction of concrete natural impressions. Under the influence of her second husband Alexander Drevin she returned to nature and began painting landscapes in the open air. Udaltsova wrote: 'My own creative urge alternated with my passive observation, experience and study of nature. My life in the winter at the city art school alternated with my life in the summer in the country amidst the virgin wildness of nature.'[22]

During 1926–34 Udaltsova and Drevin travelled widely across Russia, visiting and painting the Ural and Altai Mountains, Armenia and Central Asia. The artist was especially taken with 'the hills and valleys of the Urals, the swiftly flowing Chusova glittering in the evening glow, the bears in the pine forests, the hoary mountain-tops, the blue of the forests and fiery sunsets, the villages on the banks of the rivers and the melodious voices of the women and children.'[23] All these experiences found their way into her landscapes of this period. Particularly interesting are those depicting agricultural life in the Altai, such as *Building the Haystack* of 1931 and *On the Threshing Floor* of 1932 as well as her enchanting images of peasant life in the villages of Armenia, which include canvases such as *In an Armenian Village Garden* of 1933.

From a technical point of view the main organizational principle in her paintings of these years was colour and light. As the artist recalled: 'My trip to the

Altai region, its transparent air, its precise forms, its dazzling, omnipresent light, prompted a dramatic change in my work. Impressions came so fast and furious that I had to simply sketch them down quickly. Since it was impossible to take paint and pad with me when I went riding on long trips, I made rough notations by using strokes that only I could understand. In this way, I returned once again to painting without nature. I had, so to speak, come full circle. I was confronted with the same pictorial problems that I had encountered before, except that I now had the rich experience of having worked both on abstract form and with nature.'[24]

Udaltsova's paintings entitled *In an Armenian Village Garden* are perhaps the most lyrical of her later works. Lines are no longer hard and tense but have become soft and flowing, and here Udaltsova uses the colour possibilities of the entire spectrum. As Malevich noted, 'Udaltsova perceives nature only in terms of colour and not in drawing.'[25] In this Udaltsova pursued a similar path to other artists of the time, and in 1931 exhibited at the 'Group 13' exhibition which brought together artists of a lyrical and impressionist persuasion. Udaltsova had attuned herself to the inner necessity of her art and admitted change when change was due. She remained above all an easel artist, committed to solving purely pictorial problems with paint on canvas. In this way Udaltsova spanned the painterly hiatus caused by Constructivism and the cul-de-sac of Suprematism, until she was eventually rejoined by many of her colleagues at the birth of a new period in which the loud polemics of the avant-garde were silenced in favour of a new and more intimate approach to art.

Nadezhda Udaltsova at work, Moscow, 1937

DOCUMENTS

Udaltsova on her contemporaries
I first saw Mayakovsky in 1911 at a lecture about a little exhibition of Larionov's. He was standing in the doors, in a black shirt, with curly hair and shining, penetrating eyes. At that time he had only just started at the art school.

From 1911 to 1912 [1912–13] I went abroad. When we were young we had great confusion in our heads. I was attracted by Futurism and studied in Paris [at La Palette] with Le Fauconnier and Metzinger. Metzinger said: 'What we have discovered will be enough for a hundred years.' He was a friend of Picasso's who had started all these new ideas. Already at that time he had done some things that were wonderful in their lightness and their construction. Americans, Swedes and Russians studied in our studio: it was kept by an Englishman but the French didn't come for some reason – they considered it a mad-house.

It was a colourful time with interesting characters. In the spring of 1913 I returned to Moscow. I chanced on an exhibition which was being held in the Lemercier building. Left-wing artists were shocking the Muscovite bourgeoisie. Tatlin, for instance, exhibited a relief which was fixed in the passage-way and the public tore their shoes on its nails . . .

I remember very clearly an evening at Kulbin's at the end of December 1915. Mayakovsky read extracts from *War and Peace*. Among those present were a group of Muscovites – Tatlin, Popova and me. Khlebnikov also read his poetry – he got a bit confused and Maykovsky prompted him from the corner. He loved

Khlebnikov and knew his work by heart. The impression made by Mayakovsky's poetry was very strong . . .

Then there was the '0.10' exhibition (1915). That was a piece of Malevich's wit. He thought, everything ended in nothing and then – ten. At the exhibition Malevich hung a square, a circle, some shapes on a white surface: the flight of an aeroplane and so on. Later Malevich began to do desk-sets, then he did some very interesting abstract architectural constructions composed of planes. He dreamed of totally changing people's furniture and rooms, of repainting towns. Malevich passionately believed in his ideas. For some reason I once went to his place. Malevich opened the desk and there was an endless quantity of papers there. They were all compositions which he was transferring to canvas – the flying-motion of aeroplanes, little squares, sticks. . . . He invented his square. That was probably a moment of genius. He was simply obsessed with this square on white, with his red circle also on white. Nonetheless there was something great about this square and this circle. Whenever Malevich arrived, he had always come with a new idea. He was a businesslike man in some ways, but he was not cunning. To be more precise, all his astuteness was on the surface and in the end he was often deceived in business. He and Tatlin never became friends, but when Malevich died, Tatlin wept.[26]

M. N. Yablonskaya: As I Remember Udaltsova

To crown everything there was her ever-increasing isolation – there were no exhibitions, no sales, no recognition. But no, in the end there was her life as an artist, or rather, her life in art.

In 1952 the former Vkhutemas Building on Kirov Street, that had long been home to many outstanding representatives of pre-Revolutionary Russian and Soviet artistic life, had become a block of cramped communal flats. Besides housing the original inhabitants it was tightly packed with all sorts of Muscovites, and, most often of all, with recent arrivals from the countryside. And that's how it was with Flat No. 51. I remember a rather dark, high-ceilinged communal kitchen, with an uneven floor of black and white tiles, clean but not homely. There was a grey-haired, thin, bent old man with cottonwool in his ears, always wearing the same embroidered skull-cap. He was bending over a little saucepan, stirring something which bubbled peevishly. This was the former leader of Russian literary Futurism, now subsisting by selling books, famous in his time as a rebel and innovator, poet, artist and bibliophile – Alexei Kruchenykh. Neighbours' children ran up shouting joyfully, someone would appear in the kitchen half-dressed, drunk and swearing. More rarely a small woman would appear in a dark neat dress which was obviously the only one she possessed. This was Nadezhda Udaltsova. I have no idea what Udaltsova ate (since she was alive I presume she did eat). My strongest impression was of her complete disregard of everyday problems, her total aloofness from them. Her goodwill towards her surroundings was absolute. Later I understood that her lack of bitterness arose from her sense of fulfilment. Her painting had always been a compensation, but never more so than in the 1950s. She had a miserly pension and put aside whatever she could for the summer so that she could rent a hut in a village and live there to paint. An injury during the most difficult period of her life had left her an invalid. Not just journeys but even moving around her flat became difficult. She nevertheless found ways to continue painting, chiefly still-lifes, such as *Pizhma* and her last work, the *Kitchen Table* (1960, State Russian Museum).[27]

3 WOMEN ARTISTS AND THE 'CHAMBER ART' OF THE 1920s AND 1930s

Antonina Sofronova

Eva Rozengolts-Levina

Nina Simonovich-Efimova

Eva Rozengolts-Levina

Antonina Sofronova

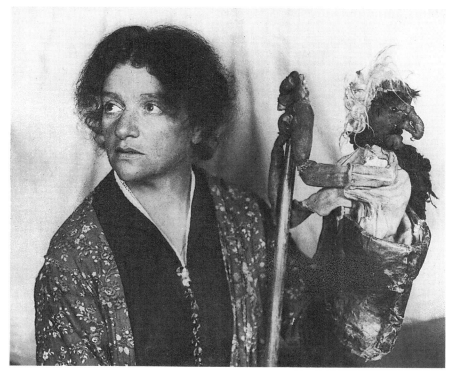

Nina Simonovich Efimova

Antonina Sofronova

An action involves choice, and by selecting one
possibility we reject others. Choosing emotion, we
reject peace of mind, choosing work, we reject
frivolity, choosing fawning, we reject creativity.

LIDYA GINZBURG[1]

Antonina Sofronova, 1916

A whole constellation of women artists came to maturity in the late 1920s and early 1930s, and it is interesting to consider their work from the viewpoint of the above quotation. It has been aptly noted that 'at the end of the 1920s culture entered a period, if not of exhaustion then of lassitude, when a whole continent of reality interposed itself between the reviled past and the bright future. The present, previously unnoticed, appeared before the artist. It was impossible to ignore it any longer. It could not be avoided but had to be lived through, seemingly for a whole life-time.'[2] This was a period in which official demands grew more restrictive and artists were faced with real-life choices.

During the 1910s and 1920s women artists had been at the forefront of artistic developments of international significance. The most radical artists such as Stepanova and Rodchenko had thrown themselves into Constructivism and production art, but many such as Udaltsova and Drevin remained tied to the easel and began to return along the path to figuration. Moreover many groups of artists in the early 1920s were directly challenging the principles of the avant-garde. Notable in this respect was the powerful 'Association of Artists of Revolutionary Russia' (AKHRR), which reaffirmed the realist approach to art. In the face of such opposition the avant-garde was forced to retreat. By the late 1920s exhibitions of non-realist art were rarely held, and experimental work was criticized as 'formalist' – a term which was applied to any art which was seen to lack social or political values. In 1932 the 'Decree on the Reconstruction of Literary and Artistic Organizations' seriously curtailed the artist's independence, and dissolved all official art groups. This measure paved the way for the formal proclamation of Socialist Realism at the 'First All-Union Conference of Soviet Writers' of 1934. It was here that Maxim Gorky described the years before the Revolution as the 'most disgraceful and shameful decade in the history of the Russian intelligentsia', and under his chairmanship the Conference endorsed Socialist Realism as the only viable form of expression for artists and writers.[3]

Within this general trend towards Socialist Realism the 'feminine face' became less evident and women artists began to lead a kind of 'counter-movement'. In the early 1930s their work became more personal and they created a 'chamber art' which, due to its intimate and poetic qualities, set itself apart from the general development. We see it in the later work of Udaltsova and even in works by Malevich and Stepanova. It is in the context of the evolution of painting in this period that Antonina Sofronova falls within our sphere of interest. Belokhvostova wrote that 'a whole generation of gifted artists who came to maturity in the 1920s and 1930s were fated to be forgotten, particularly the younger generation: Sofronova, Shchukin, Zefirov, Kazenin, Markova, Nekrasov, Morgunov, Egorov and many others'.[4] It is only today that these 'forgotten' artists are being rediscovered, and their respective contributions re-evaluated.

Antonina Fyodorovna Sofronova was born in 1892 into the family of a local doctor in the village of Droskovo in Orel Province. In 1909 she graduated from the Girls' Commercial College in Kiev and, aspiring to an artistic education, moved to Moscow in 1910. Here she began to study in the School of Feodor Rerberg, where Malevich had studied some years before. Then in 1913 she transferred to the studio of Ilya Mashkov where she continued her studies until the Revolution took place. Alexander Benois noted that 'in Mashkov you can sense something firm, thorough and peaceful, and he is just the same among his seventy pupils whom he trains not only to draw from nature but to practise all the basic techniques of painting'.[5] The atmosphere and teaching of Mashkov's studio were ideally suited to Sofronova's needs, and here she gained a lucid command of form, colour and technique. Her fellow student V. Shlezenger noted that at this time Sofronova possessed 'balance, a calm spirit and above all, an aptitude for work'.[6]

Hardly any of Sofronova's paintings have been preserved from this early period, and we can only observe that in the 'Knave of Diamonds' exhibition of 1914 Sofronova exhibited alongside works by Braque, Derain, Konchalovsky, Lentulov, Malevich, Mashkov, Morgunov and Picasso, and that in the 'World of

Antonina Sofronova (right) with friends, 1911

State Free Studios, Tver 1921. Antonina Sofronova (on the back row) and Mikhail Sokolov (centre) with their pupils

Art' exhibition of 1917 she was in the company of Rozhdestvensky, Falk, Popova, Klyun, Rozanova, Exter and Malevich. It was in 1919 that Sofronova began to paint her first mature works, and set herself her future programme: 'I must surrender my feelings to nature. I must develop powers of observation and inventiveness in myself and I must work.'[7]

120   Sofronova was clearly influenced by her contact with the Knave of Diamonds, and paintings such as *Fragrant Tobacco* of 1919 recall the magnificent still-lifes by artists such as Mashkov and Kuprin. However the discussions and disputes taking place around Sofronova forced her to pay attention to other tendencies, and her works of this year also betray certain departures from the Knave of Diamonds

121   tradition. Paintings such as *Landscape with Trees* lack the density of paint and the decorative qualities so characteristic of the Knave of Diamonds. In addition they possess a simplified approach to form and a dynamism of brushwork which indicates an interest in Expressionist tendencies. Sofronova's *Portrait of My Daughter* also of 1919 reveals her attention to colour and spatial arrangements, and represents a logical transition from her figurative paintings of the 1910s to the abstract and non-objective graphic experiments of the next decade.

During 1920 Sofronova taught at the State Art Studios in Tver (now Kalinin) with the artist Mikhail Sokolov. Here she entertained a broad approach to painting. A photograph of her studio at this time (pl. 123) shows paintings by herself and her students comprising Expressionist landscapes, Cubist portraits and a series of still-life studies which reveal investigations into the nature of form and colour. In the atumn of 1921, however, Sofronova returned to Moscow, where the arguments about easel painting versus production art were at their height. Sofronova made her own response to this dialogue by producing a substantial series of 'constructive' drawings executed with charcoal, watercolour and indian ink. Some drawings such as *Figure* of 1922 are reminiscent of the dynamism and rhythm of Stepanova's figure-compositions, while others, such as *Composition* of 1922, are completely non-objective and betray the influence of Popova's *Spatial Force Constructions* (cf. pl. 124, fig. p. 104) and the Suprematist drawings of Ivan Klyun.

For a brief period Sofronova clearly allied herself with the Constructivist aesthetic and turned towards graphic design. In this respect she is particularly noted

Antonina Sofronova
Constructive Composition, 1922

Antonina Sofronova
Moscow Landscape, 1922

for her work on the book *From the Easel to the Machine* of 1923, a major treatise on Constructivism by the art critic Nikolai Tarabukin.[8] However Sofronova's work from the mid-1920s onwards shows that Constructivism represented only a short-lived phase in her career. Her 'constructive' drawings were no more than a tribute to the most vital ideas of the day. Moreover, Sofronova never completely gave up her ties with figuration, and wrote in her diary at this time that 'non-objective art is useful only in so far as its effect on the viewer is to raise the organizing force of consciousness – to increase its intensity'.[9] Consequently from the mid-1920s Sofronova returned to a more figurative approach and became renowned as an artist of the urban landscape.

The theme of the city had preoccupied Sofronova as early as 1921 when she wrote in her diary that 'the "green world" and the world of urban culture are the same. One has come from the other and could return to it again. It is all one matter and one spirit. This idea came clear one day when I returned to Moscow after a long stay in the countryside. Moscow grew up like a forest amid the surrounding fields. I noticed a striking correspondence between the forms of Moscow and the forms of the countryside. I understood that there was no difference between them . . . If one has the skill to extract the elements from the subject, almost any kind of landscape will serve as a means of revelation.'[10]

During 1924–5 Sofronova executed a series of watercolours and indian ink drawings entitled *Moscow Street Types* in which she depicted the low-life of the city,

Antonina Sofronova
Logo for the Northern Forest Company, 1923

Antonina Sofronova
Cover design for *From the Easel to the Machine* by Nikolai Tarabukin, 1923

Antonina Sofronova
Homeless Children, from the series *Moscow Street Types*, 1924

Antonina Sofronova
Sunflowers, 1924

the homeless urchins, the drunks and the beggars, besides rural images such as *Sunflowers*. Then in the later 1920s and early 1930s she executed a large and impressive series of Moscow cityscapes including *Moscow Street* of 1928 and the wonderfully naive *Smoke of MOGES* (the Moscow Hydro-electric Station) of 1930 (pl. 127). Also belonging to this series is *The Square, White Houses* of 1930 which is surprising in its use of opalescent colour combinations, and the evocative painting *Alleys of the Arbat* of 1932 (pl. 128). All these works are approached with a delicacy and simplicity which testify to the impact on Sofronova of the French painter Maurice Utrillo, whose quiet and nostalgic cityscapes of Paris had been shown in Moscow in the large 'Exhibition of Contemporary French Art' in 1928.

Many artists were decisively influenced by this important exhibition, and those who were particularly taken with the more lyrical and impressionist trends of modern French art banded together in 1929 to form the 'Group 13'. This society took its name from the number of participants at its first exhibition, but in distinction to other societies of the period the group was essentially reserved and retrospective. As the main aim of the group was to convey their direct impressions of nature clearly and easily, their spontaneous studies were not considered as preliminaries but as complete artistic works in themselves. For them expressive drawing and rapid watercolour sketches took on a special value. 'Group 13' never issued any manifestos or declarations, and only encapsulated its approach in a letter to Lunacharsky in which its members stated: 'This group brings together the most energetic and healthy trends in Russian drawing. It primarily aspires to a healthy and joyful perception of life, free of Gothic arrangement and mental unbalance.'[11] The creative atmosphere of the group and its emphasis on Impressionist values attracted Sofronova, and in 1931 she participated in the second and last exhibition of the group.

However the 'Group 13' exhibition was badly received. Those who participated were branded 'formalists', while the critics attacked the artists on the grounds of 'aloofness, lifelessness and superficiality'.[12] Sofronova was herself implicated, and as the artist Nikolai Kuzmin remembered, 'After that Sofronova's pictures could only be seen in her attic on the Arbat. She almost stopped painting. Her pictures were never shown . . . Sofronova's art, so filled with clarity, lightness and lyricism makes us forget that the artist's creative path was thorny.'[13] Sofronova's *Self-portrait* of 1931 and her poems from that period testify eloquently to the situation in which she found herself:

132

> Icy needles of crystals,
> Hoar Frost is winter's light coat,
> The dry sparkle of your opals
> does not disperse the darkness of the heart!
>
> Though through the gloom of the troubled night
> The snowstorm spreads its sleep,
> In the silence of the solitary midnight
> The heart's groan is stronger.
>
> The blue of sapphire, the brilliance of azure!
> Frost stills the blood,
> The heart begs for a spring storm,
> The heart waits for spring thunder.[14]

Sofronova continued to paint her cityscapes until the mid-1930s, and among her best works of this period are those which forsake the enclosed areas of yards and backstreets in favour of the 'real' spaces of wide parks and avenues such as *Woodland Path* of 1933–4, or those which display a new intensity of colour such as the charming *Pink House, Blue Fence* of 1933–4. But gradually Sofronova retreated from the world. Her art became more intimate, and she concentrated on portraits and still-lifes. However her work can be seen as a complete success. To the complexity of the historical moment in which her art was formed and developed, Sofronova counterposed the world of her images. In this she found her own salvation, and like

130

129

Rozengolts-Levina and kindred painters, demonstrated the firmess of her position in relation to the growing contradictions in art.

DOCUMENTS

Sofronova: Diary – Orel 1916–17
. . . When approaching a painting we should have in mind the strongest contrasts existing in a given group of objects – whether this is the contrast between light and dark colours or between shapes; and then beginning from the biggest, or rather, the most general, one should move gradually to the lesser, constantly opposing and subordinating the latter to the former.

. . . Light and shade is formed by the aggregate of tonal contrasts, arising on the surface of an object depending on how it is illuminated and on its form.

. . . The pictorial or plastic characteristics of an object, i.e. those characteristics which could serve as the content of an artistic construction of that object, can be subdivided into characteristics that are constant and those that are transient.

Constant features – volume (quantitative)
form (qualitative)
tonality (quantitative)
colour (qualitative)

(Volume and tonality are quantitative categories, form and colour are qualitative.)

Transient features – linear perspective
light and shade
aerial perspective

. . . I have been very concerned by texture recently. I think that to achieve results one needs years of experience.

I think that if texture is not the very art of a painting then it is one of its most essential means of expression.

31 July
. . . It could be said that the whole art of painting comes down to the following: what colour and what tone should be used on a given surface in what position, and using what technical method.

4 August
Landscape with a chimney, a coloured composition. At first: blue, green, brown, reddish-violet. The reddish-violet attacks as if destroying the harmony. It turns out like an extra weight on the scales . . .

6 May
. . . To combine two starting points in a painting, the spiritual and the formal, that is the highest aim, but it is hard not to fall into the chasm of the inartistic. Keeping the balance between these two could only be done by such masters as Rembrandt and Michelangelo.

10 July
It seems to me that the desire to include in a work of art elements of the real (sticking on all sorts of things, even the article itself, beads or spoons as with Lentulov) is an extremely paradoxical demonstration of naturalism.[15]

Eva Rozengolts-Levina

All Eva Rozengolts-Levina's work is a symbol . . .
                    MIKHAIL ALPATOV

Eva Rozengolts-Levina was an artist who experienced all the pressures and processes of twentieth-century Russian culture. Her career had much in common with that of Sofronova and artists of a similar persuasion who attempted to bridge the rift between the ideological and the artistic which had opened up during the first half of the nineteenth century. As Elena Murina observed: 'When that unity between social, psychological, spiritual and artistic concerns which had sustained classical art was destroyed, then painting looked inwards to its own specifics. The human aspects of life fell outside this artistic sphere.'[1] In essence the career of Rozengolts-Levina represented an attempt to heal the breach between art and the human soul, and it was from this endeavour that her art gained its tragic inspiration and value.

Eva Rozengolts was born into a large and friendly family in Vitebsk in 1898. Initially she was inspired by the remarkable example of her mother who, as soon as Eva and her five brothers were old enough, 'became interested in drawing and attended the People's Art College which had been organized in Vitebsk'.[2] Here Eva's mother studied under the 'World of Art' painter Mstislav Dobuzhinsky and the artist Vera Ermolaeva. She also attended Malevich's school where she encountered the theories of Suprematism, and in later years taught a drawing course there. Eva was the only child in the family to share her mother's passion for art but her father insisted on a different profession. Consequently when she graduated from the Alekseev High School in Vitebsk in 1915 she worked as a hospital nurse and later entered the School of Dentistry at Tomsk University. In 1919 Rozengolts-Levina was in Moscow where she made her first contact with the art establishment. Here she became interested in the work of the sculptor Stepan Erzya (1876–1959), and she worked in his studio for a short while before returning to Vitebsk. At this time Russia was torn apart by the Civil War in which three of Rozengolts-Levina's brothers lost their lives. For the rest of the year she herself worked as a nurse on the Civil War front, caring for the soldiers of the Red Army who were dying in a typhus epidemic.

It was only in 1920 that Rozengolts-Levina returned to Moscow with the intention of becoming an artist, though initially, like Goncharova before her, she began her career as a sculptor. At first she met Anna Golubkina and joined her studio. However Golubkina considered her pupil frivolous, and a difficult and uncommunicative relationship developed between them (p. 36). Murina also

Eva Rozengolts-Levina while a student at the Tomsk School of Dentistry, 1917

Eva Rozengolts-Levina (left) as a nurse in 1916

Eva Rozengolts-Levina in Robert Falk's studio, 1928. Falk and Rozengolts-Levina are on the left in the second row

testifies to Rozengolts-Levina's capricious yet analytical nature when she declared her to be 'a charming young woman, very feminine, occasionally frivolous but at the same time extremely acute',[3] while another acquaintance sensed 'a centre of steel in her'.[4] Nonetheless Rozengolts-Levina revered her teacher, and her contact with the serious yet romantic Anna Golubkina prepared the young artist for her meeting with the painter Robert Falk later in the year.

Before the war Falk had played a prominent role within the Knave of Diamonds group, and since the Revolution he had joined the teaching staff at Vkhutemas. In 1921 Rozengoltz-Levina became his pupil and gave up a career in sculpture for a life in painting. The transition was easy for the artist, since painting appeared a more direct and responsive medium than sculpture, and Golubkina herself had repeatedly remarked upon her gifts as a colourist.[5] Rozengolts-Levina's work with Falk immediately crystallized her approach to painting, and it is said that every year throughout the rest of her life she would finish one of her works on the 1st of October and dedicate it to his memory. Falk in his turn was once heard to remark among his students that he considered Rozengolts-Levina the sole justification of his life in teaching.[6]

Rozengolts-Levina completed her training in 1925 with a first class degree and won the right to travel abroad. In 1926 she visited London where her brother was working in the Soviet Trade Delegation. Here she studied the paintings of Turner in the Tate Gallery, and paid particular attention to the works of Cézanne that were then on display. However she had already reached maturity as an artist, and her personal direction had been set by Falk's humanitarian and lyrical approach. The influence of Robert Falk upon Rozengolts-Levina is clearly evident in her first mature works. In the painting *Female Nude* of 1922 she resorts to an idealization of the human form which is in the Knave of Diamonds tradition. Moreover the

134

technique of building up the painted layer from heavily loaded and evident brushstrokes emulates that of Robert Falk himself. However the real synthesis of human and painterly concerns began with the painting *Ryazan Peasant Woman* of 1924 which is executed in a warm palette of colours. During these years Rozengolts-Levina painted a number of sympathetic character-studies of the people around her such as *Old Jews* of 1925 and *Marusya* of 1929–30 which are magnificent large-scale canvases, reminiscent, yet again, of the work of Robert Falk at this time. However this period in her development was to be short-lived, and soon the artist found a different scale and medium appropriate to her changing perception of the world.

133

136, 135

In the early 1930s Rozengolts-Levina strengthened the dramatic quality of her works, and as their scale became smaller so the power of their imagery becomes correspondingly greater. Her preferred medium in this period was pastel, and her work functioned as an expression of spiritual travail and suffering. It is interesting that during this period Rozengolts-Levina's social involvement and activity increased. She became a member of the 'Union of Social Artists' (OKHO), a group composed of Falk's former pupils whose objective was 'to take art to the people'. The opening of their exhibition in May 1928 in the October Revolution Club was accompanied by a statement entitled 'Our Path' in which they declared: 'We come from one school, the Vkhutemas, and we are seeking the forms of artistic labour which will best answer society's demands of the artist. To realize our tasks we are organizing exhibitions which will be held not in the centre of town, which is difficult for many people to reach, but in workers' clubs where they will be free to all. We wish to show our works not only to the narrow circle who always visit exhibitions, but also to the people who have not yet acquired the habit of visiting them. We want to work together with others using our own methods (painting, drawing, graphic art, sculpture) to build the new life.'[7] Rozengolts-Levina also published an article entitled 'The Theatre of the Near Future'[8] which raised the question of adapting theatre buildings in accordance with the principles of the 'new social environment'. Based on the ideas of theatrical reformers such as Meyerkhold, she suggests the destruction of the barrier between theatre and audience so as to facilitate social equality and to conform to the new democratic society. Moreover during 1931–2 Rozengolts taught at the First State Textile Print Factory in Moscow, in 1932–3 she made fabric designs for the Dorogomilovskaya Factory, and in 1934–6 she worked as a consultant designer for the People's Commissariat of Light Industry.

Eva Rozengolts-Levina
Drawing from the series 'People', 1960s

However, as if exhausted by the tensions and struggles of the decade Rozengolts-Levina slowly withdrew into herself. Her favourite subject became the cityscape, and while her works share characteristics with those of Sofronova the differences are equally apparent. For example in her pastel entitled *Chimneys* of the early 1930s the smoke-stacks which tower over the sleeping town and the dark sky lit by the city's glow convey a sense of fear and tension. These works possess a disturbing atmosphere, that 'Gothic arrangement', which 'Group 13' rejected in favour of 'a

138

joyful perception of life'. Moreover in her foreboding pastel entitled *Moscow River at Twilight* of 1934 Rozengolts-Levina forsakes the tranquil approach of Sofronova in favour of an apocalyptic, visionary quality inspired by Turner. The river has become a threatening and powerful current.

137

Eva Rozengolts-Levina was exiled in 1949. As Murina has pointed out, she suffered many deaths, but was spiritually reborn through her art. In this respect her simple graphics of the exile period are particularly expressive. She concluded her career with an extensive series of sky and figure studies executed from the late 1950s to the early 1970s in which she expressed the changes wrought in people's lives by the twentieth century. Her poems are equally evocative, and serve as a touching epigraph to her work and career:

> A familiar light has come into my memory
> And my soul has become aware of itself in joy.
> But the past has hidden itself deeply away.
> A familiar light has come into my memory
> And joy has been recalled with pain.

DOCUMENTS

Rozengolts-Levina by the poet Evgeny Vinokurov
Eva Pavlovna's drawings are severe and, in the main, dark in tone and in their lighting. Yet one of her favourite words was 'joy'. She would not sit down to work until she experienced the joy — although it might be a bitter kind of joy — which was necessary for her creativity. This was the stimulus and the source of her work.[9]

Rozengolts-Levina by the artist Oleg Vasiliev
Eva Pavlovna's graphic works are not at all aggressive. They do not say 'Stop, look at me' . . . She was an artist who broke no rules and overstepped no limits. Somehow, unobtrusively but very solidly, she found herself a place in the Russian artistic tradition of the first half of the century and was thus included in the general European line of cultural development. Her work reminds one of that of Chekrygin[10] which she never saw, and of that of Turner, which she saw in the original when she was young and loved very much.[11]

Rozengolts-Levina by the art historian Mikhail Alpatov
I got to know Eva Pavlovna when I was taken to see her as an old pupil of Falk, in hospital in the 1950s . . . She first showed me some sheets where she had drawn sky with broadly depicted clouds, seen through trees. There was something troubling in these pictures. In the foreground bare trees leaned against the wind. The knarled branches were harshly denuded. According to the old tradition, I did not ask why there were only trees and wind there. It was necessary to look and not ask questions. Then we returned to the sky again. Now it had become calm. There was not even a gentle breeze. In contrast to the previous drawings the relationships had become fine and clear. . . . I felt full of joy. . . . I felt happy that other people who had seen these works also had strong feelings about them. . . . It was then that I understood that all Eva Pavlovna's work is a symbol.[12]

120 **Antonina Sofronova** *Fragrant Tobacco in a Jug*, 1919

122 **Antonina Sofronova**
Portrait of My Daughter, 1919

121 **Antonina Sofronova** *Landscape with Trees*, 1919

123 Works by Sofronova and her pupils, Tver, 1921

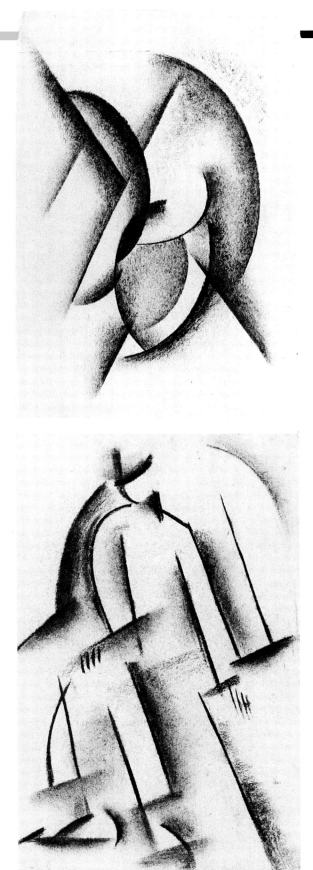

124 **Antonina Sofronova**
Composition, 1922

125 **Antonina Sofronova**
Figure, 1922

126 **Antonina Sofronova**
*Portrait of the artist Mikhail
Sokolov*, 1922

127 Antonina Sofronova
Smoke of MOGES (Moscow
Hydro-electric Station), 1930

128 Antonina Sofronova
Alleys of the Arbat, 1932

129 Antonina Sofronova
Pink House, Blue Fence, 1933–4

< 130 **Antonina Sofronova**
Woodland Path, 1933–4

131 **Antonina Sofronova**
Still-life with Red Coffee Pot, 1931

132 **Antonina Sofronova**
Self-portrait, 1931

133 **Eva Rozengolts-Levina**
Ryazan Peasant Woman, 1924

134 **Eva Rozengolts-Levina**
Female Nude, 1922

135 **Eva Rozengolts-Levina**
Marusya, 1929–30

136 **Eva Rozengolts-Levina** *Old Jews*, 1925

137 **Eva Rozengolts-Levina**
Moscow River at Twilight, 1934

138 **Eva Rozengolts-Levina**
Chimneys, early 1930s

139 **Nina Simonovich-Efimova** *Festival in Tambov Province*, 1914

140 **Nina Simonovich-Efimova** *Vision de Voyage*, 1910

141 **Nina Simonovich-Efimova** *Peasant Woman in a Red Skirt*, 1915

142 **Nina Simonovich-Efimova** *Self-portrait in an Interior, Sokolniki,* 1916–17

143 **Nina Simonovich-Efimova**
Ivan Efimov as a Faun, 1927

144 **Nina Simonovich-Efimova**
Puppet of Pushkin, 1922

145 **Nina Simonovich-Efimova**
Whore puppet, 1929

146 **Nina Simonovich-Efimova** *Poster for the Puppet Theatre: Krylov's 'Fables'*, 1929

Nina Simonovich-Efimova

All the world's a stage . . .
WILLIAM SHAKESPEARE

Nina Simonovich-Efimova, like Serebryakova before her, was born into the Russian intelligentsia. As a child she found herself at the centre of the latest developments in the artistic life of Moscow, and she enjoyed the friendship and protection of her cousin the artist Valentin Serov. In later life she married the sculptor Ivan Efimov and became friendly with the graphic artist Vladimir Favorsky. In addition, her home acted as a meeting place for artists, writers and musicians. Simonovich-Efimova left a legacy of some three thousand works including paintings, graphics, sculpture, theatre designs, puppets and typography. Moreover, specialists in each of these fields regard her contribution as considerable. In particular she is known as the founder of the first professional puppet theatre in the Soviet Union, and as the inventor of charming rod-puppets, exquisite shadow figures and expressive string-puppets. Despite her fame, however, the work of Simonovich-Efimova has yet to be properly studied and re-evaluated.

The sad neglect into which her work fell stemmed from the same bureaucratic proscriptions which affected the careers of artists such as Sofronova and Rozengolts-Levina. In addition the names which attracted most attention during the span of her career were those of artists involved in the battle between different groups, each with their own programme. Since Simonovich-Efimova belonged to none of these, and because her art was relatively traditional, it was natural that she should escape the attention of art historians. It is only recently that attention has once again focused on her career.

Nina Yakovlevna Simonovicha was born in St Petersburg in 1877. Her father, Yakov Mironovich Simonovich, was a successful paediatrician, while her mother, Adelaida Semyonovna Bergman, organized the first kindergarten in Russia in 1866. They were typical of the progressive Russian intelligentsia at this time, and even published a journal entitled *Kindergarten* devoted to teaching matters. They were an active family and according to Ivan Efimov 'laboured with hands, head and heart in the artistic, musical and teaching fields'.[1] Simonovicha's maternal aunt was the talented composer Valentina Serova, and she too testified to the family's cultural and intellectual activities: 'in the "working salon" on Kirochnaya Street drawing and music-making made way for jokes and games, and those in turn for serious discussions on art or the development of Russian painting'.[2] The family boasted another talent in the person of the famous painter Valentin Serov (1865–1911), and it was he who fostered his young cousin's artistic talents from an

Nina Simonovich-Efimova during a shadow-theatre performance, 1930s

201

early age, taking her to art classes with him and correcting her mistakes himself.

In 1896 Simonovicha graduated from High School in St Petersburg and following this worked for two years as a teacher in the Georgian capital of Tbilisi. However she continued to study painting, and attended the studio of O. Shmerling, a battle-painter of the Munich school, who worked in the 'Meisonnier style'. It was only in 1898 that she finally committed herself to a career in art, and at the same time her attention was attracted by both puppet and shadow theatre. A year later Simonovicha visited Paris where she studied in the studio of Delécluze, which was particularly popular with Russian artists at the time. Golubkina, Mukhina, Serov and Somov had all studied there but, as Golubkina reported, the only training given was technical. However, as Simonovicha readily admitted, the discipline of academic drawing was essential for her development, since her ability with line came less readily than her ability with colour.

Valentin Serov, who was inclined to consider women as more suited to painting than drawing, had sent Nina Simonovicha to Paris with the injunction to 'draw! draw! draw! – a complete curriculum expressed with his customary concision'.[3] Nevertheless her interest moved in the direction of painting. On her return to Russia in 1900 Serov encouraged Simonovicha to join the Stroganov Institute, and a year later to revisit Paris where she worked in the studio of the Symbolist painter Eugene Carrière. Here she took the opportunity to study the work of the Impressionists, Toulouse-Lautrec and Van Gogh. Nonetheless on her return home she continued to study with Serov, and his influence on her work remained paramount until her marriage to Ivan Efimov in 1906. She also joined the Moscow School of Painting, Sculpture and Architecture where Serov taught. In 1908 Simonovich-Efimova moved to France for two years. In Brittany she painted a series of landscapes and seascapes while in Paris she enrolled in the studio of Henri Matisse where she executed a number of etchings of Parisian street-scenes. The *Vision de Voyage* of 1910 is characteristic of her painting at this time – it is somewhat traditional in composition although the strong silhouettes and the active role played by the distinct areas of colour bear witness to her experimental approach.

A change of direction occurred during 1911–15 when Simonovich-Efimova discovered one of the main themes of her easel painting in the peasant women of the Tambov region in Central Russia. Whilst her subject matter is similar to that of Serebryakova and Goncharova, her figures are less symbolically rendered than Goncharova's and less idealized than Serebryakova's. They are closer to festive peasant art, as we see in *Peasant Woman in Red* or *Tambov Girl*, both of 1912 (Efimov Museum, Moscow). However, despite the evident difference in execution between the works of Simonovich-Efimova and contemporaries such as Serebryakova and Goncharova, the art-critic Yakov Tugendkhold noted an important unifying characteristic: that 'the people, rather than being conceived as objects of pity, have become the subject of a national style'.[4] This new approach finds expression in paintings such as the lively *Festival in Tambov Province* of 1914 and the bright *Peasant Woman in a Red Skirt* of 1915. All these works are executed

Nina Simonovich-Efimova
Pavel Florensky at work, 1926

Nina Simonovich-Efimova
The Duel: Pushkin, 1926

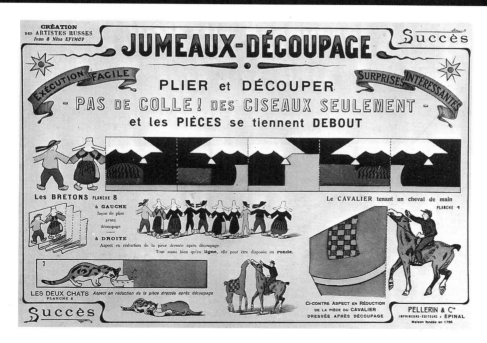

Nina Simonovich-Efimova
and **Ivan Efimov**
Book of paper cut-outs, 1910

in the pure colours of red, green, and white — those colours which had struck
Matisse as being so characteristic of the Russian icon, and which were common to a
number of very different artists in 1910.

139, 141

However Simonovich-Efimova did not entirely confine herself to this subject
matter. There are several interesting self-portraits such as *Self-portrait in an Interior,
Sokolniki* of 1916–17 which rely on the device of a reflected image in a mirror and so
recall Serebryakova's painting *At the Dressing Table* and Serov's famous portrait of
Henrietta Girshman. The density of the paint-layer is both an interesting and
distinguishing characteristic of Simonovich-Efimova's work at this time, and this
aspect of her technique may be seen to link her with the work of the Knave of
Diamonds group. However the surface of the paint is deliberately smooth, and in
turning away from the texture or 'faktura' of the painting Simonovich-Efimova
also rejects one of the key aspects of avant-garde creativity.

142

It is interesting that a number of the principles elucidated in her work on
silhouettes at this time were transferred to her painterly work. *Vision de Voyage* relies
heavily on the expressive power of dark silhouettes against a lighter ground.
Moreover a clear-cut sense of pose and gesture and a contrast between figures and
their background are features which are also evident in the Tambov cycle.
Silhouettes interested Simonovich-Efimova throughout her life. She saw them as
works of art demanding refinement and an understanding of form in that the
silhouette was a generalized image and not an imitation of reality. In Russia the
concept of the silhouette as an art form was revived by the 'World of Art' at the turn
of the century and attracted a number of painters including Somov, Benois and
Narbut. However the two most interesting exponents of this technique were
Kruglikova and Simonovich-Efimova. Here again we encounter the handicraft
tradition which had traditionally been regarded as the work of women, and a

140

Nina Simonovich-Efimova
Oak Tree, 1925

Nina Simonovich-Efimova
Pavel Florensky, 1925

natural form of female expression. Simonovich-Efimova compared her silhouettes to the graceful contours found in ancient Greek vase painting, and strove to achieve the beauty and clarity of the shadows cast by sunlight. The artist wrote that 'a silhouette is the depiction of light with shade, and perspective and even tone are possible – insofar as they are present in nature. On the other hand I do not consider it permissible to break a silhouette with collars, buttons, checked material or suchlike'. For Simonovich-Efimova the silhouette had its own expressive language, and the absence of a horizon-line allowed the figure to be projected as it were monumentally.[5]

Simonovich-Efimova painted a number of unusual portraits in the late 1920s, such as that of *Ivan Efimov as a Faun* of 1927, in which one senses an ironic attitude towards the world, and a growing feeling of unreality. For Simonovich-Efimova, Shakespeare's maxim that 'all the world's a stage, the men and women merely players' was perceived as immutable. To a large extent this defined the artist's interest in the theatre with which she was deeply involved. In particular Simonovich-Efimova and her husband were the first to turn puppetry into a professional art-form within the Soviet Union, as distinct from its previous use as a form of popular entertainment in Tsarist Russia and its propagandist function during the Revolution and Civil War. Although Simonovich-Efimova had presented puppet shows before the Revolution at an evening organized by the Moscow Society of Artists and at the famous Café Pittorèsque, it was only in October 1918 that she and her husband opened the 'Theatre of Marionettes, Petrushkas and Shadows' in Moscow. The theatre acted as an exciting focus for artistic collaboration, for puppets, being symbolic representations rather than concrete depictions, captured the imagination of the intelligentsia. Vladimir Favorsky and Pavel Florensky both worked for the theatre, as did several women artists such as Alexandra Exter and Lyubov Popova.

From this point on, Simonovich-Efimova became principally associated with the latest developments in the art of the puppet theatre and committed herself to this medium of expression until the end of her creative life. She was particularly noted for introducing rod-puppets into the Russian puppet theatre. Simonovich-Efimova executed many such puppets from the refined and thoughtful poet *Pushkin* of 1922 to the exhibitionist *Whore* of 1929. All these puppets are carefully sculpted and dressed in gorgeous costumes and plush fabrics. The method of working the puppets, in which rods were attached to the joints, ensured that the puppets peformed the most graceful of gestures in a kind of silhouette.

Between 1918 and 1936 Simonovich-Efimova organized over fifteen hundred puppet theatre performances, all of which excited and charmed the public. A poster-design which is still extant advertises performances based on Krylov's *Fables*, but Simonovich-Efimova had her greatest success with Shakespearean subjects. Of these her production of *Macbeth* stands out as being her masterpiece. Smirnova draws attention to the clever play of light which completely changed the expression on the puppets' faces as they moved around the stage, and she singles out

146

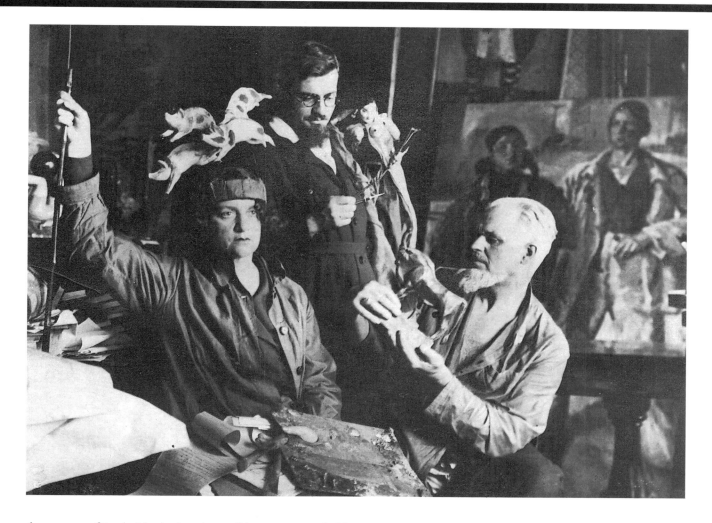

the puppet of Lady Macbeth as 'one of the most remarkable creations in which the talent of the sculptor, artist and graphic designer were embodied'.[6] In her concept of puppetry as 'moving sculpture' Simonovich-Efimova brought both culture and elegance into the art of the puppet theatre, and with the performance of *Macbeth* she completely fulfilled her aims. As one critic wrote: 'The moment Lady Macbeth appeared, red-haired and impetuous, I felt something new had occurred. A supernatural feeling was evoked which expressed her ambition and pride better than words. Through some strange device — be it art or deception — the puppets added to rather than detracted from Shakespeare's images. The Efimovs have finally realized their dream — to use puppets for serious drama. They have captured what is most essential — puppets sculptured and vivid enough to evoke strong emotion.'[7]

As an artist Simonovich-Efimova was tormented by the division between the 'left' and 'right' wings of the Russian art world and believed that this 'poisoned the atmosphere in a way that it did in no other country'.[8] It was natural therefore that in 1925 Simonovich-Efimova should join the 'Four Arts Society' which encompassed a wide variety of artistic approaches and aimed to synthesize the four arts of

Nina Simonovich-Efimova with her husband Ivan Efimov and son Adrian, surrounded by her paintings and puppets, 1935

painting, architecture, graphic design and sculpture. In this respect her puppets were a triumph, expressing as they did a perfect synthesis between these four arts. However when Socialist Realism, with its overriding emphasis on subject matter, became the prescribed form of art, her work remained outside the stream of its formation and development. Here the initially different careers of Sofronova, Rozengolts-Levina and Simonovich-Efimova converge. In paying tribute to the artist, Vladimir Favorsky pointed to her artistic diversity and 'creative richness',[9] while the art-critic Pavel Ettinger declared her to be 'one of the most interesting artists in Moscow possessing that type of creative nature which arrests the attention by its talent and individual artistic temperament'.[10] It was precisely these qualities which were to distinguish the work of her contemporaries, Vera Mukhina and Sarra Lebedeva, who were working in more orthodox sculptural fields and who made a more successful transition to the Socialist Realist approach.

DOCUMENTS

Simonovich-Efimova writing in 'Kindergarten', 1918
. . . Chinese shadows can be compared with the magic lantern which is now being more and more widely used in schools but they . . . are more accessible and their shows are merrier than those of the magic lantern . . .[11]

Simonovich-Efimova: from 'Notes of a Puppeteer'
An actor multiplies his personality with puppets. He doesn't depend on a partner, he is his own partner. After puppets, it seems to me to be impoverishing for an actor to play a role without also playing its opposite or extension . . .[12]

Notes of Simonovich-Efimova
In the years of the Revolution my artistic interests turned in another direction, to the puppet theatre. Apart from the fact that this provided me with the means for existence, it made people more cheerful. I felt that the theatre was what the people very much needed at that stormy period. They looked at it with great hungry eyes. Theatre then was like bread, and painting was not needed immediately after the Revolution. There were no exhibitions then, and artists were not painting, and I decided that the theatre was what was indispensable. I began to get involved in the theatre, and then it drew me so stongly that I spent twenty-eight years there. The two of us moved our puppets, spoke for them, designing or composing our plays ourselves. I had the idea of transferring this kind of folk-theatre to the stage of the literary theatre. In the ten years that we gave this idea publicity through our own theatre, it became general.[13]

Sarra Lebedeva

4 TWO SOVIET SCULPTORS

Sarra Lebedeva

Vera Mukhina

Vera Mukhina

Sarra Lebedeva

> The image should be constructed according to the
> harmony between the internal and the external.
> VERA MUKHINA

During the 1930s the work of Sofronova, Rozengolts-Levina and Simonovich-Efimova had either expressed the contradictions of its time or set itself completely apart. However the work of artists such as Lebedeva and Mukhina was essentially different. These artists were genuinely confident about the future under Soviet socialism, and their work bespeaks their optimism. It is too simplistic to see artists such as these as the mere tools of Soviet bureaucracy, dutifully implementing the 'triumphal aesthetics' of Socialist Realism. On the contrary, the success of their works as persuasive arguments in favour of the new régime derives from the fact that there genuinely was something to be proud of. There were indeed deep contradictions in Soviet society at this time, but a determination to make the Revolution work inspired many artists to adopt a positive approach. If aesthetic values are the test of sincerity, then it was women artists who once again expressed the perception of their times with a particular sensitivity, and especially so as sculptors. Now the stormy and emotive approach of Anna Golubkina was superseded in the work of Sarra Lebedeva and Vera Mukhina by a new objectivity, not only in style but also in the relationship between the artist and her subject.

Sarra Dmitrievna Darmolatova was born into a prosperous family of the intelligentsia in St Petersburg in 1892. She was educated at home until the age of fourteen, when she began to attend classes at the School for the Encouragement of the Arts in St Petersburg. In the years before the war Lebedeva travelled widely with her family, visiting France, Germany, Austria and Italy. Here she was introduced to the museums and galleries where she was particularly attracted by the Renaissance artists, her favourite sculptor being Donatello. She was also devoted to Cranach and Rembrandt, and at this time knew nothing whatsoever of the developments taking place in modern art. In 1910 Lebedeva began to study painting and drawing in Mikhail Bernshtein's school in St Petersburg, but in 1912 decided to commit herself to sculpture and joined the school of the well-known sculptor Leonid Shervud (1871–1954). Following this she worked with V. Kuznetsov, firstly as his pupil and then at the age of nineteen as his assistant.

Perhaps the greatest influence on Lebedeva was that of the graphic artist Vladimir Lebedev (1891–1967) whom she married in 1915. It was through studying the books in his exceptional library that Lebedeva first made the acquaintance of Picasso, Braque and Matisse.

147 **Sarra Lebedeva**
Portrait of OM, 1918

148 **Sarra Lebedeva**
Chinaman, 1918

149 **Sarra Lebedeva**
Bull, 1922

150 **Sarra Lebedeva** *Portrait of Aron Solts*, 1931

Sarra Lebedeva
151 (Top left) *Portrait of Leonid Krasin*, 1924
152 (Top right) *Portrait of the General Secretary of the Communist Party, Felix Dzerzhinsky*, 1925

153 (Above) *Portrait of the writer Vsevolod Ivanov*, 1925
154 (Right) *Portrait of Alexander Tsyurupa*, 1927

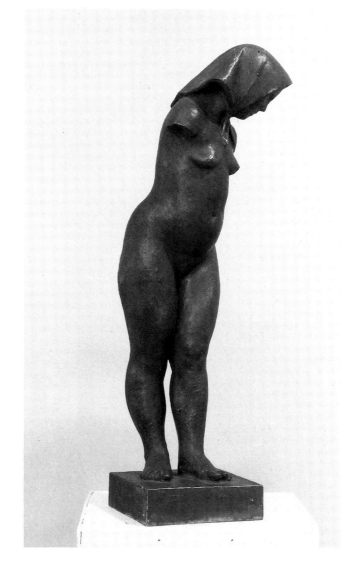

<155 **Sarra Lebedeva**
Girl with a Towel, 1931

156 **Sarra Lebedeva**
Model with Raised Arms, 1928

157 **Sarra Lebedeva**
Reclining Figure: Stasya, 1928

158 **Sarra Lebedeva**
Girl with Plaits, study, 1934

159 **Sarra Lebedeva**
Nude with Headscarf, 1930

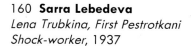

160 **Sarra Lebedeva**
Lena Trubkina, First Pestrotkani
Shock-worker, 1937

161 **Sarra Lebedeva**
Self-portrait, 1925

162 **Sarra Lebedeva**
Red Fleet Shock-worker, Vlasov,
1931

163–4 **Sarra Lebedeva**
'Hen' teapot with bowls
(top), and
fruit bowl, 1934–6

Sarra Lebedeva with her husband Vladimir and 'O.M.', 1918

At this point, however, her course was already set, and she committed herself to the portrait bust and to her most important subject – people. One of her first works to gain recognition was *Female Head – Portrait of O. M.* of 1918, which reveals a clear and precise rendering of features in contrast to the expressive approach of Golubkina. In *Chinaman* of the same year the process of modelling is more apparent in the construction of the facial muscles and the skin. In contrast to Golubkina, who used her whole hand with which to sculpt, Lebedeva preferred to work with her finger-tips to achieve a precise, smooth and steady finish to her work. The art historian Mikhail Alpatov recalled that 'Lebedeva had an exceptional gift as a portraitist. She was easily able to capture the resemblance of her model. We could recognize the portraits of the people we knew and it was easy to believe that the portraits of those whom we did not know represented them as they were.'[1]

In the immediate post-Revolutionary period Lebedeva was drawn into the literary and artistic circles which then held sway in Petrograd. Here she came to know writers and poets such as Maxim Gorky, Alexander Blok, Vladimir Mayakovsky, painters and sculptors such as Malevich, Tatlin, Alexander Matveev, Pavel Kuznetsov, Martiros Saryan, Natan Altman, and David Shterenberg as well as the theatre director Vsevolod Meyerkhold. Like many of these artists, Lebedeva's imagination was captivated by the Revolution, and in 1918 she was among the first to respond enthusiastically to Lenin's Decree on Monumental Propaganda. As the massive statues and monuments which proclaimed the power of Tsarist Russia were being pulled down, so Lenin called on Russian sculptors to play an active socio-artistic role in the physical rebuilding of the new Russia by erecting monuments to revolutionary heroes both past and present. Lebedeva's contribution included monumental busts of *Danton* and

147

148

Alexander Herzen, neither of which have been preserved, as well as a relief of *Robespierre* of 1920.

151   In 1924 Lebedeva executed her portrait bust of *Leonid Krasin*, the Soviet diplomat who negotiated the Anglo-Soviet Trade Agreement in 1921 and the Treaty of Rapallo in 1922. Her successful completion of the portrait represented the start of her long career as a sculptor of Soviet officialdom. In 1925 the artist
152   moved to Moscow and began work on the portrait of *Felix Dzerzhinsky*, the General Secretary of the Communist Party. These busts were the first to reveal her maturity as a portraitist, and were followed by many other commissions in which Lebedeva searched out the character of her sitter and gave it an external reality through attention to facial expression and surface texture.

Particularly interesting in this major series are the busts of the writer *Vsevolod*
153   *Ivanov* of 1925, with its simple and laconic composition elongated into a smile, and
154   the clever and wistful portrait of *Alexander Tsyurupa* of 1927, the director of the Commissariat of Worker-Peasant Inspection (Rabkrin). Also notable are the busts of *Semyon Budyonny* of 1925, the courageous Colonel of the Civil War and Marshal of the Soviet Union, *Pavel Dybenko* (State Tretyakov Gallery) the army commander, a forceful intellect and talent, and many others, as various in their characters as in their destinies. A portrait of the leading Party activist *Pavel Postyshev* of 1932 (Kiev Museum of Russian Art) conveys not only the sitter's
150   strength but also his light build and open nature, while the portrait of *Aron Solts* of 1931 represents a figure as unusual as his fate. However, Lebedeva's busts are not simply flattering portraits, for as Alpatov notes 'Lebedeva was a sharp-sighted observer, and her observation is sometimes ruthless and ironic'.[2]

During the 1930s, however, Lebedeva worked on portrait busts of quite a different order. In these years she turned towards the worker-heroes of the Soviet Union for her subject-matter, and through a generalized and heroic approach to the individual she attempted to convey the determination and resilience of the Russian people as a whole to the task ahead of them. Of particular importance in this series is the poised and solid bust of the *Red Fleet Shock-worker, Vlasov* of 1931. However some works in her *œuvre* do reveal momentary doubts, as with the portrait of the 'shock-worker' *Lena Trubkina* of 1937 which bears 'the stamp of contradictions' (pls 160, 162).

Lebedeva secured her place in the history of Soviet art through her portraits. However she also executed a number of lively and exciting figure-sculptures such as *Model with Raised Arms* and *Reclining Figure: Stasya*, both of 1928, and *Girl with a Towel* of 1931. Alpatov tells us that Lebedeva sculpted and drew the nude mainly as an escape from her principal genre of portraiture.[3] However the nude was virtually proscribed at this time, and these small majolica and bronze figures attracted little attention in Lebedeva's own lifetime. Yet they demonstrate a lyrical and expressive approach to both subject-matter and the medium itself, and are altogether more personal and intimate than the monumental and heroic approach that she adopted for her public commissions.

Sarra Lebedeva
Robespierre, 1919

Lebedeva was also an active participant in the many exhibitions which brought her work and her name before the public. For several years she played an important role within the Society of Russian Sculptors (ORS), and exhibited with them in 1926, 1929 and 1931. In succeeding years her work occupied a prominent place in many exhibitions. Several of her heroic portraits were shown in the commemorative exhibition 'Fifteen Years of the Workers' and Peasants' Red Army' held during 1933–4, and a year later she participated in a group exhibition in Moscow together with Vera Mukhina, Ilya Slonim, Favorsky and others. In 1941 she was honoured with a personal exhibition in the State Museum in Moscow and in 1945 she was awarded the title 'Honoured Art Worker of the RSFSR'. Exhibitions of her portrait busts continued into the 1960s, until her death in Moscow in 1967. It may seem that Lebedeva's career was an unqualified success in terms of the difficult period through which she lived, but her art did not escape accusations of formalism. Her work was considered insufficiently 'heroic', and other ideological faults were found. However her work was of such a stature that she was able not only to express the present with all its complexity but also to prophesy the future, and this power she shares with her contemporary and colleague the sculptor Vera Mukhina.

Sarra Lebedeva in her studio, 1930s

DOCUMENTS

Lebedeva on the portrait of Dzerzhinsky

During the Revolution almost all sculptors worked on portraits. It was difficult and sometimes impossible to get sittings. Attempts were made to sculpt from photographs, but I doubt whether a true portrait could be made in this way.

I had long had the idea of doing a portrait of Dzerzhinsky. I felt that he had an exceptionally interesting face, with something for the sculptor to fix on to. It is disagreeable to work from photographs, so I decided to get a sitting or else to abandon the idea of a portrait.

In February 1925 I took my materials to Dzerzhinsky's room in the GPU building for the first time. As I knew that I would not have long to work with him as a model I had already prepared my clay and made a rough start from photographs and from memory (I had once seen him briefly). Here with the living Dzerzhinsky in front of me I felt yet again the inadequacy of photographs. I destroyed all that I had prepared and made a fresh start. What immediately struck me upon seeing Dzerzhinsky, and remained with me until the end of our work, was that behind a firm, asymmetrical face, broad at the cheekbones, with fine features, I could sense inner fires.

His eyes, however strange this may seem, were the most peaceful part of his face. Perhaps this was because of the heavy tired eyelids, from under which looked out the light, piercing, almond-shaped blue eyes . . .

When Gerson once said, 'It's a good resemblance, but you've made F. E. severe,' Dzerzhinsky replied, 'Well, you sit, you don't become an angel. That's how I am.'

We had about ten sittings of two hours, or sometimes two-and-a-half hours.[4]

Lebedeva by the sculptor Ilya Slonim

A beautiful, restrained woman, light in her movements, with a penetrating blue-eyed glance, a glance that could confuse and even discourage a person new to her. Of few words, rarely giving any external show of her feelings. Severe on herself and on those close to her but the most loyal of friends. A passionate artist, constantly thinking about her work but rarely talking about it. An artist who left both a large number of varied sculptures and thousands of drawings.

In the 1930s Lebedeva became interested in ceramics and, having settled near the Konakovsky Factory, she worked on designs for tableware. From this period the splendid 'Hen' teapot and several fruit-dishes have been preserved. It is interesting that on one of these fruit dishes there is a female figure which, in its proportions, reminds one of the *Little Girl with Butterfly* [see Chronology]. Only a few examples of these objects remain and none of them, unfortunately, ever went into production.

She possessed an innate feeling for form. . . . She had the ability to arrange everything from an exhibition-hall to her own flat or studio so that a person would feel at his best there. . . . A vase or a piece of sculpture stood in such a way that not only did you not want to move it, but you felt it would be impossible. . . . It is a pity that architects did not involve her in designing parks or interiors – their cooperation with her would doubtless have been productive.

Lebedeva made three designs for monuments: Dzerzhinsky for Moscow, Pushkin for Mikhailovskoe and Chekhov for Yalta. None of the three done at different periods was ever realized. I was a witness to her work on the Dzerzhinsky monument. She worked with a talented and experienced architect A. K. Burov, a man of firm views with the ability to insist on them. Nevertheless, throughout their work together, the initiative mainly stayed with Lebedeva, who could never rest until she had found a solution . . .

Lebedeva set to work when she had a firm conviction of what she wanted to achieve. After her death we discovered numerous small sculpture-studies perfectly done from memory. Firm knowledge enabled her to complete some portraits in just two or three sittings.[5]

Truly there was something to be proud of
and something to reflect upon.

M. GERMAN

At the turn of the century the architect Feodor Rerberg had written that 'The art of women is intimate. It is rarely seen on the streets, it does not build palaces or temples, it does not decorate their walls with paintings, nor city squares with monuments.' It was therefore a remarkable testament to the revolutionary nature of the times when just three decades later in 1937 a steel sculpture entitled *Worker and Collective Farmworker* by Vera Mukhina crowned the Soviet Pavilion at the Paris Exposition. It was a striking and vibrant example of monumental sculpture which reflected the pride of Soviet Russia in the communal labour of its people, and has been recognized as a national symbol ever since. However Mukhina's unforced and idealized vision of the world was formed both by her nature and her training.

Vera Ignatievna Mukhina was born in Riga in 1889 into an old merchant family which had made its name in the hemp trade. Unhappily the family was blighted by tuberculosis. Her mother died of the disease before Vera was two. Shortly afterwards her father, in search of a more healthy climate, took his children to Kiev, where Vera studied in the Feodosisky High School and took private drawing lessons at home. When she was fourteen Mukhina's father died, and for several years she lived in Kursk where she continued to study painting and drawing. In 1910 she moved to Moscow and was introduced to the large circle of rich merchant families that included famous art patrons and collectors such as the Morozovs and Ryabushinskys. Here she attended Konstantin Yuon's school where Popova and Udaltsova were students. Her meeting with Popova was particularly important for Mukhina, and for the next decade Popova would be her closest friend and guide.

Mukhina recalled that Popova was 'enthusiastic in turns about Gauguin, Van Gogh and Cézanne. She had a marvellous sense of colour and was in general very talented. She taught me to look at colour and the colour relationships in Russian icons. Popova played an important role in my development, I began to question things and became aquainted with the 'Knave of Diamonds' – Exter, Mashkov, Lentulov, Tatlin – and Cubism for the first time.'[1] At this time Mukhina also attended Sinitsyna's sculpture studio, which provided a model but no instruction, and she began to study drawing in Mashkov's school. It was Mashkov who advised Mukhina to 'look at things whole', for he realized that the young artist's talent was spoiled by her concentration on details. His advice to her 'to educate your eye to take in the whole model' and to 'catch movement and character' proved particularly useful, and one can trace it in her later monumental works.[2]

In 1912 Mukhina realized her desire to study in Paris, and entered Bourdelle's studio at the Académie de la Grande Chaumière. Although Bourdelle had once been Rodin's pupil and assistant, his work represented a new sculptural generation and his studio attracted many young artists. It was here that Mukhina met her future biographer the sculptor Boris Ternovets. The system of instruction at the studio was particularly free. On her first day at the studio (the students called it the Day of Judgement) Mukhina had the opportunity to observe the great master: 'A little Nibelung, shorter than myself, with an enormous shining high forehead, thick, bushy brows and a black wedge-shaped beard. He was in a velvet-ribbed suit of the sort normally worn by workers and artists. He went round everybody. He would look at one thing attentively, at another cursorily. He would begin to talk about it and then wander off the point and talk about something else. The first subject was always the most interesting. Although my knowledge of French was not bad, it was difficult for me to understand him. He spoke so philosophically.'[3]

At this time Bourdelle's fame was at its peak. He was a temperamental but inspiring teacher who increased his pupils' awareness and opened up new perspectives for them. If his teaching was sometimes contradictory then it served to discourage blind acceptance. It was from Bourdelle that Mukhina first heard about the negative influence of Impressionism on sculpture. In Bourdelle's view Impressionism was anti-sculptural. For him the true foundation of sculpture was clarity of construction, vigour of form, inner discipline and observance of the laws of materials.

Although Mukhina broadly accepted Bourdelle's guidance her receptive nature began to assimilate other traditions. Bourdelle's rejection of Impressionism encouraged her to study both Classical and Egyptian sculpture in the Louvre. Ternovets recalled that she was particularly attracted by a bronze walking Horus and a seated Pharaoh carved from pink granite which taught her about 'the architectonics of form and concision of expression'.[4] Mukhina herself wrote at the time that 'a large statue should be simple, it should express itself "in a word", so as to add to the visual and psychological impact upon the viewer's perception'. It is interesting that Matisse had made the same point in his famous essay 'Notes of a Painter', in which he cites Egyptian sculpture as an art-form which adopts a simplicity of means to add to the overall expressiveness of the composition. It is no surprise therefore that Mukhina was also attracted to the work of the sculptor Maillol, who was friendly with the Fauves and whose works were distinguished by a relative simplicity and expressive strength.

Among Renaissance sculptors Mukhina admired Michelangelo for his power to 'create titans', and this became her own aspiration. However when Bourdelle expressed his astonishment that 'all Russians sculpt illusionistically and not constructively' Mukhina began to attend anatomy lectures at the Académie des Beaux-Arts where the lecturer painted the musculature directly on to the model. She soon realized, though, that such anatomical realism was not her objective. At this point Mukhina, like many of her compatriots who were working in Paris,

could have given way to the impact of Cubism which concentrated on structure and form. However her fiercely independent spirit set her apart from Russians such as Chagall, Shterenberg, Altman, Archipenko and Lipchitz who were all in varying ways close to the Cubist aesthetic. Mukhina even went so far as to reject Cubism on the basis that 'Cubists reveal form, but skeletally, losing what is most dear, the image. When they try to depict a living person they are defeated.'[5]

Mukhina's portrait busts of her friends and studio colleagues in Paris seemed completely traditional, but everything that she had assimilated became apparent after her return to Moscow. One of her earliest Russian works was the *Pietà* of 1916 (not extant) which recalls archaic forms of stylization but as yet lacks unity of approach. In many ways the *Pietà* is an experimental piece, showing Mukhina's interest in various idioms without having truly discovered her own. In Moscow Popova introduced Mukhina to avant-garde artists such as Alexandra Exter, who in turn introduced her to Tairov, the director of the famous Chamber Theatre. Shortly afterwards Mukhina was commissioned to sculpt two masks for the Theatre, but beyond this she rarely exhibited and was virtually unknown outside this narrow artistic circle.

In the following year, however, the Revolution provided a new creative impetus. Mukhina participated with Sarra Lebedeva in the implementation of the

Bourdelle's studio, Paris, with Bourdelle at front left, Iza Burmeister second row, second left, and Vera Mukhina half hidden by Boris Ternovets, who is standing second from the right

166

Plan for Monumental Propaganda, and became more widely known. She took part in the competitions of 1919–22, and together with her friend Ternovets joined the 'Monolith' group, a society of sculptors which was dedicated to the execution of monumental sculptural projects.

Mukhina's first work within the society was a model for a monument to Nikolay Novikov, a writer and journalist from the time of Catherine the Great who fought against the principle of serfdom. Her model was enthusiastically acclaimed by the commission but like many such works it has not survived due to the fact that these sculptures were made of cheap and makeshift materials that disintegrated in rain and frost. However, a small study by Mukhina of 1919 (State Tretyakov Gallery), featuring a seated woman in a Phrygian cap with a hammer in her hand, which was designed as a Revolutionary monument for the town of Klin, is still extant to testify to the nature of her Revolutionary work. The power of her conception is evident even in this small study, and here for the first time Mukhina succeeded in fusing the various lessons which she had learned from her studies in Paris.

Mukhina's first mature work, however, was her remarkable sculpture *Flame of the Revolution* of 1922. The sculpture was conceived as a design for a monument to the famous Bolshevik revolutionary Yakov Sverdlov who had died suddenly in 1919. It was this event which provided Mukhina with her chance to attempt the titanic. Initially her designs were based on the Classical legend of the birds of Stymphalus which were destroyed by Hercules, but in the final model these were passed over in favour of a winged female figure bearing a torch in her hand. As an image of dynamism and flight, which symbolizes the revolutionary whirlwind which had swept through Russia, the model clearly recalls the work of the Italian Futurist sculptor Boccioni. Yet once again Mukhina reveals the independence of her approach by employing a readily recognizable imagery in distinction to the abstract and dislocated forms of both the Cubist and Futurist sculptors.

At this time Mukhina also became interested in design work. She collaborated with Alexandra Exter on the design for the film *Aelita* of 1924, and worked closely with her in the field of theatrical design. Mukhina also associated with Nadezhda Lamanova, the leading fashion designer of the day, and made many sketches for hats and clothing which Lamanova produced. It was only in the mid-1920s however that Mukhina fully returned to sculpture, pursuing the theme of the female nude. Representative of this series is her sculpture *Yulia* of 1926 which was executed in wood. Here her previous symbolism is less apparent, though the fact that the sculpture resembles the Venus de Milo may point to how far removed the present troubled time was from that of Classical harmony. The vitality and power of Mukhina's sculpture in these years was a rare phenomenon, and we can find it again in works such as *Wind* of 1927, in which Mukhina stated that she wished to show 'two forms in dynamic inter-relationship with everything else subordinate to them'.[6]

We can agree with art historians such as Suzdalev who regard Mukhina's work at this time as promoting a new and idealized view of the beauty of the Soviet

165 **Vera Mukhina**
Wind, 1927

224

166 **Vera Mukhina**
Pietà, 1916

167 **Vera Mukhina**
Study for *Revolution*, 1919

168 **Vera Mukhina**
Yulia, 1926

169 **Vera Mukhina**
Flame of the Revolution, 1922
Design for the monument
to Yakov Sverdlov

170–1 **Vera Mukhina** Above: Designs for women's hats, 1925.
Below: Nadezhda Lamanova's illustration of a dress designed by Mukhina, 1920s

ДОМАШНЕЕ ПЛАТЬЕ из ГОЛОВНОГО ПЛАТКА

37. « Abito da casa ricavato da uno scialle »
— il disegno è completato dalle istruzioni per la
sua esecuzione.

В этом платье за основу взят квадрат головного каше-
мирового платка, и поэтому весь план его построен на квадрате.
Добавочная черная материя—такой же кашемир, как и платок.
Требуется ее 3½, до 4 метров. Зеленые полосы сделаны из
легкой шелковой материи; можно делать их и из шерстяной.
Излишнюю ширину кафтана в бедрах надо их заколоть в складку
с левой стороны или опоясать узким черным кушаком (отнюдь
не над талией).

На рисунке 1—пунктиром обозначена форма нижней
рубахи, верхнюю часть которой можно делать из более
легкой материи. Для более худой фигуры рукав можно делать
приблизительно на ладонь уже и ставить ластовицу зеленого
цвета. Один рукав показан нами в плане, другой—сшитый.

Это платье можно делать также из бумажной материи
с применением бумажных головных платков.

172–3 **Vera Mukhina**
Peasant Woman, 1927–8

174 **Vera Mukhina**
Drawings for *Peasant Woman*,
1927

175 **Vera Mukhina**
The architect S. A. Zamkov, 1934

176 **Vera Mukhina**
Woman with a Pitcher.
Figure for the Fountain
of the Nations, 1935

177 **Vera Mukhina**
Peasant Woman with Sheaves, 1935

working woman of the 1920s. This was an approach which Mukhina subsequently developed in her monumental bronze sculpture *Peasant Woman* of 1927–8 which celebrated the tenth anniversary of the Revolution. Many of Mukhina's colleagues were surprised by her choice of a peasant theme, since she was considered an urban artist. However the subject had no special connotation for Mukhina, but represented a new heroic type. Here Mukhina had at last achieved a mastery of concept and expression. She exaggerated the strong legs and the weight of the figure, played with proportion, light and shadow and arbitrarily moulded the folds of the clothing. When *Peasant Woman* was exhibited it was received with wide artistic and popular acclaim. Ternovets recorded that the sculpture embodied 'the healthy, flourishing strength of the earth' while Mashkov congratulated his former pupil in his direct way saying 'women such as she give birth standing and do not even grunt'.[7] Lunacharsky, reviewing the work in the press, wrote that 'It is impossible not to rejoice that sculpture has attained such a height, for soon we shall see great construction, and this construction will achieve its ideological significance in so far as the great language of architecture is combined with the great language of sculpture.'[8]

172–3

In the same period Mukhina also executed a number of portrait busts, such as that of *The architect S. A. Zamkov* of 1934. In this series the artist concerned herself with heightening individual characteristics, so that several of these portraits border on caricature, especially those of *Professor Kotlyarevsky* (State Russian Museum) and *Professor Koltsov* (State Tretyakov Gallery), both of 1929. Mukhina explained her unusual approach to portraiture when she declared that 'the image should be constructed according to the harmony between the internal and the external', but noted that 'artists have the right to use their model's appearance as is necessary to embody the sense of the image in the way that the artist understands the individual being depicted'.[9] If these images are more programmatic than those by Sarra Lebedeva then they are still powerful. However other works by Mukhina from this period seem unexpectedly lifeless, and it is not difficult to understand why these received official praise. *Woman with a Pitcher* of 1934 commissioned for the 'Fountain of the Nations' by the Trust for Town Design is an example of such a work. From a technical point of view, however, we can agree with Ternovets that even here Mukhina 'aspires to a richness of relief and an expressiveness of detail which the artist achieves with absolute precision'.[10]

175

176

It was this 'expressiveness of detail' combined with Mukhina's energetic and powerful approach which contributed to the success of her famous *Worker and Collective Farmworker* of 1937 for the Paris Exposition. The sculpture was closely related to the architecture of the pavilion which it surmounted, and hence fulfilled Lunacharsky's prophecy that sculpture and architecture would unite to create constructions of ideological significance. Nonetheless the work had an independent life which was due, as Ternovets noted, to 'the artist's heightened interest in form combined with the bright imagery of her art'.[11] In these years of official demands and restrictions on artistic activity it was this 'bright imagery' which

178
179

179 Vera Mukhina
The Soviet Pavilion with Worker and Collective Farmworker,
Paris Exposition, 1937

saved Mukhina from the formalist critics, while her remarkable technical capabilities called forth the admiration of her contemporaries, and marked her out as playing an unique role in the development of Soviet monumental sculpture at a time when there was quite simply no other sculptor of equal calibre.

Vera Mukhina was a sculptor whose attitude and approach were enthusiastically responsive to her time. Throughout the 1930s and 1940s she was frequently invited to execute public commissions, and her work was exhibited both at home and abroad. In distinction to artists such as Sofronova, Rozengolts-Levina and Simonovich-Efimova, who retreated from the social, political and economic context in which they found themselves, Mukhina readily affirmed it in her work. She was an artist who was not afraid to stride out and deal with the contemporary world, and it is not surprising that the unique perception she brought to it and the unusually bold and inspiring imagery which sprang from the encounter should be adopted as representative of the aims and aspirations of the young Soviet state. If the careers of Russian women artists in the late nineteenth and early twentieth centuries were prescribed by their struggle against the conventions of their time, then the career of Vera Mukhina witnessed a late triumph in the battle, and when *Worker and Collective Farmworker* crowned the Soviet Pavilion in Paris it crowned not only the achievements of the Soviet state but also the achievements of two generations of Russian women artists who had seized the freedom of the period to express the times in which they had lived.

NOTES ON THE TEXT

NOTE ON ACRONYMS

Inkhuk   *Institute of Artistic Culture*

Narkompros   *People's Commissariat for Enlightenment*

IZO Narkompros   *People's Commissariat for Enlightenment, Visual Arts Dept*

Proletkult   *Proletarian Culture*

Svomas   *Free State Studios (The former Moscow School of Painting, Sculpture and Architecture and Stroganov Institute combined, 1918–20)*

Vkhutemas   *Higher Artistic and Technical Studios (The former Svomas renamed, 1920–7)*

Vkhutein   *Higher Artistic and Technical Institute (The former Vkhutemas renamed, 1928–30)*

NOTE ON REPRESENTATION

The 14 artists who are the subjects of the chapters of this book are chosen as representative and do not exhaust the list of notable women artists of the period, among whom the following may be listed:

Tatiana Borisovna Alexandrova, 1907–87
Elena Bebutova, 1892–1970
Xenia Boguslavskaya, 1892–1972
Alisa Bruschetti-Mitrokhina, 1872–1942
Natalya Danko, 1892–1942
Sonia Delaunay, 1885–1979
Maria Ender, 1897–1942
Xenia Ender, 1894–1955
Vera Ermolaeva, 1893–1938
Lyubov Gauche, 1887–1943
Olga Gildebrandt, 1897–1980
Alisa Golenkina, 1892–1970
Elena Guro, 1877–1913
Nadezhda Kashina, 1896–1977
Nina Kashina, b.1903
Valentina Khodasevicha, 1894–1970
Ekaterina Kobro, 1898–1951
Elizabeta Kruglikova, 1865–1941
Valentina Kulagina, b.1902
Nadezhda Lamanova, 1881–1941
Maria Lebedeva, 1895–1942
Eugenia Lenyova, b.1898
Anna Leporskaya, 1900–82
Tatiana Mavrina-Lebedeva, b.1902
Vera Nikolskaya, 1890–1964
Khanna Orlova, 1878–1968
Anna Ostroumova-Lebedeva 1871–1955
Vera Pestel, 1887–1952
Ekaterina Petrova-Trotskaya, 1900–32
Elena Samokish-Sudkovskaya, 1883–1924
Alexandra Shchekotikhina-Pototskaya, 1892–1967
Lyubov Silich, b.1907
Maria Sinyakova, b.1898
Maria Vasilieva, 1884–1957
Sofia Zaklikovskaya, 1899–1975
Lyubov Zalesskaya, 1905–1979
Ekaterina Zernova, b.1900

NOTE ON ALTERNATIVE USAGES

There is no standardized nomenclature. Instances of variation include:

Chamber/Kamerny Theatre, Moscow
Knave/Jack of Diamonds
Rayonism/Rayism
The Old Style (rather than New Style) calendar is used throughout

INTRODUCTION

1 F. I. Rerberg (1865–1938) was one of the founding members and participants in the 'Moscow Association of Artists' and was well known as the founder (in 1905) and director of a private art school in Moscow where Kazimir Malevich, Antonina Sofronova, etc., studied in their early years.
2 F. I. Rerberg, 'On Women's Creativity', manuscript. Central State Archives of Art and Literature, fond 2443/I/27, pp. 52–93. Transcribed by M. Potapova.
3 The Russian employs a subtle but clear differentiation here which the English does not have. A male artist is *khudozhnik*, a female artist is *khudozhnitsa*.
4 A. Blok, 'Without Deity, Without Inspiration', *Collected Works (Sobranie sochinenii)*, Vol. 6, Moscow-Leningrad 1962, pp. 175–6.
5 M. Tsvetaeva, 'The Poet and Time', January 1932, published in *Youth (Yunost')*, 1987, No. 8, pp. 57–80.
6 Ya. Polonsky, cited by Tsvetaeva in 'The Poet and Time', op. cit.

1 ON THE BRINK OF MODERNISM

Maria Yakunchikova

1 V. Bryusov: 'Keys of the Secret' in *The Scales (Vesy)*, 1904, No. 1, p. 20.
2 Cited in M. Kiselev: *M. V. Yakunchikova*, Moscow 1979. p. 7.
3 K. Korovin, cited in Kiselev, op. cit., p. 11.
4 Letter from M. Yakunchikova to N. Polenova, 26 October 1888, cited in Kiselev, op. cit., p. 17.
5 Letter from M. Yakunchikova to N. Polenova, March 1889, cited in Kiselev, op. cit., p. 21.
6 Continuation of the above letter.
7 M. Yakunchikova, extract from diaries. Cited in Kiselev, op. cit., p. 33.
8 M. Yakunchikova, letter to N. Polenova, 1894, cited in Kiselev, op. cit., pp. 62–3.
9 M. Yakunchikova to N. Polenova, 1894, op. cit.
10 K. Balmont, cited in Mashtkits-Verov, *Russian Symbolism and the Path of Alexander Blok*, Kuibyshev 1969, p. 12.
11 W. Salmond, 'The Solomenko Embroidery Workshops', *Journal of Decorative and Propaganda Arts*, Summer 1987, No. 5, p. 135.
12 M. Yakunchikova, letter to N. V. Polenova, June 1887. Cited in Kiselev, op. cit., pp. 12–14.
13 A. Benois, 'Letter from the Exposition Universelle', *The World of Art (Mir iskusstva)*, 1900, Nos 17–18, p. 109.
14 See the special memorial issue of *The World of Art (Mir iskusstva)*, 1904, No. 3, with reproductions and articles on her work.
15 S. Glagol, 'The Union of Russian Artists', *Russkoe slovo*, 22 February 1905, No. 51.
16 Letter cited in Kiselev, op. cit., p. 24.

17 Letter cited N. Bovin in *The World of Art (Mir iskusstva)*, 1904, No. 3, p. 106.
18 Sakharova Archive. Cited in Kiselev, op. cit., p. 144.
19 Sakharova Archive. Cited in Kiselev, op. cit., p. 35.
20 Manuscripts Dept., State Russian Museum, fond 133, d. 193, 23–25. Cited in Kiselev, op. cit., p. 125.

Anna Golubkina

1 E. Murina, 'Anna Semyonovna Golubkina', *Decorative Art (Dekorativnoe iskusstvo)*, 1964, No. 6, cited in the introduction to *A. S. Golubkina: Letters and Recollections*, Moscow 1983, p. 7.
2 M. Voloshin, *Apollo (Apollon)*, 1911, No. 6, p. 11.
3 A. Golubkina, letter to E. Ya. Golubkina, the artist's mother, 1894, St Petersburg, cited in *A. S. Golubkina*, op. cit., pp. 22–3.
4 A. Golubkina, letter to E. Ya. Golubkina, December 1895, Paris, cited in *A. S. Golubkina*, op. cit., p. 25.
5 E. Murina, in *A. S. Golubkina*, op. cit., p. 5.
6 A. Golubkina, *Some Words on the Sculptor's Craft (Neskolko slov o remesle skulptora)*, Moscow 1923.
7 Dossier No. 472 of The Chamber of Justice for 1907 (preserved in the Central State Archives of the USSR, fond 131/71/1) provides the following details of Golubkina's case: 'In March 1907 Golubkina was imprisoned in Zaraysk prison where, as a protest, she announced a hunger strike. After several days of illness she was granted bail. On the 12 and 25 September there was a closed trial in Ryazan where Golubkina was sentenced to one year in prison but for health reasons it was agreed to curtail this.
8 A. Golubkina, letter to Auguste Rodin 1907. The original is in the Musée Rodin, Paris. The full text is printed in *Masters of Art on Art (Mastera iskusstva ob iskusstve)*, Moscow 1970, pp. 287–8.
9 I. Efimov, op. cit., p. 364.
10 V. Ern, letter to his wife, 11 May 1914, in *A. S. Golubkina*, op. cit., pp. 290–1.
11 See editorial article 'The Spark', *Illustrated Literary-Artistic Journal*, 4 January 1915, No. 1.
12 E. Murina, op. cit., p. 5.
13 *A. S. Golubkina*, op. cit.
14 op. cit., p. 79.
15 op. cit., p. 87.
16 Manuscript in Yablonskaya Archive.
17 Manuscript in E. Levina Archive.

Zinaida Serebryakova

1 A. Benois, 'Zinaida Serebryakova' in *Aleksandr Benois Reflects (Aleksandr Benua razmyshlyaet)*, Moscow 1968, pp. 219–22.
2, 3 A. Benois, 'Zinaida Serebryakova', op. cit.
4 A. Benois, *My Recollections (Moi vospominaniya)*, Moscow 1980, Vol. 1, p. 215.
5 A. Benois, 'Artistic Letters: The 'Union' Exhibition', *Discourse (Rech)*, 13 March 1910.
6 A. Benois, 'Artistic Letters', op. cit.
7 In 1916 Benois had been commissioned to decorate the Kazan Station in Moscow and invited Evgeny Lanceray, Boris Kustodiev, Mstislav Dobuzhinsky and Serebryakova to contribute to the project. Serebryakova took the subject of the Orient and depicted Persia, Siam, Turkey and India. Her tempera studies for these paintings are now in the State Tretyakov Gallery.
8 A. Benois, 'Zinaida Serebryakova', op. cit.

9 A. Ostroumova-Lebedeva, *Autobiographical Notes* (*Avtobiograficheskie zapiski*), Moscow 1974, Vol. 3. Cited in *Zinaida Serebryakova*. Catalogue, Leningrad-Moscow 1984, p. 26.
10 Z. Serebryakova, letter to T. B. Serebryakova, 23 January 1947, in *Zinaida Serebryakova*, op. cit., pp. 29-44.
11 T. Serebryakova, the artist's daughter, *Zinaida Serebryakova*, op. cit., p. 29.
12 D. Sarabyanov, 'On the Self-portraits of Z. Serebryakova', *Zinaida Serebryakova*, op. cit., p. 9.

2 THE AMAZONS OF THE AVANT-GARDE

Natalya Goncharova
1 M. Tsvetaeva. Manuscript, Meudon, March 1929.
2 D. Sarabyanov, 'Talent and Hard Work' (*Dar i trud*). Manuscript, p. 2. Sarabyanov Archive.
3-5 M. Tsvetaeva. Manuscript, op. cit.
6 M. Tsvetaeva, 'Natalya Goncharova, Life and Work' ('*Zhizn' i iskusstvo*'), in *Prometheus* (*Promety*), Moscow 1969, Vol. 7, p. 201.
7 M. Tsvetaeva, 'Natalya Goncharova', op. cit., pp. 178-9.
8 N. Goncharova, Preface to the catalogue *Natalya Sergeevna Goncharova 1900-1913*, Moscow 1913.
9 M. Tsvetaeva. Manuscript, op. cit.
10 D. Sarabyanov, op. cit., p. 7.
11 G. Apollinaire, Preface to the catalogue *Exposition Gontcharowa et Larionow*, Paris 1914.
12 M. Fokine, *Memoirs of a Ballet Master*, London 1961, pp. 227-8.
13 Letter from E. V. Polenova to V. D. Polenov of 14 May 1914, Manuscripts Department, State Tretyakov Gallery, fond 54/3798, 24.
14 D. Sarabyanov, *New Trends in Russian Art 1900-1910* (*Noveyshie techeniya v Russkom iskusstve 1900-1910*).
15 V. Mayakovsky, in *Collected Works*, 1933, Vol. 1, p. 353.
16 A. Blok, *Three Questions* (*Tri voprosa*), Moscow.
17 Manuscript Department, State Tretyakov Gallery, fond 54/3807.
18 'Kubizm', text from B. Livshits, *The One-and-A-Half-Eyed Archer* (*Polutoraglazy strelets*), Leningrad 1933, pp. 80-81. Trans. as 'Cubism', J. Bowlt, *Russian Art of the Avant-Garde, Theory and Criticism*, London, New York, rev. edn. 1988, pp. 77-8.
19 Extract from preface to second solo exhibition, *Natalya Sergeevna Goncharova*, Moscow, August to October 1913. Trans. Bowlt, op. cit., pp. 54-60.

Olga Rozanova
1 A. Blok, *Collected Works* (*Sobranie sochinenii*), Vol. 2, Moscow-Leningrad 1962, p. 308.
2 O. Rozanova, 'The Bases of the New Creation and the Reasons Why It is Misunderstood' ('*Osnovy novogo tvorchestva i prichiny ego neponimaniya*'), Union of Youth (*Soyuz molodezhi*) 3, St Petersburg, March 1913, p. 12. Trans. J. Bowlt in *Russian Art of the Avant-Garde, Theory and Criticism*, London, New York, rev. edn. 1988.
3 V. Rakitin, 'Illusionism is the Apotheosis of Vulgarity' in the catalogue *Women-Artists of the Russian Avantgarde*, Galerie Gmurzynska, Cologne 1979-80, p. 254.
4 Some Western scholars, such as M. Calvesi below, believe that Rozanova visited Paris and Rome in 1914 but as yet there is no evidence to substantiate this claim.
5 A. Benois, 'Cubism or Ridiculism?' ('*Kubizm ili kukishizm*'), *Discourse* (*Rech*), 23 November 1912.
6 B. Livshits, *The One-and-A-Half-Eyed Archer* (*Polutoraglazy strelets*), Leningrad 1933. Trans. J. Bowlt, Oriental Research Partners, Newtonville, Mass., 1977, p. 128.
7 Varst (V. Stepanova), 'Posthumous Exhibition of Olga Rozanova', in *Art* (*Iskusstvo*), 1919, No. 1, p. 8.
8 *Dissonance* is reproduced in colour in M. Calvezi, 'Il

Futurismo Russo' in *L'Arte Moderna*, 1967, Vol. 5, No. 44, p. 304.
9 Varst, op. cit., p. 2.
10 N. Khardzhiev, *The Russian Avant Garde*, Stockholm 1976, p. 61.
11 O. Rozanova to A. Shemshurin, Manuscripts Dept., State Lenin Library, Shemshurin fond 5/14.
12 A. Kruchenykh, *Declaration of the Word as Such*, Moscow 1913, pp. 5-8.
13 V. Kandinsky, *Concerning the Spiritual in Art*, Moscow 1915, p. 11.
14 Cited in N. Punin: 'Flat No.5', Manuscripts Department, State Tretyakov Gallery, fond 4/1568.
15 O. Rozanova: 'The Bases of the New Creation', op. cit. Trans. Bowlt, *Russian Art of the Avant-Garde*, op. cit., p. 109.
16 V. Markov, *Principles of the New Art: Texture*, St Petersburg 1914, p. 42.
17 Extract from 'The Bases of the New Creation', op. cit., pp. 14-22. Trans. Bowlt, op. cit., pp. 102-10.
18 *Supremus* magazine, No. 1 (unpublished). Trans. Bowlt, op. cit., p. 148.

Lyubov Popova
1 V. Mukhina, cited in P. K. Suzdalev, *Vera Ignatievna Mukhina*, Moscow 1981, p. 85.
2 L. Popova, manuscript notes in the archive of D. Sarabyanov. Cited in Sarabyanov's own manuscript 'The Painting of Popova', ('*Zhivopis Popovoy*'), p. 9.
3 D. Sarabyanov, op. cit., p. 12.
4 L. Popova, letter of 1916 from Samarkand to A. Vesnin. Sarabyanov Archive, cited in Sarabyanov, op. cit., p. 10.
5 Cited in *Izvestiya*, 9 April 1922, No. 800.
6 A. Gan, 'Constructivism' in M. Bush and A. Zamoshkin, *The Path of Soviet Art 1917-1932*, Ogiz-Izogiz, 1933, p. 24.
7 I. Ehrenburg, in M. Bush and A. Zamoshkin, op. cit., p. 24.
8 Ya. Tugendkhold, 'Notes on Contemporary Art' in *Russian Art* (*Russkoe iskusstvo*), Nos 2-3, p. 95, and also A. Skvortsov and D. Shterenberg, *Art for the Workers* (*Iskusstvo-trudyashchimsya*), 10-15 February 1925. No. 11, p. 5.
9 A. Fedorov-Davydov, 'Tendencies in Contemporary Russian Painting in the Light of Social Analysis', *Red Virgin Soil* (*Krasnaya nov*), 1924, No. 6, p. 329.
10 D. Aranovich, 'Ten Years of Art', *Red Virgin Soil* (*Krasnaya nov*), 1927, No. 11.
11 Unsigned article in *The Shows* (*Zrelishcha*), 1923, No. 67, p. 8.
12 D. Sarabyanov and N. Adaskina: *Lyubov Popova*, London 1990.
13 From Rodchenko's memoir 'On Tatlin' ('*O Tatline*'). Manuscript, 1940. Rodchenko-Lavrentiev Archive.
14 Trans. J. Bowlt, *Russian Art of the Avant-Garde. Theory and Criticism*, London, New York, rev. edn. 1988, pp. 146-8.

Alexandra Exter
1 B. Livshits, *The One-and-A-Half-Eyed Archer*. Trans. J. Bowlt, Oriental Research Partners, Newtonville, Mass., 1977, pp. 128-9.
2 B. Livshits, op. cit., p. 36.
3 B. Livshits, op. cit., p. 129.
4 G. Kovalenko, 'Alexandra Exter' *Creativity* (*Tvorchestvo*), 1987, No. 10, p. 30.
5 A. Exter, text in 5 × 5 = 25, exhibition catalogue, Moscow, September 1921, p. 13.
6 A. Nakov, 'Painting and Stage Design: A Creative Dialogue', *Alexandra Exter: Artist of the Theatre*, New York 1974, p. 9.
7 J. Bowlt, 'Some Very Elegant Ladies', in the catalogue *Women-Artists of the Russian Avantgarde*, Galerie Gmurzynska, Cologne 1979-80, p. 37.

8 Ronny Cohen, 'Alexandra Exter's Designs for the Theatre', *Artforum*, Summer 1981, p. 49.
9 J. Bowlt, 'The Marionettes of Alexandra Exter', *Alexandra Exter Marionettes*, Hutton Galleries, New York 1975-6, p. 8.
10 '*Prostota i praktichnost v Odezhde*' in *Red Cornfield* (*Krasnaya niva*), No. 21.

Varvara Stepanova
1 O. Brik, 'From Pictures to Textile Prints', *LEF*, Moscow 1924, No. 2, pp. 27-34.
2 V. Stepanova, 'Concerning My Graphics at the Exhibition', ('*O vystavlennykh grafikakh*'), *The Tenth State Exhibition: Non-objective Creation and Suprematism*, Moscow 1919.
3 E. Kovtun, 'Varvara Stepanova's Anti-book', *From Surface to Space, Russia 1916-1924*, Galerie Gmurzynska, Cologne 1974, pp. 57-64.
4 V. Stepanova, 'Non-objective creation' ('*Bespredmetnoe tvorchestvo*'), in *The Tenth State Exhibition: Non-objective Creation and Suprematism*, op. cit., p. 9.
5 V. Stepanova, Diary, 1920, cited in A. Lavrentiev, *Stepanova: A Constructivist Life*, London 1988, pp. 44-7.
6 A. Rodchenko, text in 5 × 5 = 25, exhibition catalogue, Moscow, September 1921, unpaginated.
7 Varst (Stepanova), text in 5 × 5 = 25, op. cit.
8 M. Rowell and A. Rudenstine, *Art of the Avant-Garde in Russia: Selections from the George Costakis Collection*, exhibition catalogue, Guggenheim Museum, New York 1981, p. 276.
9 V. Stepanova, from a lecture given at Inkhuk, cited in T. Strizhenova, *The History of Soviet Costume* (*Iz istorii sovetskogo kostyuma*), Moscow 1972, p. 84.
10 O. Brik, 'From Pictures to Textile Prints', op. cit.
11 V. Meyerkhold, *Vsevolod Meyerkhold: Articles, Letters, Discourses, Conversations* (*Statii, pisma, rechi, besedy*), Vol. 2, Moscow 1968, p. 79.
12 V. Stepanova, 'The Death of Tarelkin' ('*Smert' Tarelkina*'). Manuscript, 1934, Rodchenko-Lavrentiev Archive, Moscow.
13 A. Law, 'The Death of Tarelkin', *Russian History*, 1981, Vol. 8, Parts 1-2, p. 145.
14 O. Brik, 'From Pictures to Textile Prints', op. cit.
15 O. Brik, 'From Pictures to Textile Prints', op. cit.
16 Letter in the Rodchenko-Lavrentiev Archive.
17 Solomon Telingater, 1903-1969, typographer and graphic designer.
18 Diary. Manuscript in the Rodchenko-Lavrentiev Archive, Moscow.
19 V. Stepanova, 'From Costume to Designs and Fabric' ('*Ot kostyuma k risunku i tkani*'), *Evening Moscow* (*Vechernyaya Moskva*), 1929, No. 49, p. 3.

Nadezhda Udaltsova
1 N. Udaltsova, 'My Autobiography' ('*Moya avtobiografiya*'), manuscript written in 1933, E. Drevina Archive, Moscow. Trans. in *Women-Artists of the Russian Avantgarde, 1910-1930*, Galerie Gmurzynska, Cologne 1979-80, pp. 311-12.
2 Udaltsova was born on 30 December 1885 (Old Style calendar) but some authorities cite the New Style date of January 1886.
3-5 N. Udaltsova, op. cit.
6 N. Udaltsova, conversation with the author, 1952.
7-9 N. Udaltsova, op. cit.
10 N. Udaltsova, letters to Alexander Udaltsov, 1912-13, E. Drevina Archive, Moscow.
11-13 N. Udaltsova, op. cit.
14 N. Udaltsova, 'How Critics and the Public Relate to Contemporary Russian Art', 1915, trans. in *Women-Artists of the Russian Avantgarde*, op. cit., p. 307 ff.
15 A. Rodchenko, 'On Tatlin' ('*O Tatline*'). Manuscript, 1940, p. 5, Rodchenko-Lavrentiev Archive.
16 A. B. Nakov (Ed.), *Malevich: Ecrits*, Paris 1975, p. 67, No. 1.

17 K. Malevich, Record of a report on Udaltsova given at Inkhuk, 1924. Trans. in *Women-Artists of the Russian Avantgarde*, op. cit., p. 302.
18 *Anarchy (Anarkhiya)*, 2 April 1918, cited in M. Bush and A. Zamoshkin, *The Path of Soviet Art 1917–1932*, Ogiz Izogiz, 1933, p. 19.
19 Ya. Tugendkhold, 'Painting of the Revolutionary Decade', in *Art of the October Epoch*, Leningrad 1930, pp. 36–9.
20, 21 K. Malevich, op. cit.
22–4 N. Udaltsova, op. cit.
25, 26 K. Malevich, op. cit.
27 M. V. Yablonskaya, *Light*, 1987–8.

3 WOMEN ARTISTS AND THE CHAMBER ART OF THE 1920s AND 1930s
Antonina Sofronova
1 Lidya Ginzburg, 'Variations on an Old Theme', *Notes on the Twenties and Thirties*. First published in *Neva*, Leningrad 1987.
2 I. Uvarova, 'The Force of Gravity', *Decorative Art of the USSR*, 1987, No. 11, p. 16.
3 M. Gorky, cited in I. Luppol, M. Rozental and S. Tretyakov (Eds.), *The First All-Union Congress of Soviet Writers 1934 (Pervy vsesoyuzny sezd Sovetskikh pisatelei 1934)*, Moscow 1934, p. 12.
4 N. Belokhvostova, *The Creativity of Antonina Sofronova*, Diploma thesis, Moscow State University 1986, p. 4.
5 A. Benois, cited in I. S. Bolotina and A. V. Shcherbakov, *Osmerkin*, Moscow 1981, p. 13.
6 Cited in M. Nemirovskaya, 'Some Features of Soviet Easel Drawing of the 1920–1930s', *Soviet Drawing 75–76*, Sovetsky khudozhnik, 1977, p. 201.
7 A. Sofronova, Diary, May 1919, Efstafyeva Archive, Moscow.
8 N. Tarabukin, *From the Easel to the Machine (Ot molberta k mashine)*, Rabotnik prosveshcheniya, Moscow 1923.
9 A. Sofronova, Diary, May 1921, Efstafyeva Archive, Moscow.
10 Diary, September 1921, Efstafyeva Archive, Moscow.
11 Group 13, letter to A. Lunacharsky, cited in M. Nemirovskaya, *The Artists of the Thirteen*, Moscow 1986, p. 131.

12 Editorial article, 'Exhibition of "The Thirteen"', *Evening Moscow (Vechernyaya Moskva)*, 4 May 1931, p. 4.
13 N. Kuzmin, 'Our Guests', cited in M. Nemirovskaya, op. cit., p. 196.
14 A. Sofronova, 'Moscow 1929–1930', from a manuscript album of poems, Efstafyeva Archive, Moscow.
15 Diary. Efstafyeva Archive, Moscow.

Eva Rozengolts-Levina
1 E. Murina, address given at an evening dedicated to Rozengolts-Levina, 2 January 1978, Moscow.
2 Biography of Rozengolts-Levina. Manuscript. E. Levina Archive, Moscow.
3 E. Murina, op. cit.
4 Biography of Rozengolts-Levina, op. cit.
5 E. Rozengolts-Levina, account of Golubkina, E. Levina Archive, Moscow.
6 From the reminiscences of the artist E. Bulatova, a pupil of Robert Falk.
7 'Declaration by OKHO' in *Panorama iskusstv*, No. 4, Moscow 1981, p. 34.
8 E. Rozengolts-Levina and R. Izelson, 'The Theatre of the Near Future: The Question of the Theatre in the Socialist City', *Revolution and Culture (Revolutsiya i kulttura)*, 1930, No. 13–14.
9 Manuscript in E. Levina Archive, Moscow.
10 Vasily Chekrygin (1897–1912), a member of the World of Art group, a mystical painter whose religious subjects were based on the philosophy of Fedorov, a friend of the poets Mayakovsky and Khlebnikov.
11 Manuscript in E. Levina Archive, Moscow.
12 Manuscript in E. Levina Archive, Moscow.

Nina Simonovich-Efimova
1 I. Efimov, *On Art and Artists*, Moscow 1977.
2 V. S. Serova, *How My Son Grew Up (Kak poc moy syn)*, Leningrad 1968.
3 N. Simonovich-Efimova, *Note Books 1926–1948*, Central State Archives of Art and Literature, cited in N. Potapova, *The Creativity of Simonovich-Efimova 1877–1948*, thesis, Moscow State University 1987, p. 37–8.
4 Ya. Tugendkhold, 'Contemporary Art and the People', *Northern Notes (Severnye zapiski)*, 1913, p. 195.
5 N. Simonovich-Efimova, *Notes on Petrushka and Articles on the Theatre of Marionettes*, Leningrad 1980, pp. 170–80, 207–34, 226.

6 N. Smirnova, *Soviet Puppet Theatre 1918–1932*, Moscow 1963, p. 312.
7 John van Zant, 1933, cited in Simonovich-Efimova, *Notes on Petrushka*, op. cit., p. 243.
8 N. Simonovich-Efimova, *My Account of Life as an Artist*. Manuscript, Efimova Archive, Moscow.
9 Cited in *Simonovich-Efimova 1877–1948*, exhibition catalogue, Moscow 1968, p. 7.
10 P. Ettinger, in Simonovich-Efimova, *Notes of an Artist*, Moscow 1982, p. 325.
11 'Chinese shadows' ('Kitayskie teni'), in A. S. Simonovich, *Kindergarten (Detsky sad)*, Moscow 1907, pp. 250–8.
12 In *Notes on Petrushka*, op. cit., p. 43.
13 Extracts from 'Notes' published in *Simonovich-Efimova 1877–1948*, exhibition catalogue, Moscow 1968, pp. 15–18.

4 TWO SOVIET SCULPTORS
Sarra Lebedeva
1 M. Alpatov, 'On Sarra Lebedeva', *Sarra Lebedeva*, album, p. 7.
2 M. Alpatov, op. cit., pp. 7–8.
3 M. Alpatov, op. cit., p. 9.
4 'Some words on the portrait of F. Dzerzhinsky', *Projector (Prozhektor)*, 1926, No. 17, p. 18.
5 I. Slonim, 'Sarra Lebedeva', *Soviet Artist*, Moscow 1973, p. 11.

Vera Mukhina
1 V. Mukhina, cited in P.K. Suzdalev, *Vera Ignatievna Mukhina*, Moscow 1981, p. 7.
2 I. Mashkov, cited in Suzdalev, op. cit., p. 10.
3 V. Mukhina, cited in Suzdalev, op. cit., pp. 17–18.
4 B. Ternovets, *V. I. Mukhina*, Moscow and Leningrad 1937, p. 13.
5 V. Mukhina, cited in Suzdalev, op. cit., p 25.
6 B. Ternovets, op. cit., p. 40.
7 B. Ternovets, op. cit., p. 42.
8 A. Lunacharsky, Commissar for Enlightenment, cited in Suzdalev, op. cit., p. 66.
9 V. Mukhina, cited in Suzdalev, op. cit., p. 82.
10 B. Ternovets, op. cit., p. 62.
11 B. Ternovets, op. cit., p. 76.

SELECT BIBLIOGRAPHY

General
Barron, S., and M. Tuchman, *The Avant-Garde in Russia 1910–1930: New Perspectives*, Los Angeles County Museum of Art, 1980.
Bowlt, J., *Russian Stage Design: Scenic Innovation 1900–1930*, Mississippi Museum of Art, 1982.
—, *Russian Art of the Avant-Garde: Theory and Criticism, 1902–1934*, London, New York, rev edn. 1988.
Compton, S., *The World Backwards: Russian Futurist Books 1912–1916*, British Museum Publications, London 1978.
Lodder, C., *Russian Constructivism*, London 1983.
Paris – Moscou, Parizh – Moskva, Centre Georges Pompidou, Paris, 1979.
Rudenstine, A. (Ed.), *Russian Avant-Garde Art: The George Costakis Collection*, New York, London 1981.
Künstlerinnen der russischen Avantgarde/Women Artists of the Russian Avantgarde 1910–1930. Exhibition catalogue. Galerie Gmurzynska, Cologne, 1979–1980.

Maria Yakunchikova
Barok, N. (N. V. Polenova), 'M. V. Yakunchikova', *Mir iskusstva*, 1904, No. 3.
S. D. (Diaghilev), 'M. V. Yakunchikova', *Mir iskusstva*, 1902, No. 12.
Izgoy, R., 'Our Artistic Affairs' ('Nashi khudozhestvennyi dela'), *Iskusstvo i khudozhestvennaya promyshlennost*, 1899, No. 6.
Kiselev, M., *Maria Vasilievna Yakunchikova*, Moscow 1979.

Mir iskusstva, 1900, Nos 21–22 (reproduced headpieces); 1901, No. 4 (works).
Octav, Uzanne, 'Modern Colour Engraving with Notes on Some Work by Marie Yakounchikoff', *The Studio*, 1895, Vol. 6, No. 6.
Sakharova, E., and V. Polenov, *Elena Dmitrievna Polenova: Chronicle of an Artist's Family (Elena Polenova, Khronika sem'i khudozhnika)*, Moscow 1974.
Voloshin, M., 'The Creativity of M. Yakunchikova' ('Tvorchestvo M. Yakunchikovoy'), *Vesy*, 1905, No. 1.

Anna Golubkina
Exhibition of the Sculptor A. S. Golubkina: 80th Anniversary of her Birth 1864–1944 (Vystavka skul'ptora A. S. Golubkinoy. 80 let so dnya rozhdeniya 1864–1944), Moscow 1944.
Golubkina, A., *Letters, Some Words on the Sculptor's Craft, Contemporary Reminiscences (Pis'ma, Neskol'ko slov o remesle skul'ptora. Vospominaniya sovremennikov)*, Moscow 1983.
Kamensky, A., *The Knight's Victory: A Book about Anna Golubkina's Sculpture (Rytsarsky podvig. Kniga o skul'pture Anne Golubkinoy)*, Moscow 1978.
Konenkov, S., and S. Gerasimov, *Anna Golubkina: Jubilee Exhibition (Anna Golubkina. Yubileynaya vystavka)*, Moscow 1964.
Kostin, V., *Anna Semyonovna Golubkina 1864–1927*, Moscow and Leningrad 1947.
Nikolaev (Ternovets), B., 'Anna Semyonovna Golubkina', *Iskusstvo*, 1939, No. 3, pp. 117–21.

Rozanov, V., 'The Success of Our Sculpture' ('*Uspekhi nashey skulptury*'), *Mir iskusstva*, 1901, Nos 1–3, pp. 111–13.

—, 'The Work of Golubkina' ('*Raboty Golubkinoy*'), *Sredi khudozhnikov*, Moscow, 1914, pp. 341–3.

Zinaida Serebryakova

Benois, A., 'Zinaida Serebryakova', *Aleksandr Benois Reflects* (*Aleksandr Benua razmyshlyaet*), Moscow 1968.

Dmitriev, V., 'Women Artists' ('*Khudozhnitsy*'), *Apollon*, 1917, Nos 8–10.

Ernst, S., *Z. E. Serebryakova*, Petrograd 1922.

Knyazeva, V., *Zinaida Serebryakova*, Moscow 1979.

Lapshin, V., *Serebryakova*, Moscow 1969.

Savinov, A., *Zinaida Serebryakova*, Leningrad 1973.

Zinaida Serebryakova: Exhibition of Works from Museums & Private Collections (*Zinaida Serebryakova: Vystavka proizvedeniy iz muzeev i chastnykh sobraniy*), Moscow 1965.

Zinaida Serebryakova, catalogue, exhibition to mark the centenary of the artist's birth, Moscow 1986.

Natalya Goncharova

Apollinaire, G., 'Nathalie de Gontcharowa et Michel Larionow', *Exposition Gontcharowa et Larionow*, Galerie Paul Guillaume, Paris, 1914.

Chamot, M., *Gontcharova*, Paris 1971.

—, *Goncharova: Stage Designs and Paintings*, London 1979.

Eganbyuri, E., *Nataliya Goncharova Mikhail Larionov*, Moscow 1913.

Khardzhiev, N., 'In Memory of Natalya Goncharova and Mikhail Larionov' ('*Pamyati Natalii Goncharovoy i Mikhaila Larionova*'), *Iskusstvo knigi 1963–1964*, Vol. V, Moscow 1968, pp. 306–18.

Larionov, M., N. Goncharova et al., *The Donkey's Tail and Target* (*Osliny khvost i Mishen*), Moscow 1913.

Loguine, T., *Gontcharova et Larionov*, Paris 1971.

Parnack, V., *Gontcharova Larionow: L'Art Décoratif Théâtral Moderne*, Paris 1919.

Olga Rozanova

Calvesi, M., 'Il Futurismo Russo', *L'Arte Moderna* (Milan), 1967, No. 44, Vol. 5, pp. 281–320.

Dmitrieva, N., *Image and Word* (*Izobrazhenie i slovo*), Moscow 1982.

Exhibition of Paintings, Studies, Sketches and Drawings by O. V. Rozanova (*Vystavka kartin, etyudov, eskizov i risunkov O. V. Rozanovoy*), exhibition catalogue, Moscow 1919.

Kovtun, E., 'Experiments in Book Design by Russian Artists', *Journal of Decorative and Propaganda Arts*, Summer 1987, No. 5, pp. 46–59.

Rowell, M., and A. Rudenstine: 'Olga Rozanova', *Art of the Avant-Garde in Russia: Selections from the George Costakis Collection*, New York 1981.

Rozanova, O., 'Verses' ('*Stikhi*'), *Iskusstvo*, Moscow, 1919, No. 4, p. 1.

'Olga Rozanowa', *Russische Avantgarde 1910–1930: Sammlung Ludwig, Köln*, Munich, 1986, pp. 150–5.

Voinov, V., *Russian Lithographs of the past 25 Years* (*Russkie litografii za poslednie 25 let*), Moscow 1923.

Lyubov Popova

Adaskina, M., 'The Question of Production Art in the Work of L. S. Popova' ('*Problema proizvodstvennogo iskusstva v tvorchestve L. S. Popovoy*'), *Artistic Problems of the Object and Spatial Environment* (*Khudozhestvennye problemy predmetno-prostranstvennoy sredy*), Moscow 1978.

—, 'Lyubov Popova. The Way to become an Artist-Constructor' ('*Lyubov Popova. Put stanovleniya khudozhnika-konstruktora*'), *Tekhnicheskaya estetika*, 1978, No. 11.

Bowlt, J., 'From Surface to Space: The Art of Liubov Popova', *The Structurist*, 1975–76, Nos 15–16, pp. 80–88.

—, 'Liubov Popova, Painter', *Transactions of A.R.A.S.*, New York, 1982, Vol. 15, pp. 227–51.

Murina, E., 'Popova's Materials' ('*Tkani L. Popovoy*'), *Dekorativnoe iskusstvo SSSR*, 1967, No. 8.

Posthumous Exhibition of the Work of L.S. Popova (*Posmertnaya vystavka proizvedenii L.S. Popovoy*). Exhibition catalogue, Moscow, 1924.

Rakitina, E., 'Lyubov Popova, Art and Manifestos' ('*Lyubov Popova, Iskusstvo i manifesty*'), *Artist, Stage, Screen* (*Khudozhnik, stsena, ekran*), Moscow, 1975.

Zhadova, L., 'Lyubov Popova', *Tekhnicheskaya estetika*, 1967, No. 11.

Alexandra Exter

Bowlt, J., 'Alexandra Exter: A Veritable Amazon of the Russian Avant-Garde', *Art News*, September 1974, pp. 41–3.

Cohen, R., 'Alexandra Exter's Designs for the Theatre', *Artforum*, Summer 1981, pp. 46–9.

—, *Alexandra Exter. Marionettes*, Hutton Galleries, New York, 1975.

Artist of the Theatre. Exhibition catalogue, New York Public Library at Lincoln Centre, New York, 1974.

Khaydykov, R., 'On Three Artists of The Kamerny Theatre: Exter, Vesnin, Yakulov' ('*O tryokh khudozhnikakh Kamernogo teatra. Exter, Vesnin, Yakulov*'), *Iskusstvo*, 1975, No. 5.

Nakov, A., *Alexandra Exter*, Galerie Chauvelin, Paris, 1972.

Strizhenova, T., 'The Costume Designer Alexandra Exter' ('*Avtor kostyuma Alexandra Exter*'), *Dekorativnoe iskusstvo*, 1967, No. 1.

Tugendkhold, Ya., *Alexandra Exter*, Berlin 1922.

Varvara Stepanova

Kovtun, E., 'Das Antibuch der Warwara Stepanova/Varvara Stepanova's Antibook', *Von der Flache zum Raum/From Surface to Space. Russland/Russia 1916–1924*, Galerie Gmurzynska, Cologne, 1974, pp. 57–64.

Lavrentiev, A., 'Poeziya graficheskogo dizaina v tvorchestve Varvary Stepanovoy', *Tekhnicheskaya estetika*, 1978, No. 12, pp. 22–6.

—, *Varvara Stepanova: A Constructivist Life*, London 1988.

Law, A., 'The Death of Tarelkin': A Constructivist Vision of Tzarist Russia', *Russian History*, 1981, Vol. 8, Parts 1–2, pp. 145–98.

Rodchenko, A., *Articles, Recollections, Autobiographical Notes, Letters* (*Statii, Vospominaniya, Avtobiograficheskie zapiski, Pisma*), Moscow 1982.

'Varvara Stepanova', *Sieben Moskauer Kunstler/Seven Moscow Artists 1910–1930*, Galerie Gmurzynska, Cologne, 1984, pp. 248–89.

Strizhenova, T., *The History of Soviet Costume* (*Iz istorii sovetskogo kostyuma*), Moscow 1972.

Trospolskaya, N., 'The Constructor "Varst"' ('*Konstruktor "Varst"*'), *Rabotnitsa*, 1987, No. 11, pp. 37–9.

Nadezhda Udaltsova

Exhibition of Paintings by A.D. Drevin and N.A. Udaltsova (*Vystavka kartin A.D. Drevina i N.A. Udaltsovoy*). Exhibition catalogue, Leningrad 1978.

Myasina, M., *The Oldest Soviet Artists on Central Asia and the Caucasus* (*Stareyshie sovetskie khudozhniki o Sredney Azii i Kavkaze*), Moscow 1973.

Salko, O., 'In Front of Udaltsova's Pictures' ('*U kartin Udaltsovoy*'), *Iskusstvo*, 1966, No. 4.

'Nadezhda Udaltsova', *Sieben Moskauer Kunstler/Seven Moscow Artists 1910–1930*, Galerie Gmurzynska, Cologne, 1984, pp. 290–339.

Antonina Sofronova

Nemirovskaya, M., 'Images Born of Time' ('*Obrazy rozhdyonnye vremenem*'), *Tvorchestvo*, 1978, No. 12.

—, 'On Certain Characteristics of Soviet Easel Graphics in the 1920s and early 1930s' ('*O nekotorykh osobennostyakh sovetskoy stankovoy grafiki 1920-kh nachala 1930-kh gg*'), *Sovetskaya grafika 77*, Moscow, 1979.

—, 'Sofronova's Works in the State Tretyakov Gallery' ('*Raboty Sofronovoy v GTG*'), *Muzey 1*, Moscow, 1980.

—, *The Artists of the Thirteen* (*Khudozhniki gruppy 'Trinadtsat'*), Moscow 1986.

Eva Rozengolts-Levina

Falk, R., *Conversations about Art, Letters, Memories of the Artist* (*Besedy ob iskusstve. Pis'ma. Vospominaniya o khudozhnike*), Moscow, 1981.

Roytenberg, O., 'On the Border of the 1920s and 1930s' ('*Na rubezhe 1920–1930-kh godov*'), *Panorama iskusstv*, No. 4, Moscow, 1981, 306–40.

Shashkina, M., 'Everything is Degree . . . Towards a Portrait of Eva Levina-Rozengolts' ('*Vse est stepen . . . K portretu Evy Levinoy-Rozengolts*'), *Panorama iskusstv*, No. 7, Moscow, 1984, pp. 237–46.

Touring Exhibition of Paintings, Graphics and Drawings (*Peredvizhnaya vystavka zhivopisi, grafiki i risunka*). Exhibition catalogue, Moscow, 1928.

Nina Simonovich-Efimova

Efimov, I., *On Art and Artists* (*Ob iskusstve i khudozhnikakh*), Moscow 1977.

N. Simonovich-Efimova 1877–1948. Exhibition catalogue, Moscow, 1968.

Simonovich-Efimova, N., *Zapiski petrushechnika*, Moscow and Leningrad 1980.

Smirnova, N., *Soviet Puppet Theatre 1918–1932* (*Sovetsky teatr kukol 1918–1932*), Moscow, 1963.

Sarra Lebedeva

Ternovets, B., 'Sarra Lebedeva', *Iskusstvo*, 1935, No. 3, pp. 62–84.

—, *Sarra Lebedeva*, Moscow and Leningrad 1940.

S. D. Lebedeva. Exhibition catalogue, Moscow, 1969.

Sarra Lebedeva: Album (*Sarra Lebedeva. Albom*), Moscow 1973.

Vera Mukhina

Klimov, R. (Ed.), *V. Mukhina: The Literary-Critical Heritage* (*Literaturno-kriticheskoe nasledie*), Vols. 1–3, Moscow, 1960.

Suzdalev, P., *Vera Mukhina*, Moscow 1980.

Ternovets, B., *V. I. Mukhina*, Moscow and Leningrad 1937.

Voronova, O., *V. I. Mukhina*, Moscow 1976.

GENERAL

Publisher's note: the general chronology (and some text interpolations) have been provided editorially. For more detailed general background readers are referred to *New Worlds: Russian Art and Society 1900–1937* by David Elliott (1986).

1870 Foundation of the Society of Circulating Art Exhibitions, in rebellion against the teaching of the St Petersburg Academy of Art. The artists became known as *Peredvizhniki* (Wanderers), and the work they showed in touring exhibitions depicted contemporary social conditions in critical realist style. Members included Ilya Repin, Vladimir Makovsky, Abram Arkhipov.

1870s Revival of Russian arts and crafts. Pavel Tretyakov began to form his collection of Russian art; the railway magnate Savva Mamantov and his wife Elizaveta organized an arts-and-crafts colony at his estate of Abramtsevo, while Princess Maria Tenisheva formed a similar colony at her estate of Talashkino, among many such communal enterprises.

1880s–1907 Russia's 'Silver Age', a period characterized by a rapid progression through the styles of European art: Impressionism, Post-Impressionism and Symbolism (followed 1908–14, see below, by Fauvism, Cubism and Futurism).

1897 Lev Tolstoy's *What Is Art?* stressed the function of art as communication, great art being art accessible to all.

1898–9 Foundation of 'The World of Art' group, a loose association of artists, writers and musicians led by Sergei Diaghilev, who edited its journal, also named *The World of Art*, first published in 1898. Based on St Petersburg, its participants included Leon Bakst, Alexander Benois, Mstislav Dobuzhinsky, Dmitri Filosofov, Evgeny Lanceray, Isaac Levitan, Nicholas Roerich, Konstantin Somov, Anna Ostroumova-Lebedeva and Zinaida Serebryakova. Diaghilev drew into its compass the Symbolism of Mikhail Vrubel, the Neo-nationalism of Victor Vasnetsov, French Impressionism, interest in ancient Russian icons, as well as numerous other European and Russian sources. In 1899, the second 'World of Art' exhibition, held at the Steiglitz Institute, St Petersburg, showed more than 300 modern European works.

1904 War with Japan, the destruction of the Baltic Fleet and Russian defeat. Deteriorating political stability, industrial discontent, strikes.

1905 9 January: 'Bloody Sunday'. Peaceful march to the Winter Palace fired on by troops. October: General Strike. The Tsar conceded a 'Constitutional Manifesto'.

1906–10 Period of growing discontent, nihilism, and a sense of foreboding that found expression in all the arts.

1906 Sixth and final 'World of Art' exhibition, including the Symbolists Borisov-Musatov and Vrubel, anticipated the formation of the Symbolist 'Blue Rose' group in Moscow in the following year. (The 'World of Art' group ceased in this year, but was revived in 1910, and in its second stage attracted several members of the avant-garde.)

1907 'The Wreath' exhibition, Moscow, exhibited Goncharova, Larionov, Exter, and the organizers David and Vladimir Burlyuk. The 'Blue Rose' group was taken up by the wealthy financier Nikolai Ryabushinsky, who produced a de-luxe art journal, *The Golden Fleece*.

1908 'The Golden Fleece' exhibition showed 197 modern French paintings by Impressionist, Post-Impressionist, Symbolist and Fauve artists. This exhibition had a dramatic impact on the artists of the Russian avant-garde such as Goncharova and Larionov, and decisively altered the course of Russian art. 'The Link' exhibition, Kiev, organized by the Burlyuk brothers, Exter, Goncharova and Larionov, represented the first avant-garde manifestation in Russia, and like the 'Knave of Diamonds' exhibition in 1910 (below) was a response to the 'Golden Fleece' show.

1909 Goncharova's and Larionov's 'primitive'-style paintings heralded the Neoprimitive aesthetic.

1910 Formation of the large avant-garde group the 'Union of Youth', which organized exhibitions in 1910 in St Petersburg and Riga, and thereafter each year till 1914 in St Petersburg (1913 in Moscow also). Members included David Burlyuk, Chagall, Exter, Pavel Filonov, Ivan Klyun, Kazimir Malevich, Waldemar Matvejs (Markov), Rozanova, Vladimir Tatlin and Udaltsova. Revival of 'The World of Art', which subsequently exhibited, usually twice yearly, in St Petersburg and Moscow until 1917. Formation of the 'Knave of Diamonds' group, which included 'the Russians' around Larionov and Goncharova, and 'the French' led by Lentulov. The playing-card imagery of the group's name referred to their interest in the popular print, and also to the diamonds stamped on convicts' clothing. Members included Robert Falk, Piotr Konchalovsky, Alexander Kuprin, Ilya Mashkov. Exhibited in Moscow each year to 1914, then again in 1916 and 1917.

1912 'The Russians' broke away from the Knave of Diamonds to form 'The Donkey's Tail' group, so named by Larionov in reference to a French artist who had hoodwinked the public by tying a paintbrush to a donkey's tail and successfully submitting the result (entitled *Sunset over the Adriatic*) to the 1910 Salon des Indépendants. Goncharova's and Larionov's illustrations for Futurist books (1912–13).

1913 'The Target' exhibition organized by Larionov showed his own and Goncharova's 'Rayonist' paintings. The Moscow 'Hylea' group (also known as 'Cubo-Futurists') centred round David Burlyuk and the poets Klebnikov, Kamensky, Kruchenykh and Mayakovsky, published their manifesto entitled *A Slap in the Face for Public Taste*. Larionov and Goncharova organized a large exhibition of Russian icon-paintings and popular prints in Moscow.

1913–14 Futurists, including David Burlyuk and Mayakovsky, and 'Rayonists', including Goncharova and Larionov, stirred up disorder with frenzied public debates on the New Art, and exhibitionistic appearances on the streets with painted faces. Member of the 'Union of Youth' Malevich adopted Cubism, experimented with collage. Rozanova's, the Burlyuk brothers' and Malevich's illustrations for Futurist books.

1914 'No. 4' (Futurist) exhibition organized by Larionov. A Futurist film made, starring Larionov and Goncharova (now lost). The Italian Futurist Marinetti's first visit to Russia. Outbreak of war, followed by a number of patriotic exhibitions.

1915 February/March: 'Tramway V' exhibition (the 'First Exhibition of Futurist Painting'), Petrograd. April: 'The Year 1915: Exhibition of Pictures', Moscow. December: 'The Last Futurist Exhibition: 0.10'. In the course of these 3 important exhibitions leadership of the avant-garde passed from the Futurists centred on Goncharova and Larionov to the metaphysical idealists (Suprematists) around Malevich and the materialists around Tatlin. Goncharova and Larionov left Russia.

1916 'The Store' exhibition (so-named because it was held in a vacant shop) showed Tatlin's counter-reliefs as well as non-objective works by Popova, Exter, Udaltsova, Alexander Rodchenko, etc. 'Knave of Diamonds' exhibition showed Suprematist work by Malevich, Rozanova, Popova, Exter, Udaltsova and Ivan Puni.

1917 Following the October Revolution, the Bolshevik Central Committee announced the members of Lenin's new government. Anatole Lunacharsky, writer and intellectual, became head of the new 'People's Commissariat for Enlightenment' (Narkompros). He pursued a policy of multiplicity in the arts, sponsoring both avant-garde and traditional artists until his forced resignation in 1929.

1918 Free State Studios (Svomas) set up in Moscow. Lenin's Decree on Monumental Propaganda, prescribing revolutionary sculpture, was implemented by sculptors with designs for monuments to heroes such as Danton and Robespierre. Revolutionary and Bolshevik agit-prop (agitational propaganda) art took the government's message to the people with poster-cartoons in the streets and 'agit-trains' to the provinces, decorated by artists such as Exter and her pupils. 'Proletkult', the organization centred round Alexander Bogdanov, novelist, medical doctor, Revolutionary of 1905, advocated suppression and even destruction of pre-Revolutionary art. (This iconclasm offended the intelligentsia, and was checked in 1920 by a Decree of the Central Committee removing Proletkult's independence and subordinating it to Lunacharsky's Narkompros). Proletkult ran literary, theatre, arts and music workshops, and published journals and books such as *Shockworker Poetry*, 1918. IZO Narkompros, industrial art department, headed by Rozanova and Alexander Rodchenko, organized crafts and industrial workshops, and state exhibitions.

1919–21 Civil war, followed by famine.

1919 The State Publishing House (Gosizdat) set up. Malevich, teaching in Vitebsk Free Workshops, formed 'Unovis' (the Union of New Art) and proposed to 'integrate Suprematism with life'. His followers sewed a black square on their sleeves to testify their allegiance to the Suprematist revolution in art. (In 1923 Malevich moved to Petrograd, and 'Unovis' came under the aegis of 'Inkhuk', see below.) 'Tenth State Exhibition: Non-objective Creation and Suprematism' held in Moscow. In this, Malevich 'broke the boundaries of colour' with *White on White*, Rodchenko stated of his *Black on Black* that 'as a basis for my painting I put nothing'.

1920 Foundation of the Institute of Artistic Culture (Inkhuk) directed by Kandinsky as a section of Narkompros, first functioning as a centre for aesthetic debate in Moscow, then in 1921 (Kandinsky having resigned) becoming identified with Constructivism and the Production art movement.

1921–8 New Economic Policy co-incided with a brilliant flowering of the arts dedicated to the building of the new state. This embraced production and applied and also traditional art, as with the Realist 'New Society of Painters' (1922) who were chiefly former pupils of Tatlin, Malevich and Exter, the 'Society of Young Artists' with exhibitions organized by the Higher Artistic and Technical Studios (Vkhutemas) and the exhibition society 'Association of Artists of Revolutionary Russia' (AKHRR). The last-named, formed in response to the '47th Exhibition of *Pererdvizhniki*' (Wanderers) in Moscow, organized Realist shows from 1922 until (like all such associations) it was dissolved by Decree in 1932.

1921 September: '5 × 5 = 25' exhibition, organized by Inkhuk. In this 5 artists (Popova, Alexander Vesnin, Stepanova, Rodchenko and Exter) showed 5 works each, and it was announced there that the last easel painting had been painted. Thereafter, easel art was abandoned in favour of Constructivism and Production art dedicated to building the new society. Industrial art was advocated by Nikolai Tarabukin's book *From the Easel to the Machine* and other publications.

1922 Robotism and technology were combined with Constructivism in Meyerhold's avant-garde theatre-productions *The Magnanimous Cuckold* and *The Death of Tarelkin* at the newly opened Actor's Theatre, Moscow, designed by the Constructivists Popova and Stepanova respectively.

1923 Leadership of the avant-garde was taken over by the writers, critics and artists centred on the magazine *LEF* ('Left Front of the Arts'), led by Osip Brik and Vladimir Mayakovsky. The artists, who were mainly affiliated to Vkhutemas (including Stepanova, Rodchenko, Popova, Tatlin, El Lissitsky, Vesnin, and Moise Ginsberg), worked directly with industry, on architecture, fabric-design, ceramics, typography, using photomontage, photography etc. *LEF* (1924) illustrated Popova's and Stepanova's designs for the First Moscow Textile Print Factory; *Red Virgin Soil*, a similar publication, showed Lamanova's, Exter's and Mukhina's designs for practical clothing. Vkhutemas which had pioneered a Basic Course and acted as a powerhouse of art and design, just as did the Bauhaus in Germany, was now declared by its *LEF*-group teachers to be 'cut off from the ideological and practical tasks of the present', and to be overweighted with 'purists' (painters).

1924 Death of Lenin. Formation of Society of Moscow Artists (OMKH), largely of former Knave of Diamonds artists. Its first exhibition in the following year included Alexander Drevin, Kuprin, Konchalovsky, Lentulov, Mashkov, Sofronova, Udaltsova, Vera Favorskaya, and was accompanied by a declaration which denied the proposition that painting and sculpture were 'chamber art'. In 1926 OMKH merged with AKHRR; in 1927, most of its former members left AKHRR and merged with members of the former 'Union of Artists and Poets' (Makovets), as 'The Wing'.

1925 Formation of 'Four Arts Society', so-named because it included painters, graphic artists, architects and sculptors. It embraced both young and old, ranging from 'Blue Rose' and 'World of Art' artists to 'leftists'. Exhibited 1925, 1926 and 1929 in Moscow, 1928 in Leningrad. Members included Vladimir Favorsky, Konstantin Istomin, Ivan Klyun, Vladimir Lebedev, El Lissitsky, Mukhina, Ostroumova-Lebedeva, Simonovich-Efimova, Nikolai Ulyanov. Successful showing by Vkhutemas at the Paris Exposition Internationale des Arts Décoratifs et Industriels Modernes.

1928 The All-Union Party Conference on Propaganda and Agitation condemned 'formalism' (i.e. art based on style rather than on ideologically approved subject-matter), Constructivism and nihilism. Writers such as Mayakovsky were criticized as élitist by the Russian Association of Proletarian Writers (RAPP), founded in 1922. Commencement of the first Five Year Plan for collectivization and industrialization. (The Plan led to great hardship, and was declared completed in only 4 years.)

1929 'Group 13' formed: conservative, French-influenced, it held 2 exhibitions, published 3 catalogues, 1929, 1930, 1931, issued no manifesto. Exhibitors included David Burlyuk, Alexander Drevin, Tatiana Mavrina-Lebedeva, Sofronova and Udaltsova. The 1931 exhibitors were criticized for formalism. Resignation of Lunacharsky. Commencement of Stalin's 'Cultural Revolution'.

1930 Suicide of Mayakovsky. The former Vkhutemas (by now an 'Institution', known as Vkhutein) divided. *New LEF* journal denounced. Rodchenko's sharply angled photographs criticized in *Soviet Photography*. Many artists were converted to celebrating Soviet labour and achievements in Socialist Realist style, with genuine fervour and commitment, while others withdrew into private opposition, as the content of exhibitions became subject to control.

1931 Malevich returned to figure-painting and portraits with Renaissance references. Avant-garde artists who embraced traditional easel painting included Stepanova and Tatlin.

1932 Decree of the Party Central Committee abolished the artistic and literary organizations, substituting 'Unions' for each discipline.

1934 At the All Union Congress of Soviet Writers (former members of AKHRR), Stalin's son-in-law Andrei Zhdanov and Maxim Gorky specified 'Socialist Realism' as the sole acceptable form of expression. December: following the assassination of Stalin's political rival Sergei Kirov, Stalin's supreme power became unchallenged.

1935– Start of the period marked in the arts by conformity, accusations of formalism and leftism, and prosecutions affecting whole-hearted Party supporters and traditional artists as well as the former avant-garde. The former leader of RAPP, L. Averbakh, shot for 'leftism' in 1938, the theatre-director Meyerhold arrested and shot in 1939, the painter Eva Rozengolts-Levina exiled in 1949, and the poet Osip Mandelstam who died in a transit camp, were among many writers and artists who were exiled or perished.

ARTISTS

Maria Yakunchikova

1870 Born in Wiesbaden where her parents were on holiday. Childhood spent in Moscow.

1883 Began to study painting and drawing privately with N. A. Martynov.

1885 Attended the Moscow School of Painting, Sculpture and Architecture as an unregistered student. Home studies supervised by S.S. Golushev (Sergey Glagol).

1887–9 Began to form a folk-art collection.

1887 Travelled to the Crimea with her father and Vasily Polenov.

1888 First works in oils. Visited Austria and Italy.

1889–90 Travelled to France and Germany (Biarritz, Paris, and Berlin). Entered the Académie Julien, the studios of the salon painters Bouguereau and Fleury.

1890–3 In Paris winter and spring, Russia summer and autumn. Worked at the Polenov estate, Bekhova, and at the Mamontovs', Abramtsevo.

1892–3 First experiments with colour etching.

1894 Return to Paris. Organized an exhibition of applied art by women artists.

1895 Polenova came to Paris. Encouraged Yakunchikova to organize an exhibition of folk art. Executed first series of panels in pokerwork and oils. Return to France in the autumn.

1896 Participated in 'Exhibition of Experiments in Artistic Creativity (Sketches) by Russian and Foreign Artists and their Pupils', St Petersburg, organized by Ilya Repin. Married the doctor of medicine L. N. Weber.

1897 First book illustrations.

1898 Sergei Diaghilev commissioned a cover for the journal *Mir Iskusstva* (*The World of Art*). Began to design textiles and toys. Death of Elena Polenova.

1899 At Yakunchikova's estate at Nara, near Moscow, she carried out Polenova's project of assembling a Russian handicrafts collection for the 1900 Exposition Universelle, Paris. Began using appliqué techniques. Took charge of the embroidery workshops at Abramtsevo in succession to Polenova.

1900 Returned to Paris. Worked with Princess Tenisheva there. Sketches for an illustrated alphabet.

1901 Birth of her second son affected her health.

1902 Died in Switzerland, at Chêne Bougerie near Geneva, aged thirty-two.

Anna Golubkina

1864 Born in Zaraysk, Ryazan Province.

1889–90 Studied with the artist and architect A. O. Gunst in Moscow. Supervised by the sculptor S. M. Volnukhin.

1891–4 Studied with the painter S. I. Ivanov at the Moscow School of Painting, Sculpture and Architecture.

1894–5 Worked at the Higher Art Institute, attached to the St Petersburg Academy of Arts, in the studio of the sculptor V. A. Beklemishev.

1895–6 Spent 14 months in Paris. Worked in Filippo Colarossi's studio. Returned to Moscow.

1897 Visited Paris for 3 months. In contact with Auguste Rodin.

1899 Awarded a medal (3ème classe) by the Académie for her contribution to the Salon de Printemps.

1901–3 Taught sculpture in classes which she organized together with the painter N. P. Ulyanov, and also at the Moscow Commercial Institute.

1902 Sculpted a panel above the entrance to the Moscow Art Theatre, commissioned by Savva Morozov.

1903 Visited Paris to study the techniques of working in marble.

1904 To London; returned to Moscow.

1905–7 Took an active part in the Revolutionary movement.

1907 Imprisoned at Zaraysk for distributing literature on behalf of the RSDRP (Bolsheviks); freed because of ill-health. Rented a studio in B. Levshinsky Street (now Shchukin Street) where she continued to work to the end of her life.

1913 Taught sculpture courses for Presnensky workers. Contributed to 'Thirty-Second Exhibition of the Moscow Society of Art Lovers', Moscow; 'World of Art', St Petersburg; 'Twentieth Exhibition of Watercolours', Moscow.

1914 First one-woman exhibition, 'in aid of the war-wounded', Museum of Fine Arts, Moscow.

1917 Exhibited with, and an elected member of, the 'Moscow Salon'.

1918–20 Taught sculpture at Svomas.

1920–1 Professor of sculpture at Vkhutemas.

1923 Published *Some Words on the Sculptor's Craft*. Awarded third prize in a competition for a monument to A. N. Ostrovsky. Exhibited in the 'Seventeenth Moscow Salon'.

1924 Affected by ill-health; worked on small-scale sculpture and cameos. Participated in the Exhibition of Russian Art, New York.

1925 Exhibited 'Women in Russian Art', Moscow, and 'Drawings by Contemporary Russian Sculptors', Moscow. Became a member of the Commission of the Tolstoy Museum, Moscow.

1926 Took part in the organization of the Society of Russian Sculptors (ORS).

1927 Died at Zaraysk.

Zinaida Serebryakova

1884 Born on the Neskuchnoe Estate, near Kharkov.

1901 Briefly studied at Princess Maria Tenisheva's art school at Talashkino.

1902–3 Travelled to Italy (Rome, Capri).

1903–5 Worked in O. E. Braz's studio. Copied the Old Masters in the Hermitage.

1905–6 Married a relative, the railway engineer Boris Serebryakov. Went to Paris. Studied drawing and watercolour in the Académie de la Grande Chaumière (tutors Simon and Danet).

1906 Returned to Russia (St Petersburg and Neskuchnoe). Joined the World of Art group.

1910 First exhibitions, participated in 'The Contemporary Female Portrait', and 'Seventh Exhibition of Paintings Organized by the Union of Russian Artists'. Travelled to the Crimea (Yalta, Gurzuf).

1910–13 Regularly contributed to the second series of 'World of Art' exhibitions in Moscow and St Petersburg.

1914 Travelled through Switzerland and northern Italy (Milan, Florence, Padua, Venice).

1916 Paintings for Kazan Station, Moscow (together with her uncle Alexander Benois and brother Evgeny Lanceray).

1918 'The Russian Countryside' exhibition, Petrograd. Fire destroyed her home at Neskuchnoe.

1918–20 Lived in Kharkov working at the University Archaeological Museum (making archaeological drawings).

1919 'First Exhibition of the Arts organized by the Kharkov Soviet Worker Deputies', Kharkov. Death of her husband.

1920 Exhibition of paintings by members of the House of Arts, Petrograd.

1921 Served in IZO Narkompros, Education Department.

1922 Participated in the 'World of Art' exhibition, held in the Anichkov Palace, Petrograd.

1924 Participated in the 'World of Art' exhibition, Leningrad; 'The Peasant in Russian Painting, VIII–XXth Centuries', at the Tretyakov Gallery, Moscow.

1924–5 Represented in travelling exhibition of Russian Art, New York and Canada.

1925 To England (London). In this year and later, painted many commissioned portraits.

1926 Travelled to England, then to Brittany where she began a series of pastel portraits of fishermen, and landscapes.

1927–55 Continued to paint, travelled widely.

1967 Died in Paris.

Natalya Goncharova

1881 Born at Negaevo.

1898–1901 Studied sculpture at the Moscow School of Painting, Sculpture and Architecture, where she met the young artist Mikhail Larionov.

1906 Contributed to the 'World of Art' exhibition in Moscow, and sent works in impressionist style to the Russian Art section of the Salon d'Automne in Paris.

1907 Exhibited landscapes in 'The Wreath' exhibition organized by Larionov, Exter and the Burlyuk brothers.

1908 Collaborated on the organization of the famous 'Golden Fleece' exhibition in Moscow which introduced Post-Impressionist and Fauve paintings into Russia, and on 'The Link' exhibition, Kiev.

1909 Developed the style that became known as Neoprimitivism.

1910 One-woman exhibition in Moscow. Her paintings were confiscated for their alleged 'pornography'. Became a founder-member of the Knave of Diamonds group.

1910–11 Contributed to the 'Knave of Diamonds', 'Union of Youth' and 'World of Art' exhibitions.

1912 Publicly dissociated herself from the Knave of Diamonds. With Larionov founded the rival 'Donkey's Tail'. Illustrated Russian Futurist books. Exhibited with Kandinsky's Blue Rider Group in Munich, and in Roger Fry's 'Second Post-Impressionist Exhibition' in London.

1913 Organized a personal exhibition in Moscow, showing 768 works. Contributed to Larionov's 'The Target' exhibition in Moscow, and to the 'Der Stürm' Autumn exhibition in Berlin. With Larionov, organized exhibition of 'Original Icon Paintings and Popular Prints' in Moscow. Experimented with abstraction and non-objectivity in her Rayonist and Cubo-Futurist paintings. Engaged in Russian Futurist activities. Published manifestos, and made a Futurist film with Larionov.

1914 Contributed to Larionov's 'No. 4' exhibition in Moscow. Visited Paris to supervise her designs for Diaghilev's production of *Le Coq d'Or*. Held a joint exhibition with Larionov at the Galerie Paul Guillaume, Paris. (Apollinaire provided the introduction to the catalogue.) Returned to Russia and published the album of lithographs *Mystical Images of War*.

1915 Made designs for the Chamber Theatre production of Goldoni's *The Fan*. Joined Diaghilev in Switzerland and made designs for the unstaged ballet *Liturgie*.

1916–17 Toured Spain and Italy with the Ballets Russes. In Rome at the time of the October Revolution.

1919 Settled permanently in Paris. Theatrical designs exhibited at the Galerie Barbazanges.

1920s Exhibited on an international scale. Worked as an easel painter, graphic artist and stage designer. Noted for her work on the Diaghilev ballets *Les Noces*, 1923, and *L'Oiseau de Feu*, 1926.

1938 Became a French citizen.

1955 Married Larionov.

1962 Died in Paris.

Olga Rozanova

1886 Born in the town of Malenki, Vladimir Province.

1904–10 Studied painting in Bolshakov's studio-school in Moscow, and attended the Stroganov Institute, Moscow.

1911 Moved to St Petersburg, where she became a leading member of the newly-formed Union of Youth. Met Waldemar Matvejs (Vladimir Markov), Mikhail Matyushin, and became a friend of Kazimir Malevich. The subsequent exhibitions of the Union of Youth, in which Rozanova participated, introduced the avant-garde artists of Petersburg to those of Moscow.

1912–13 Attended Zvantseva's art school, St Petersburg.

1913 Her manifesto 'The Bases of the New Creation and the Reasons Why It Is Misunderstood' published in the *Union of Youth* almanach. Engaged in a wide variety of avant-garde activities.

1913–16 Painted in Futurist and Cubist styles.

Illustrated Futurist and transrational books by the poets Alexei Kruchenykh and Velimir Khlebnikov.

1914 Participated in the First Free Futurist Exhibition, Galleria Sprovieri, Rome (April–May).

1915 At 'Exhibition of Leftist Tendencies', showed paintings inspired by playing-card imagery. With Malevich and Tatlin contributed to the exhibition 'Tramway V' and sent her first non-objective paintings to 'The Last Futurist Exhibition: 0.10', in Petrograd.

1916 Linocuts for *War*. Married Kruchenykh. Contributed collages paralleling Kruchenykh's poems for the album *Universal War*. Exhibited Suprematist works at the 'Knave of Diamonds' exhibition. Helped organize the 'Supremus' group, and was appointed editorial secretary of its magazine (unpublished).

1918 Member of IZO Narkompros and of Proletkult. With Rodchenko appointed head of a special Industrial Art sub-section of IZO Narkompros, set up at her instigation. Helped to organize Svomas in several provincial towns, and assisted in the study and reorganization of a number of important centres for the applied arts.
Died of diptheria in November aged thirty-two. Solo exhibition of her work organized by IZO Narkompros.

1919 Works shown in at 'First State Exhibition', Moscow.

1922 Represented at the 'Erst Russische Kunstausstellung', Van Diemen Gallery, Berlin.

Lyubov Popova

1889 Born in the village of Ivanovskoe, near Moscow. Childhood spent at the family estate of Krasnovidovo, then at Rostov.

1907–8 Attended the studios of Stanislas Zhukovsky and Konstantin Yuon in Moscow. Introduced to Impressionist landscape and still-life painting.

1909–11 Visited Kiev, and in 1910 Italy, and 1910–11 ancient Russian cities such as Novogorod and Pskov, making studies of church art and architecture. Set up a studio in Moscow with Udaltsova, Udaltsova's sister Prudkovskaya and Vera Pestel.

1912 Worked in Tatlin's Tower studio with Viktor Bart and Alexander Vesnin. Under Tatlin's influence paid particular attention to drawing and analyzing the form of the nude.

1912–13 Worked in Paris at the Académie 'La Palette' with the Cubist painters Henri Le Fauconnier and Jean Metzinger. Friendly with Udaltsova and Mukhina.

1913 Returned to Russia and worked with Tatlin, Udaltsova, Morganov and Vesnin. Painted in a mature Cubo-Futurist style.

1914 Travelled through France and Italy with Mukhina and Iza Burmeister. Exhibited for the first time with the 'Knave of Diamonds'.

1915–16 Experimented more fully with both Futurism and Cubism. Executed several 'Sculpto-paintings' and showed her works in the leading avant-garde exhibitions including 'Tramway V', '0.10', 'Knave of Diamonds' and 'The Store'.

1916–18 Executed her series of 'Pictorial Architectonics'. Identified with Suprematism and a member of the Supremus group.

1918 Married the art historian Boris von Eding. Professor at Svomas, then Vkhutemas (after 1920).

1919 Her husband died in Rostov. Popova herself was taken seriously ill there. Contributed to 'Tenth State Exhibition: Non-objective Creation and Suprematism'.

1920 Member of Inkhuk. First designs for the theatre.

1921 Took part in the Constructivist exhibition '5 × 5 = 25', Moscow. Executed her series of

'Spatial Force Constructions', then abandoned easel painting for Production art. Executed designs for Lunacharsky's play *The Locksmith and the Chancellor* performed at the Comedy Theatre, Moscow. Experimented with the design of books, ceramics, texiles and clothing.

1922 Constructivist stage designs for *The Magnanimous Cuckold* produced by Meyerhold. Represented at the Erste Russische Kunstausstellung, Van Diemen Gallery, Berlin.

1923 Made stage designs for Meyerhold's production of Trotsky's *Earth in Turmoil*. Appointed Head of Design at the First State Textile Print Factory in Moscow.

1924 Died in Moscow, aged thirty-five.

Alexandra Exter

1882 Born in Belostok, near Kiev.

1906–7 Attended Kiev Academy of Fine Arts.

1908 Married a solicitor, Nikolai Evgenievich Exter. Studied at the Académie de la Grande Chaumière, Paris, in K. Delval's studio. First contact with the Cubist painters and poets, including Picasso, Braque, Apollinaire and Max Jacob. Organized 'The Link' exhibition in Kiev with David Burlyuk, Larionov and Goncharova.

1910 Exhibited at the Izdebsky Salon in Odessa, Riga, St Petersburg and Moscow. Participated in the first 'Knave of Diamonds' exhibition (and continued to show with the group regularly until 1914). Exhibited with the 'Union of Youth'.

1910–14 Moved between Kiev, Moscow, St Petersburg and Paris. In close contact with both the Russian and European avant-garde. Adopted a Cubo-Futurist style. Collaborated with the Union of Youth and with the poets of David Burlyuk's Hylaea group (*see General Chronology: 1913*).

1914 Exhibited at Larionov's and Goncharova's 'No. 4' Futurist exhibition in Moscow, at the Salon des Indépendants in Paris and in the 'First Free Futurist Exhibition' in Rome.

1915–16 Grew close to Malevich and Tatlin. Contributed to 'Tramway V' and 'The Store' exhibitions.

1916 Made designs for Tairov's production of *Famira Kifared* staged at the Chamber Theatre, Moscow.

1917 Designed costumes and sets for Oscar Wilde's *Salome* at the Chamber Theatre.

1918 Established her own teaching-studio in Kiev. With her pupils decorated agit-prop trains. Death of her husband.

1920 Ballet designs: *Spanish Dancers*.

1921 Taught at Vkhutemas. Designed clothing and textiles. Participated in the Constructivist exhibition '5 × 5 = 25', Moscow. Designs for Tairov's production of *Romeo and Juliet* and for the Moscow Children's Theatre.

1922 Participated in the 'Erste Russische Kunstdusstellung', Van Diemen Gallery, Berlin.

1923–4 Costumes for the film *Aelita* (1924). Assisted in the design of the 'First Agricultural and Handicrafts Exhibition', Moscow. Designed books.

1924 Emigrated to Paris. Taught stage and design and painting at Fernand Léger's 'Académie d'Art Moderne' until 1930s. Exhibited at the International Biennale, Venice.

1925 Contributed to the Exposition Internationale des Arts Décoratifs, Paris.

1926 Designed forty marionettes, executed by Nechama Szmuszkovicz, for a film by Peter Gad (not issued). Participated in 'International Theatre Exhibition', Steinway Building, New York.

1927 One-woman exhibition of theatrical designs and marionettes at Der Stürm Gallery, Berlin. Designs for *Othello*, Jibertini's *La dama sullo scudo*, and for Anna Pavlova's ballet company *Don Juan*.

1928 Moved to Fonténay-aux-Roses on the outskirts of Paris.

1930 Participated in the exhibition 'Cercle et Carré', Paris. Designs for *Prologue de Revue*, Théâtre des Nouveautés, Paris.

1937 One-woman exhibition including marionettes, Prague.

1938 'Fold-outs' for children for Paul Faucher, Flammarion, Paris.

1949 Died at Fonténay-aux-Roses.

Varvara Stepanova

1894 Born in Kaunas (Kovno).

1911 Attended Kazan School of Art, where she later met her future life-companion the artist Alexander Rodchenko.

1912 Moved to Moscow.

1913–14 Attended the Stroganov Institute, Moscow. Exhibited at the 'Moscow Salon'.

1915–17 Book-keeper and then secretary at a metal-products factory. Worked in the studio of Ilya Mashkov and Konstantin Yuon, and in Mikhail Leblan's studio.

1917 Involved with IZO Narkompros. Began writing transrational poetry.

1918 Created books of graphic poems: *Rtny khomle, Zigra ar*.

1919 Illustrations for Alexei Kruchenykh's play *Gly-gly*. 'Anti-book' *Gaust chaba*. Exhibited graphics in the 'Tenth State Exhibition', Moscow.

1919–20 Series of abstract figure-paintings.

1918–22 Deputy head of IZO Narkompros. Participated in the debate (1919) on workers' clothing.

1920–3 Stepanova and Rodchenko members of Inkhuk, Stepanova Secretary to the Group of Objective Analysis and the Group of Constructivists, among other administrative and teaching posts.

1920–5 Taught in the Fine Arts Studio of the Krupskaya Academy of Communist Education.

1921 Contributed (as 'Varst') to the Constructivist exhibition '5 × 5 = 25', Moscow. Turned to Productivism and design.

1922 Collages for the magazine *Cine-Photo*. Sets and costumes for Meyerhold's production of *The Death of Tarelkin*. Represented at the 'Erste Russische Kunstausstellung', Van Diemen Gallery, Berlin. Series of wood-engravings on the theme of Charlie Chaplin.

1923–5 Designer (with Popova and Rochenko) at the First State Textile Print Factory, Moscow. Regular contributor to the journal *LEF* and (1927–8) *New LEF*.

1924 Professor in the Textile faculty of Vkhutemas. 'Evening of the Book' at the Krupskaya Academy of Communist Education.

1925 Designed posters to accompany Mayakovsky's texts. Contributed with Rodchenko to the Exposition Internationale des Arts Décoratifs, Paris.

1926–32 Designs and the costumes for the film *Isolation*. Graphic design for many contemporary journals such as *Soviet Cinema, Literature and Art*. Designed books such as *Cruel Laughter* by Mayakovsky and *From Merchant Moscow to Socialist Moscow*. Worked for the Fine Arts Publishing House Ogiz-Izogiz.

1933–4 Art editor for the Party Publishing House, designing books such as *Lenin's Testaments, To the Women of the World* and *Results of the First Five-Year Plan*, and also *Collective Farm Newspaper*.

1934–8 Worked with Rodchenko on a series of photographic albums.

1938–45 Worked extensively as a graphic designer.

1945 Art editor and designer for the magazine *Soviet Woman*.

1945–55 Worked closely with Rodchenko as a graphic designer to produce photographic albums

such as *15 Years of Soviet Cinema, 25 Years of the Kazakh S S R* (1947), *The Moscow Underground* (1948), *300 Years of Union between the Ukraine and Russia* (1955), as well as posters for the publishing houses 'Art' and 'Goskultprosvetizdat'.

1956 Death of Rodchenko.

1958 Died in Moscow.

Nadezhda Udaltsova

1885 (Old Style) Born in Orel.

1892 Family moved to Moscow.

1905–9 Attended the Moscow School of Painting, Sculpture and Architecture.

1906 Studied under Nikolai Ulyanov at Konstantin Yuon's school.

1908 Travelled to Germany, visiting Berlin and Dresden. On her return to Moscow became acquainted with Shchukin's collection of modern French art. Married Alexander Udaltsov.

1909–11 Worked in various studios including that of Karol Kish, became acquainted with Vladimir Favorsky.

1912 Visited Paris with Popova. Studied at the Académie 'La Palette' under Le Fauconnier, Metzinger and Dunoyer de Segonzac.

1913 Returned to Moscow, worked in Vladimir Tatlin's 'Tower' studio with Popova, Alexander Vesnin and Alexei Grishchenko.

1914 Contributed to the 'Knave of Diamonds' exhibition.

1915 Exhibited Cubist and Cubo-Futurist paintings at the exhibitions 'Tramway V', 'Leftist Tendencies' and '0.10'. Tatlin bought her Cubist canvas *Bottle and Glass*. Edited the text for the pamphlet *Vladimir Efgrafovich Tatlin* published by 'The New Magazine for Everyone' in Petrograd.

1916 Exhibited among the Suprematist painters at the 'Knave of Diamonds' exhibition, and in 'The Store'. 1916–17 member of the 'Supremus' group.

1917–19 Active on the Moscow Arts Board of IZO Narkompros and in other social and state organizations.

1918–20 Taught as assistant to Malevich at Svomas; later with her own studio.

1920 Married the artist Alexander Drevin.

1921 Their son the future sculptor Andrei Drevin born.

1921–30 Taught the Basic Course and led workshops in painting and textiles at Vkhutemas (after 1928 known as Vkhutein). Member of Inkhuk until in 1921 it endorsed Constructivism.

1922 Participated in the 'Erste Russische Kunstausstellung', Van Diemen Gallery, Berlin. Her works were acquired by the 'Societé Anonyme' (Katherine Dreier and Marcel Duchamp).

1923 Participated in the 'Exhibition of Paintings' alongside former members of the Knave of Diamonds. Turned away from non-objectivity to investigate the principles of Cézanne.

1926 Travelled with Drevin to the Ural Mountains. Painted impressionist landscapes.

1927–8 Member of Society of Moscow Artists.

1928 Works of the Urals period shown in her one-woman exhibition in the State Russian Museum, Leningrad. Travelled with Drevin to the Altai Mountains.

1930 Travelled with Drevin to the Altai Mountains.

1931 Paintings from this journey exhibited at the 'Group 13' exhibition.

1932–3 Travelled to Armenia.

1934 Joint exhibition with Drevin in State Cultural and Historical Museum, Erevan.

1938 Death of Drevin.

1941–5 Worked in Moscow with a group of artists painting portraits of pilot heroes of the Second World War.

1945 One-woman exhibition in the Moscow State

Gypsy Theatre. Personal exhibition in the halls of the Moscow Section of the Union of Artists of the USSR.
1961 Died in Moscow.
1965 Posthumous exhibition in the halls of the Moscow Section of the Union of Artists of the USSR.

Antonia Sofronova
1892 Born in the village of Droskovo, Orel Province.
1909 Graduated from Kiev Girls' Commercial College.
1910 Arrived in Moscow. Studied in Feodor Rerberg's Art School.
1913–17 Studied in Ilya Mashkov's studio.
1914 Participated in the 'Knave of Diamonds' exhibition.
1915 Married Genrikh Matveevich Blyumenfeld (1893–1920), artist and theorist working in Mashkov's studio.
1916 Participated in the exhibition of Moscow artists in aid of the war-wounded.
1917–18 Participated in 'World of Art' exhibitions, 'Fifth State Exhibition' of IZO Narkompros.
1919–21 Taught drawing in schools in Orel Province, and in Tver (now Kalinin) State Art Studios. Exhibited there. Returned to Moscow. Fine arts instructor in the Political Department of the Moscow military region.
1922 Series of 'constructive' drawings.
1923–27 Designs for Tarabukin's book *From the Easel to the Machine*. Executed drawings for newspapers and journals such as *Red Virgin Soil* and *Club*, also posters and book-covers for Soviet and foreign authors for the publishing houses 'Earth and Factory', 'Young Guard' and 'Moscow Community of Writers'.
1924–5 Series of Moscow street-scenes and people.
1928–34 Series of Moscow cityscapes.
1931 Contributed to the exhibition 'Artists of the RSFSR Over Fifteen Years', Moscow.
1935–8 Worked on the series *The Zoo*.
1937 Member of the Moscow Department of the Union of Artists. Contributed to the 'First Exhibition of Watercolours by Moscow Artists', Moscow.
1938 Participated in 'Exhibition of Painting, Graphics and Sculpture by Women Artists', Moscow.
1939 Lived and worked in Gudauta. Series of paintings and graphic works, *Gudauta*.
1940 Series, *Actresses*.
1966 Died in Moscow.

Eva Rozengolts-Levina
1898 Born in Vitebsk.
1915 Graduated from the Alekseev High School in Vitebsk.
1915–18 During the war worked as a hospital nurse. Entered the Tomsk University Dental School.
1919 Encountered the sculptor Stepan Erzya in Moscow and worked in his studio. Moved to Vitebsk and nursed soldiers on the Civil War front.
1920 Returned to Moscow. Met Anna Golubkina and worked as her student at Svomas. Met Robert Falk.
1921 Studied painting in Robert Falk's studio at Vkhutemas.
1923 Married the writer P. Levin.
1925 Graduated from Vkutemas as an 'artist of the first class'.
1926 Visited London. Attracted by the paintings of Turner.
1928 Exhibited with 'Union of Social Artists' in Moscow.
1930 Article with R. Izelson 'The Theatre of the Near Future'.

1931–2 Taught at the First State Textile Print Factory, Moscow.
1932–3 Fabric Design Artist at the Dorogomilovskaya Factory, Moscow.
1934–6 Senior design consultant at the People's Commissariat of Light Industry. Worked on sketches for fabrics based on children's drawings.
1940 Her husband died at the front in the Finnish War.
1942 Lived in Chistopol. Organized an artistic collective to provide work for the wives of writers at the front.
1942–9 Lived in Moscow. Worked in the foundry workshop of the Moscow Community of Artists.
1946 Exhibited with the 'Moscow Community of Artists', Moscow.
1949–54 Exiled because of her family connections. Lived in the Krasnoyarsk region, and then in Kazakhstan.
1954 Moved to Karaganda. Worked as a stage designer in the Kazakh regional theatre.
1956 Rehabilitated, and returned to Moscow.
1974 The Pushkin Museum of Fine Arts acquired 11 of her works.
1975 Died in Moscow.

Nina Simonovich-Efimova
1877 Born in St Petersburg.
1896–8 Worked as a teacher in Tiflis (now Tbilisi).
1899 First visit to Paris. Studied in Delécluze's studio.
1900 Studied at the Stroganov Institute, Moscow. Attended E. Zvantseva's studio and studied with her cousin the painter Valentin Serov.
1901 Paris. Studied in the studio of Eugene Carrière.
1902 Taught drawing in Tver.
1904–10 Worked at the Moscow School of Painting, Sculpture and Architecture.
1905–7 Took part in the strike at the School, working in the infirmary and canteen for strikers.
1906 Married the sculptor Ivan Efimov.
1908–10 Lived in France (Brittany and Paris). Worked in Matisse's studio. Painted landscapes, sea-scapes, Parisian street-scenes. With Efimov produced children's paper cut-outs.
1909–11 Exhibited at the Salon des Indépendants and the Salon d'Automne in Paris.
1911 Paintings of peasant women from the Tambov region. Began working on silhouettes.
1914–15 Member of the 'World of Art' group.
1918 Began working on puppet theatre. October: with her husband opened the Theatre of Marionettes, Petrushkas and Shadows in Moscow, the first professional puppet theatre in Russia.
1922 Member of the short-lived 'Makovets' society (*see* General Chronology: 1924).
1923 Illustrated children's and adult books. Worked on exhibitions for the Museums of Ethnology, for the Agriculture exhibition in Moscow.
1925 Joined the 'Four Arts' society.
1926–9 Regular exhibitor with 'Four Arts'.
1927 Participated in the 'Tenth Anniversary of the October Revolution' exhibition.
1928–9 Taught courses for workers on puppet theatre.
1945 One-woman exhibition, Moscow.
1948 Died in Moscow.

Sarra Lebedeva
1892 Born in St Petersburg.
1906–14 Attended the School for the Encouragement of the Arts, St Petersburg. Visited Paris, Berlin, Vienna and Italy (up to 1914).
1910–12 Studied painting and drawing in Mikhail Bernshtein's school, St Petersburg, and sculpture in Leonid Shervud's studio.
1912 Transferred to Shervud's school and specialized in sculpture.

1914 Worked with V.V. Kuznetsov as pupil and assistant.
1915 Married the artist Vladimir Lebedev.
1918 Participated in the 'World of Art' exhibition, Petrograd. Worked for the realization of Lenin's Decree on Monumental Propaganda in Petrograd.
1919–20 Taught in the Stieglitz Institute, Petrograd.
1920–4 Worked on stage design and on ceramics, as well as portrait sculpture (1924).
1925 Moved to Moscow. Worked on the portrait of F.E. Dzerzhinsky.
1925–30s Executed portrait busts of Party officials and heroes of socialist labour.
1926 Joined the Society of Russian Sculptors (ORS). Took part in the 'State Exhibition of Sculpture' (the first ORS exhibition), in Moscow.
1928 Participated in 'Tenth Anniversary of the October Revolution' exhibition. Exhibited at the Sixteenth International Biennale, Venice, and at subsequent Biennales.
1929 Participated in the 'Third Sculpture Exhibition' (ORS) and 'Soviet Art Exhibition', New York.
1931 Participated in the 'Fourth Sculpture Exhibition' (ORS).
1931–5 Made studies of nudes, and designed pottery for the Konakovsky Factory.
1933 Exhibition: 'The Artists of the RSFSR Over Fifteen Years', Moscow.
1933–4 Showed in 'Fifteen Years of the Workers' and Peasants' Red Army' in Moscow, Leningrad, Kiev and Kharkov.
1935 Group exhibition in Moscow with A. E. Zelensky G. I. Kepinov, Vera Mukhina, Ilya Slonim, Vladimir Favorsky, I. G. Frikh-Khar and I. M. Chaykov.
1936 *Little Girl with Butterfly* placed in Gorky Park, Moscow. From this date on, executed many portrait busts and three designs for monuments (unrealized).
1937 Paris, Exposition Universelle, awarded silver medal for pottery (the table-service 'Hen').
1939 All-Union art exhibition, 'The Industry of Socialism', Moscow.
1941 One-woman exhibition, State Museum of Modern Western Art, Moscow.
1942–3 Portraits of Soviet Generals, cultural workers, musicians and writers; participated in exhibitions of work of artists during the war.
1943 Participated in group exhibition together with S. V. Gerasimov, A. A. Deyneika, P. P. Konchalovsky, Vera Mukhina and D. A. Shmarinov in Moscow.
1945 Awarded the title 'Honoured Art Worker of the RSFSR'.
1948 Participated in the international exhibition 'Woman, Her Life and Aspirations', Paris (with a portrait-sculpture of Vera Mukhina).
1958 At the World Exhibition in Brussels won a silver medal for her portrait of Chkalov.
1963 Participated in 'Soviet Art' exhibition, Berlin.
1964 Represented in 'Russian and Soviet Art' exhibition, Malmo and Bucharest.
1967 Died in Moscow.
1969 Posthumous exhibition, State Tretykov Gallery, Moscow, and State Russian Museum, Leningrad.

Vera Mukhina
1889 Born in Riga.
1891 Mother died, the family moved to Kiev.
1903 Father died. Vera moved to Kursk.
1910 Moved to Moscow. To Konstantin Yuon's school which Popova and Udaltsova had attended.
1911 Entered Sinitsyna's sculpture studio, and studied drawing in Mashkov's studio school.
1912 Following a disfiguring tobaggan-accident, her relatives granted her wish to study in Paris. Entered the Académie de la Grande Chaumière. Worked

in Bourdelle's studio. Became friendly with Popove and Udaltsova.

1914 Together with Popova and Iza Burmeister, travelled through France and Italy (Genoa, Pisa, Naples, Capri, Pompeii, Amalfi, Paestum). Returned to Russia for the summer.

1915–17 Experimented in different sculptural styles. Executed masks of Apollo and Dionysius for the first building of the Chamber Theatre, Moscow. In the circle of avant-garde artists. Met Exter.

1918 Took part in carrying out Lenin's Decree on Monumental Propaganda (with design for the monument to N. Novikov).

1919–20s Member of the 'Monolith' group. Joined the 'Four Arts' group and participated in their exhibitions. Joined the 'Society of Russian Sculptors'.

1921 Participated in the 'World of Art' exhibition, Moscow.

Early to mid-1920s Engaged in design-work for theatre, film (with Exter), and of clothing (with Nadezhda Lamanova).

1927–30 Taught at the Higher Artistic and Technical Institute (Vkhutein) until its sculpture faculty transferred to Leningrad. Designed the 'Jubilee Exhibition of the Arts of the Peoples of the USSR', to mark the tenth anniversary of the Revolution, Moscow.

1930 Lived and worked in Voronezh.

1932 Designs for a Palace of Culture. Took part in a competition to design a monument to Shevchenko for the town of Kharkov. Returned to Moscow. Designs for fountains and public monumental sculpture for Moscow, and portrait sculptures.

1934 Participated in the design of the Moscow Soviet Hotel.

1936 Design for *Worker and Collective Farmworker*, for the Soviet Pavilion, Paris Exposition, 1937, accepted by Government Commission.

1930s–50s Participated in numerous exhibitions in the Soviet Union and abroad.

1963 Died in Moscow.

LIST OF ILLUSTRATIONS

For each artist, plates are listed by plate number, the text illustrations by page number (p.). Dimensions of works are given in centimetres followed by inches, height preceding width.